GUARDIANS OF THE GAME

A LEGACY OF LEADERSHIP

By Dr. James E. Krause

Foreword By
Mike Krzyzewski

GUARDIANS
OF THE GAME

NABC

Requests for permission should be addressed Ascend Media, LLC, Attn: Rights and Permissions Department, 7015 College Blvd., Suite 600, Overland Park, KS 66211.
10 9 8 7 6 5 4 3 2 1

Printed in the United States of America
ISBN-13: 978-0-9817166-0-2
ISBN-10: 0-9817166-0-1
Library of Congress Cataloging-in-Publications Data Available Upon Request.

Editor: Matt Fulks
Dust Jacket and Book Design: Lorel K. Fox and Lynette Ubel
Project Manager: Abby Biggers
All photographs courtesy of the National Association of Basketball Coaches unless otherwise noted.

www.ascendmediabooks.com

DEDICATION

In a review of the *NABC Bulletins* going back to the days of Phog Allen and Doc Carlson, there was always a section or an article written for or by a coach's wife. The message was always well prepared and well received because there was a message to deliver.

The dedication of this book goes to the coach's wife in this family. Elizabeth Currie Krause and I celebrated our 30th anniversary in 2008. We met at a basketball game at Elmira College and have been together ever since.

Like most coaches, I tried everything to drive her off. Weeks away recruiting or scouting, entertaining or supporting someone else's children, and/or moving her 11 times in a 28-year career. She was there every step of the way. She raised our two beautiful daughters, Mackenzie and Katie, and tolerated the constant quest for "quality time." When needed, she would move to the next stop, find the perfect house, school and church, and make the transition as seamless as possible.

She and the girls spent days and nights in gyms and arenas around the country and were always there to share the good times, and her strength and commitment was what kept us together when times were tough. This coach's wife was always a major part of whatever success this coach might have had.

Many of the NABC member coaches know this beautiful lady as Betty in the VIP registration area at the NABC convention. She has worked to support all of you with the same dedication that was present in our home for all these years. Dedicating this book to her is but a token of the gratitude that I have for the sacrifice that she has made choosing to be this coach's wife.

TABLE OF CONTENTS

TABLE OF CONTENTS (CONTINUED)

GUARDIANS
OF THE GAME

NABC

FOREWORD

During my days as a cadet at the United States Military Academy, history, service, and leadership were major components in the curriculum. Any lessons I had learned in those areas before going to West Point were magnified as I studied the people and events of our history and the monumental impact they have had on our lives and our future.

As a young head coach at Army and in my long career at Duke, I have always relied on those lessons of history, service and leadership to make my teams better, both on and off the court.

In the pages that follow, you will not only have the opportunity to learn about the history of the National Association of Basketball Coaches (NABC), but you will also see how the principles of service and leadership are part of the fiber of college basketball. Dr. James Naismith invented our game and his foundation has been built upon over the years by the coaches. Among them were our "founding fathers"—John McLendon of Tennessee State, Henry Iba of Oklahoma State, Kentucky's Adolph Rupp and the coach credited with founding the NABC in 1927, Kansas' Forrest "Phog" Allen.

I learned about the NABC while working for my Army coach, Bob Knight, when he was at Indiana. Coach Knight was on the NABC Board of Directors and was passionate about giving back to the game. As a result, I was fortunate enough to be exposed to some of the game's greatest teachers. When I was asked to become a member of the NABC Board, I knew it was the right thing to do. It's a long commitment—a period of more than 10 years—but it's important to have an impact on our profession and to help preserve the integrity of our game.

Much has changed through the years, but it remains evident that college basketball has a unique purity and that the NCAA Basketball Championship is one of the greatest sporting events in the world. When you read about the history of the tournament and how the NABC had to borrow money in the first years of its existence, it's remarkable to see its evolution. Beginning in Detroit in 2009, the NCAA Final Four® will have some 70,000 people in attendance and millions more watching on television.

Likewise, the duties and responsibilities of coaches have grown and evolved. There is considerably less time for the coach to teach both his players and the young coaches who want to learn more about the profession. Coaches today have so many obligations away from the basketball court, including many that come as a result of the game's growth and the extensive media coverage.

The high visibility of coaches has had a positive effect on our ability to champion significant charitable efforts. The NABC has been very successful in its creation of the Coaches vs. Cancer program several years ago. I'm proud to be involved with it and with numerous other causes, including the Jimmy V Foundation for cancer research established by my good friend and fellow coach, Jim Valvano. I currently serve as president of the NABC Foundation, the charitable arm of the association. The NABC Foundation was created in 2002 in an effort to replicate what college basketball coaches do best—encourage and motivate students to achieve at the highest possible level. The Foundation set out to use NABC coaches' motivational skills and the celebrity of college basketball to stimulate students in setting meaningful academic goals that could be measured and rewarded.

Throughout its existence, the NABC has been blessed with outstanding leadership. Many of our game's greatest coaches, at all levels of college basketball, have taken the time to serve on the Board of Directors. The guiding forces of the NABC have been four former college coaches who have served as full-time executive directors, beginning with Cliff Wells, followed by Bill Wall, Joe Vancisin, and our present Executive Director, Jim Haney. All of these men not only did a remarkable job in facilitating the growth of basketball, but were also visionaries in the evolution of our coaching profession.

I sincerely hope that this book will provide a meaningful history of the NABC. For those who would like a hands-on, state-of-the-art look at men's college basketball and a detailed historical presentation on the sport, visit the College Basketball Experience at the Sprint Center in Kansas City, Missouri. The NABC Foundation opened this magnificent facility, which is also home to the National Collegiate Basketball Hall of Fame, in October 2007, as a permanent place to celebrate our great game!

— **Mike Krzyzewski**
August 2008

ACKNOWLEDGEMENT

The publishing of this book represents the end of my college basketball career. The closure that I have been looking for was simply among the pages of *Guardians of the Game – A Legacy of Leadership*. This project was only a thought at the convention in 2006, when Joe and Elizabeth Vancisin encouraged me to consider moving forward. Without their support, it would never have gotten off the ground. Teaming with the Vancisins was the motivation I needed to present a formal proposal to the NABC. I was surprised and grateful for the support of Jim Haney, Reggie Minton and the NABC Board for embracing the project. I am most thankful for my family; wife Betty, daughters Mackenzie and Katie, sons-in-law Cliff and Brent who inspired me to go forward and then lifted me when it got tough.

Preparing for a season, a game, or a tournament requires very careful planning and I had no plan. Unsure of the NABC's willingness to move forward, the proposal was a labor of love and the granting of approval came faster than expected. At that point, Bill Wall, former NABC Executive Director, opened his home, garage and storage unit for me, and the personality of the book began to bloom. Happily for me, unhappily for his wife Marilyn, Bill has never thrown anything away. In his files, boxes and bookshelves were hand-written notes by James Naismith and Phog Allen; every manual and document used by the NABC; and about 500 books dating back to the earliest days of the game. I had hit the mother lode.

My son-in-law Cliff Ellis, a high school English teacher and basketball coach offered expertise and labor in manuscript review, vocabulary, grammar and flow. His early efforts set the course and kept the project on point.

Many people participated in the research for the text. Rick Leddy, Matt Fulks, Michael Scarano, Steve Moore, Rebecca Schulte, Timothy W. Sprattler, Gary Ellis, Mark Heatherman, Kip Fonsh and Jim McGary provided vital parts of the research. Executive Directors Joe Vancisin, Bill Wall and Jim Haney provided valuable time, effort, contacts, interviews and leadership to the project.

Finally, and with a standing ovation, I want to acknowledge Publisher Bob Snodgrass, Editor Matt Fulks and all the folks from Ascend Media. Led by Abby Biggers, Meggan Cowan and Lorel Fox, they supported a rookie author without hesitation or reservation. The book and CD are the result of the level of professionalism that these people demanded and delivered from day one.

Special thanks, in alpha order, to all of the people that agreed to be interviewed for this project. The book does not compete without their commitment: Ladell Andersen, Gene Bartow, David Berst, Ed Bilik, George Blaney, Jim Boeheim, Walter

Byers, Jim Calhoun, John Chaney, Barry Collier, Denny Crum, Vincent Cullen, Hugh Durham, Jessie Evans, Eddie Fogler, Tom Ford, Travis Ford, Bill Foster, Jim Haney, Jud Heathcote, Jim Hyneman, Mike Jarvis, Tom Jernstedt, Mike Johnston, Ben Jobe, Milton Katz, Floyd Keith, Herb Kenny, Ernie Kent, George Killian, Bob Knight, Scott Knisley, Mike Krzyzewski, Phil Martelli, Glenn Marx, James McGary, Reggie Minton, Dennis Mishko, Ted Owens, George Raveling, Nolan Richardson, Herb Sendek, Norm Stewart, Jerry Tarkanian, Joe Vancisin, William Wall, Rudy Washington, Glenn Wilkes, Tex Winter and John Wooden.

These organizations gave support to the project; Naismith Memorial Basketball Hall of Fame, College Basketball Experience, National Collegiate Basketball Hall of Fame, NABC, NCAA, NAIA, NJCAA, University of Kansas Library, University of Oregon Library, Andover Academy, Black Coaches Association and the Illinois State High School Athletic Association.

TO ALL ABOVE, I AM FOREVER IN YOUR DEBT!

Joe Vancisin opens the first NABC office to welcome all college basketball fans.

INTRODUCTION

Prior to your reading the chapters that follow, I need to provide some direction. First, please understand that this is not a history book. It is a compilation of stories told by the coaches involved and the reporters who followed them. For reasons of organization, the book will use the National Association of Basketball Coaches (NABC) as the spinal column of the story, but the "Guardians" themselves will determine any meanderings right or left of center. Going back in time revealed so many answers, but raised so many new questions. Many of the Guardians of college basketball identified in the book had connections dating back to Dr. James Naismith, the "father" of basketball, and so, eventually, the book had to start at the very beginning.

Second, the English Language was considerably different in the early 1900s and the written word, punctuation use and sentence structure were not the same as what we are used to reading today. In an attempt to report things as accurately as possible, every effort is made to present the information as it was written at that time. In the days after the invention of basketball, the game was actually represented as two words (basket ball) and then sometime later it became a hyphenated word (basket-ball). As you read through shared stories and accounts directly from the early days of the game, those are not typos that you are experiencing. You will find several items, strategies and situations that have simply changed names since the game's beginnings. The game itself was actually going to be called "Naismith ball," if friends of the inventor had been able to convince him to allow it.

Finally, the intense research that went into building the foundation for this book uncovered some noteworthy inconsistencies. In many cases, an event, a game or a significant person were reported differently, depending on the material being reviewed. Every effort was made to report the information with as much factual basis as humanly possible, but there continues to be several different accounts of the same things. For example, the list of people who made up the first committee assigned to develop one set of rules for amateur basketball is never the same. Names are added, names are missing and in some cases, even multiple first names are recorded for the same person, so please be patient. If I found a letter or newspaper report written directly about an event, then I went with the letter from the day rather than the accounts reprinted years later. I am certain some inaccuracies exist, but in an age when accounts were often shared by word of mouth, some slippage is not uncommon.

The following chapters will provide you with an insider's view of the development of this very influential American game, and the nurturing organization. Some obscure individuals responsible for building the profession of coaching and the spectacular game of college basketball will share their stories. I think many will be astonished to read that our earliest coaches actually provided the mold for the coaches practicing today. Many were making a living hawking their talents, their products and their speaking acumen. There is little going on in the coaching world today that was not present when Forrest "Phog" Allen and Walter Meanwell were facing off in the entrepreneurial marketplace.

In the very beginning of basketball coaching, the practice of sharing information and taking responsibility for teaching the next generation of coaches was taken very seriously. Even the powerful African-American influence in college basketball can be traced through Kansas with John McLendon, who was a student and mentor of James Naismith and "Phog" Allen.

Much of what has been accomplished in college basketball can be traced back to elected members of the Naismith Memorial Basketball Hall of Fame and inspirational leaders of the NABC. The NABC Past Presidents' list is a virtual who's who of coaching basketball. What is also important is the impact these people had on other aspects of sports and society. The NABC continues to emphasize the long-supported issues originally outlined in the Constitution of 1927:

- *I BELIEVE that basketball has an important place in the general education scheme and pledge myself to cooperate with others in the field of education to administer it that its value never will be questioned.*
- *I BELIEVE that other coaches of this sport are as earnest in its protection as I am, and I will do all in my powers to further their endeavors.*
- *I BELIEVE that my own actions should be so regulated at all times that I will be a credit to the profession.*
- *I BELIEVE that the members of the National Basketball Rules Committee are capably expressing the rules of the game, and I will abide by these rules in both spirit and letter.*
- *I BELIEVE in the exercise of all patience, tolerance, and diplomacy at my command in my relations with all players, co-workers, game officials, and spectators.*
- *I BELIEVE that the proper administration of this sport offers an effective laboratory method to develop in its adherents high ideals of sportsmanship; qualities of cooperation, courage, unselfishness and self-control; desires for clean, healthful living; and respect for wise discipline and authority.*
- *I BELIEVE that those admirable characteristics, properly installed by me through teaching and demonstration, will have a long carry-over and will aid each one connected with the sport to become a better citizen.*
- *I BELIEVE in and will support all reasonable moves to improve athletic conditions, to provide for adequate equipment, and to promote the welfare of an increased number of participants.*

The NABC membership has occasionally taken an inappropriate step, but the degree of respect that is identified with the title "Coach" has remained consistent. Much like basketball and James Naismith's 13 Original Rules, the organization still rests comfortably on the building blocks created by our founders and identified in this text.

One appropriate step by the NABC is recognizing its coaches as "Guardians of the Game." The moniker seems to capture the modern philosophy and the direction of the organization in a very few words. Moving forward from a philosophy aimed at organizing and educating coaches to a more businesslike approach has been received with both applause and bitterness. With growing influence, the NABC has expanded into efforts including philanthropy, professional development and cancer research while turning from the traditional staples of advocacy, teaching "coaching" and publishing the *Bulletin*.

A careful review of documents revealing the evolution of basketball development clearly identifies a number of individuals whose dedication, vision and stalwart personalities envisioned and put in motion the necessary goals and objectives to create basketball's foundation and protect its legacy. The NABC was founded by coaches, for coaches, and has been in place for 80-plus years. During that time it was rarely silent as the membership patrolled the game of basketball for inconsistencies, ethics issues and rules anomalies. The NABC was founded after an alarm was sounded when evidence surfaced that a wrong was being imposed upon the sport of basketball. With a "call to arms," the first effort to mobilize national coaches and confront an issue became a reality. George Raveling, long-time coach and past president of the NABC describes it best: *"We are an advocacy organization and an advocacy organization should never be quiet."*

Dr. Allen was an unconventional and, at times, controversial leader who often questioned practice and tradition. A close evaluation of the total work of the organization's 81 years (in the year 2008), will reveal a historical ledger filled with controversy and disagreement, but always absolute respect for the game of basketball.

The NABC was formed in 1927 and the organization maintained an eerie traditional consistency until the country began bracing for the turn of the century. Almost 70 years after the organization was founded, a major change in philosophy and approach was taking place. This change of doctrine and attitude was announced at the 1993 NABC convention in New Orleans and was received with mixed emotions. Although the change involved the hiring of a new leader for the organization, the new direction began with the following speech given by incoming President, George Blaney (Holy Cross head coach). As he received the gavel signifying the beginning of his presidency, Blaney told the membership:

"For over 40 years I have been lucky enough to have either played or coached this wonderful game of ours. Basketball has given me everything I have, has taken me to all parts of the world, and has allowed me to work with some of the best kids any coach could ever ask for.

"During that time, it has always been the game that has intrigued me. The beauty of the game and the beauty of college basketball in its diversity:big schools, small schools, urban schools, rural schools, the Big Ten, the Ivy League, the ACC, the Southland and the game is diversified in a similar fashion: Kentucky and Tubby Smith play at a fast tempo; Pete Carril and Princeton do not; Jim Calhoun and Connecticut press the entire game while Eddie Sutton and Oklahoma State play half-court man;. Roy Williams at Kansas runs motion and Gary Williams at Maryland runs the flex. Basketball is the street and it is the suburbs; it is New York and French Lick. What other game can be played by yourself, one-on-one, five-on-five or any combination in-between. It can be played indoors or out. It can be played in a small high school gym or even the Louisiana Super Dome.

"The game is about dilemmas; quickness and slowness, inside play and outside shooting, pressure and patience, tall and small, selfishness and unselfishness, power and finesse. No other game offers those differences. The game makes us heroes one night and goats the next. If we win, we must come back and try to win again. If we lose, it _allows_ us to come back again and try to win.

"The coaches are as diverse as the game– Dean Smith (North Carolina) was the innovator, Bob Knight (Indiana, Texas Tech) is the teacher, John Chaney (Temple) is the zone, Rick Pitino (Louisville) is pressure, Jim Calhoun (UConn) is intensity, George Raveling (Southern California) is our conscience and Mike Krzyzewski (Duke) is the model.

"From all of this emerges the constant thought that it is up to us to maintain the game, to improve the game, to effect change for the game…

"As we enter this new era of the NABC, I would like us to redefine teamwork by keeping the best interest of the student-athlete as our priority, and instill in them that same love of the game we all share.

"Make today an opportunity!"

Coach Blaney provided little detail, but left no doubt that change was in the wind. He was also able to use just a few words to emphasize the influence coaches have and have had in the development of basketball. The NABC was heading into uncharted water and the aforementioned coaches would have to pay particular attention each step of the way.

Throughout the book and regardless of the era, there will be numerous examples of how the great coaches were sensitive to the game's potential and preparing the next generation of coaches for the coming responsibility.

"First, try to understand that you have a job that, first of all, entails the kid that you have recruited obtaining a degree," Bob Knight remarked, when asked about new coaches today. He continued, "Secondly learn how to use different kinds of talent. Thirdly, look to put a teaching method together that enables your players to play the game efficiently and effectively." Valuable words, from the winningest coach in basketball history, on what a young coach should point toward.

So, enjoy the journey, embrace the traditions and recognize the incredible partnership that has been the National Association of Basketball Coaches of the United States and the game of college basketball.

Although an association dedicated to basketball coaches wasn't necessary at the beginning of the game, plotting the lifelines of the National Association of Basketball Coaches would be incomplete without including the origins of the game of basketball. This truly American game, invented by a Canadian-born, naturalized U.S. citizen, has become the only sport able to compete on an international level with soccer (football over most of the globe). The game's inventor, Dr. James Naismith, NABC Honorary President, 1929-present, was simply trying to satisfy a teaching weakness when he actually created a monster.

In fact, the game caught on so quickly—and probably seemed so bizarre at the time—that according to the *Springfield (Massachusetts) Republican* newspaper on March 12, 1892, more than 200 people watched from a balcony as the YMCA teachers played the students. That is assumed to be the first time basketball was played in front of the public.

GUARDIAN
DR. JAMES NAISMITH
(TEACHER, INVENTOR, MENTOR)

"Do not be afraid to serve humanity and wait for your reward."

— Dr. James Naismith

Dr. Naismith's story as somewhat of a renaissance man has been told in countless articles and books, including stories of Naismith the doctor, the soldier, the professor, the minister, the administrator and the coach.

James Naismith was born in Canada and sadly lost his parents as an eight–year-old. He was raised by a bachelor uncle on a rural farm, and it was there he developed his quiet demeanor and intense work ethic. Little is shared regarding his interest in leaving the rural setting or his motivation for personal education. Shortly after completing his local education, he set his sights on earning a degree from McGill University in Canada, and followed that with a move to the YMCA Christian Workers College in Springfield, Massachusetts. His McGill experience introduced him to the relatively new study of physical education and his degree requirements required some experience teaching physical education, often cited as the motivation that became his life's work.

As he said in a speech in 1932: *"Going into physical education in 1890 was a very different proposition than it is now. When I decided to enter physical work and spoke to a young man that I expected to be my brother-in-law, he asked, 'What are you going to do now?' I replied, 'I am going to Springfield and take up athletics.' Then he said, 'Athletics to the devil.'"*

Naismith received a degree in Physical Education, which became the focus for the remaining years of his teaching life. Early on, he showed more than a passing interest in spreading a Christian message, and did occasionally preach. Interestingly, he also pursued a degree in medicine at the University of Colorado, but never joined the ministry or practiced medicine. Instead, he worked all of his life to preach the YMCA doctrine of "Muscular Christianity," the belief that physical activity enhances the mind, body and spirit. The medical degree supported his resolve to interject anatomy, physiology and psychology into the physical education classes he taught in his pursuit of the scientific physical educator. Throughout this impressive pursuit of personal education, he developed and staunchly maintained an intense belief in physical development within the human form.

During his more impressionable days in Springfield, there were numerous unfounded theories about why James Naismith invented the game of basketball. The game was actually invented in the fall of 1891 while Naismith was teaching at the YMCA Christian Workers College (Springfield College). Frankly, the spirited young men needed an activity to satisfy their high energy levels during the harsh winter season. Naismith's superior at Springfield, Dr. Luther Gulick, gave Naismith the charge of finding that "athletic distraction."

Naismith noted in a letter to T.J. Brown in 1898: *"...there was a revolt against the introduction of Swedish Educational Gymnastics to take the place of children's recess. This led to a question about games."* Evidently, he was thinking about something new before the invention became a mandate. Additional evidence to his thinking became clear in a speech he gave titled "The Origins of Basketball" in 1932.

"In 1890, when I first entered this institution, there was practically no games with the exception of football, baseball and track; football in the fall, baseball and track in the spring. Soccer was played very little," he said. "From the time that we stopped playing football in the fall until baseball in the spring, we had nothing but work on the horse, buck, and different pieces of apparatus, along with calisthenics. We needed some sort of game that would be interesting and could be played indoors."

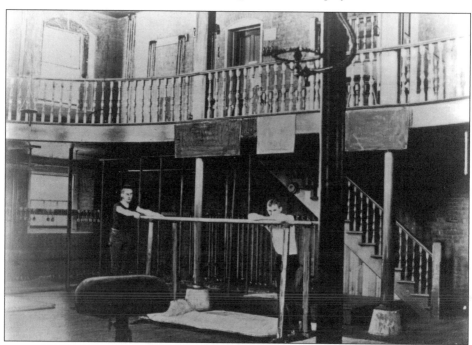

The original Naismith Gymnasium, note the balcony where he hung the baskets. Also showing are the pieces of apparatus that encouraged the game to be invented.

The game appeared to grow at an unusual pace within the Springfield community. As early as 1892, basketball was spreading to both young men and women, with the Young Men's Christian Association (YMCA) sponsoring this early introduction. Naismith himself noted that the game's invention was undertaken in the late fall, and after having a few days to enjoy and embrace the game, students were sent home for the Christmas holidays, where they introduced it to friends and families. This fortunate occurrence obviously established intrigue among a wider audience than only the students attending the school.

The YMCA, which was recognized as the governing body of basketball through 1905, marketed the game and published the first set of basketball rules. Dr. John Brown, 1940 National Council of the YMCA, wrote that the *"YMCA originated it (basketball) and carried it 'round the world."*

"The 13 Original Rules" governed the early game, and Naismith fought diligently to preserve the game within the format that he envisioned with his invention. Originally he launched the game having unlimited participants and being a staple of the winter recreation and conditioning program.

Years later, long after Naismith's death, Dr. Forrest "Phog" Allen would continuously tell this story when speaking to groups about basketball and his good friend James Naismith:

"It was Naismith's theory that 50 or 100 people could play on each side and throw the ball into the hoop. He had no conception of basketball being broken up into the small numbers and intricate passing and set plays that are now indulged in. His idea was more like the game of cage ball that used to be played in the army where the large ball was handled by a group and tossed into a net high above their heads."

Gradually, over the years, the rules were refined, resulting in the game we have today, but Naismith continued to persuade all that would listen, that the game was a recreational event that should allow for unlimited participants. With all of the rules adjustments made during his lifetime, Naismith was always pleased to report that the game continued to reflect the core values of his "13 original rules."

13 ORIGINAL RULES OF BASKETBALL

1. The ball may be thrown in any direction with one or both hands.
2. The ball may be batted in any direction with one or both hands. (Never with the fist)
3. A player cannot run with the ball. The player must throw it from the spot on which he catches it, allowances to be made for a man who catches the ball when running, if he tries to stop.
4. The ball must be held by the hands. The arms or body must not be used for holding it.
5. No shouldering, holding, pushing, tripping or striking in any way the person of an opponent shall be allowed; the first infringement of this rule by any player shall come as a foul, the second shall disqualify him until the next goal is made, or, if there was evident intent to injure the person, for the whole of the game, no substitute allowed.
6. A foul is striking the ball with the fist, violation of rule 3, 4 and such as described in rule 5.
7. If either side makes 3 consecutive fouls it shall count as a goal for the opponents (consecutive means without the opponents in the meantime making a foul)
8. A goal shall be made when the ball is thrown or batted from the grounds into the basket and stays there, providing those defending the goal do not touch or disturb the goal. If the ball rests on the edges and the opponent moves the basket, it shall count as a goal.
9. When the ball goes out of bounds, it shall be thrown into the field of play by the person touching it. He has a right to hold it unmolested for five seconds. In case of a dispute, the umpire shall throw it straight into the field. The thrower-in is allowed five seconds; if he holds it longer it shall go to the opponent. If any side persists in delaying the game, the umpire shall call a foul on that side.
10. The umpire shall be the judge of the men and shall note the fouls and notify the referee when three consecutive fouls have been made. He may have the power to disqualify men according to rule 5.
11. The referee shall be the judge of the ball and decide when the ball is in play, in bounds, to which side it belongs, and shall keep the time. He shall decide when a goal has been made and keep account of the goals, with any other duties that are usually performed by a referee.
12. The time shall be two fifteen minute halves, with five minutes rest between.
13. The side making the most goals in that time shall be declared the winner. In the event of a draw the game may, by agreement of the captains, be continued until another goal is made.

While the YMCA and others were jockeying for position as designated governing leader of basketball, the first basketball game between two colleges occurred—but, by which schools? Yale University had the honor of the first recorded victory, defeating the University of Pennsylvania 32-10. But others will argue that the first official game between colleges took place in Wisconsin; or was between the University of Chicago and the University of Iowa; or even in Canada between the University of Toronto and the Toronto YMCA School. Frankly, no one really knows who played first, when or where, but does it really matter? The game at the collegiate level simply started exploding in popularity.

It was at this point of his work that Naismith faced a crossroads in his personal life and career. The YMCA was his conduit for promoting the importance of physical fitness around the country, but a desire to return to teaching and the fertile ground that was the university campus was calling. When the University of Kansas offered him a position as assistant director of the gymnasium and coordinator of the campus convocations and prayer program, he was afforded an opportunity to explore his internal level of interest in both the areas of ministry and physical education. As his efforts at KU gained momentum, he made the decision to take his ideas and his dedication to the human form to the University of Kansas Physical Education program. It would be years before Naismith became involved with the game of basketball again.

Throughout his time at KU, Naismith shared many responsibilities, and following a two-year sabbatical in France as the nominated and elected Secretary of the International YMCA, he returned to spend 15 years as the Director of Physical Education at the university. In 1909, he became a full professor of physical education. These years were committed to concentrating on teaching physical education and sending his graduates into the world to promote the healthy lifestyle. Even with his focus on teaching and the effort to separate himself from his invention, many students and coaches would approach Naismith about basketball.

"Dr. Naismith taught us more than just basketball, but we were always jumping on him to talk more basketball. He just didn't want to do it," wrote John McLendon, who learned the game from Naismith before becoming a legendary coach years later. However, McLendon couldn't play at KU because he was black. "Naismith is the reason I went to Kansas. I heard that's where he was teaching and I wanted to learn the game from the inventor. But he was more into physical education. He couldn't imagine anybody coaching basketball unless they had studied kinesiology, sociology, social pathology, and anatomy. He wanted a person prepared to develop the entire individual."

The umbilical cord between Naismith and the game would never be completely severed and, continuing his role as the consummate professional, he was convinced once again to take an active role in basketball. For several years, he added the responsibilities of athletic director and head coach to his teaching responsibilities. (Although he laughed at one of his students, Phog Allen, when Allen brought up the idea of "coaching" the game of basketball.)

Since the coaching concept was foreign to Naismith, in the storied history of Jayhawks basketball, he is the only coach to leave KU with a coaching record showing more losses (60) than wins (55). Naismith would often choose to officiate the games that his team played because he was much more concerned how the game was administered than how it was played in competitive settings.

After two more years of coaching the team, officiating the games and performing his administrative duties, Naismith had had enough. His administrative record at KU was growing more impressive. With many excellent appointments, the development of many lesser-known sports and the building of the state-of-the-art physical education building, he was ready once again to focus his attention on his physical education duties. With the completion of Robinson Hall, the new $100,000 complex that featured state of the art locker rooms, a swimming pool, a 3,000-seat basketball gymnasium and a training area for the football team, Naismith took his leave. He was now a full professor in physical education with the finest teaching and athletics facility west of the Mississippi River.

In spite of a lifetime of modesty and some efforts to the contrary, Naismith's legacy at Springfield College and the University of Kansas has grown with the passage of time. He was always surprised at the popularity of basketball and did not really live long enough to experience the impact the game of basketball had at so many different levels.

"Basket ball is especially adapted for high schools, as it develops those traits which should be developed at that time of life," he wrote. "It is individualistic and at the same time it encourages cooperation; it develops the reflexes which must be developed at that time, if at all, in the ordinary individual. It can be played with few men and is inexpensive."

Naismith refused to allow the game to be named in his honor (many wanted it to be called "Naismith-ball") and would choose not to patent the game that he had invented. In all of his lifetime, he lived to a meager standard, but rather than gain any monetary reward, he willed the game to the players and coaches who followed. Thanks largely to a year-long effort, Naismith was honored for his invention at the 1936 Olympic Games in Germany.

"The happiest moment of my life," Naismith once told Phog Allen, "came in 1936, when I attended the Olympic Games in Berlin and saw the game of basketball played for the first time in international Olympic competition."

A year later, in 1937, Naismith and Emil Liston, Athletic Director at Baker University, were asked by Kansas City business leaders to develop an activity that might showcase college basketball. They developed a plan for a basketball tournament that would feature small colleges and universities from around the nation. This tournament would quickly grow in stature and would actually be the flagship event for the National Association of Intercollegiate Basketball (NAIB) that would later become the National Association of Intercollegiate Athletics (NAIA).

This event, which integrated college basketball in 1948, remains an annual tournament that continues to attract thousands of fans from Kansas City and the nation with great fanfare. Although it has moved locations—both in terms of arenas in Kansas City as well as a brief stint in Tulsa, Oklahoma—the NAIA men's basketball tournament is still played in the same building where it began in 1937, Municipal Auditorium.

On November 28, 1939, Dr. James Naismith died at his home in Lawrence, Kansas, from a heart attack.

As you read through this book, you will occasionally come across profiles of coaches who are presently working a college basketball sideline. These coaches will have coached anywhere from 200 to 1,200 games in their careers and will have taken at least one team to the NCAA Elite Eight or beyond. Some of these coaches will be easily recognized and some will be little known to the casual fan, but they are all successful at the elite level of college basketball.

Several years in the future, when someone writes a sequel to this book, this group will provide the next wave of GUARDIANS OF THE GAME. Coaches who have excelled on and off the court, provided mentoring to young coaches and worked diligently within the NABC to provide a level of leadership exhibited by their mentors: Allen, Meanwell, Rupp, Iba, Wooden, McLendon, Holman, Bunn, Smith, Knight, Thompson and others that set the level of excellence for them to emulate as young coaches.

SPLITTING THE POST

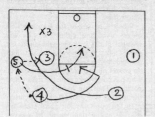

When 4 cuts right toward the right guard 2, the split is up the middle. The left forward 5 is the third cutter, because the ball was passed in from his side of the court. We have the first cutter 4 going right, the second cutter 2 going left, and the third cutter 5 coming back right. The weak side forward 1 comes back as a safety. The fourth step is to a third cutter instead of a guard. Also, we want to insure that the weak side forward 1 comes out on defense when both guards cut.

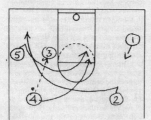

The last step — putting the five offensive men out on the court and letting them run through dummy scrimmage without a defense. We have them weave and exchange places to learn the cuts from the guard and forward positions. The center can be on the same side of the ball, or he can be opposite, and move to meet it. We also add a weak side play. The line-up is the same. Then too, we add inside and outside rolls, where the guards follow their passes after they pass into the forward. The guards and forwards are doing exactly what they did in warm-up drills. If they go inside, the forward drives over the middle and the center comes high to give the forward another pick. Then the center rolls to the basket. When the guard goes outside the forward he gets a return pass. The center comes high again, and the forward uses him as a block. He comes low to receive a pass from the guard if he is open. Finally, we add variations by inserting some picks, but the resultant changes are minor. ∎

So You Really Want To Be A Coach?

Bill Foster, Utah.

The title and the picture speak for themselves.
1973 NABC *Coaches Clinic* magazine

"BASKETBALL IDES OF MARCH"

By H. V. Porter
1940's

The gym lights gleam like a beacon beam
And a million motors hum
In a goodwill fight on a Friday Night;
For basketball beckons, "Come!"
A sharp-shooting mite is king tonight.
The Madness of March is running.
The winged-feet fly, the ball sails high
And field goal hunters are gunning.

The colors clash as silk suits flash
And race on a shimmering floor.
Repressions die, and partisans vie
In a goal acclaiming roar.
On Championship Train toward a holy grail,
All fans are birds of a feather.
It's fiesta night and cares lie light
When the air is full of leather.

Since time began, the instincts of man
Prove cave and current man kin.
On tournament night the sage and the wight
Are relatives under the skin.
It's festival time sans reason or rhyme
But with nation-wide appeal.
In a cyclone of hate, our ship of state
Rides high on an even keel.

With war nerves tense, the final defense
Is the courage, strength and will
In a million lives where freedom thrives
And liberty lingers still.
Let dictators clash and empires crash
'Neath a bloody victory arch!
Let our boys tread where hate is dead,
In the happy Madness of March!

Courtesy of Illinois State High School Athletic Association

Dr. Forrest "Phog" Allen
(The Father of Basketball Coaching)

BOOK ONE

THE BEGINNING

PHOG ALLEN AND THE FORMATION OF THE NATIONAL ASSOCIATION OF BASKETBALL COACHES OF THE UNITED STATES (NABC)

In 1927, unlike similar sports organizations, the National Association of Basketball Coaches became nationally prominent almost immediately and virtually by accident. This is quite remarkable when considering the era and what was important to Americans in those days. National news at that time spread according to urgency and interest, with news moving west to east generally in a slower process than east to west.

The journey, if you will, of the news of the NABC, started in Independence, Kansas, just after the turn of the century.

Dr. Forrest "Phog" Allen, the NABC founder and first president, is often identified as a cantankerous, unbending entrepreneur with a priority list that included him first, and everything and everybody else second. There is a great deal of truth to him being cantankerous and certainly to him as an entrepreneur, but more importantly, there is no doubt in his love for basketball and for the players he coached at Independence High School, Baker University, Central Missouri State, Haskell Indian School, and the University of Kansas.

"The year after I graduated, I had the opportunity to serve as assistant coach with Dick Harp to Dr. Allen," said legendary North Carolina coach Dean Smith. "Those two had a tremendous influence on my thinking as a beginning basketball coach. I could never be the motivator that Dr. Allen demonstrated to be time and time again. Well before I became one of his students in the early 1950s, he served as a hero to thousands and thousands of Kansans. My father, Alfred Smith, coached all sports at Emporia High School. When I was in junior high, Dad invited Dr. Allen to speak at the athletic banquet. I had never heard a man talk the way he could and move people to action as he did in that banquet speech. Dr. Allen was a gifted individual, who made the most of his gifts to help others in his many, many years of influence."

Phog Allen is recognized in basketball circles as the pioneer, the "father," of basketball coaching. Some argue that Allen even invented basketball coaching. In addition, he designed the mold for the coaching "rock stars" in the years that followed. He is said to be the first person "paid" to coach basketball in the United States, have the first shoe contract with shoes that were actually named after him, and was instrumental in establishing college basketball as a marketable "big event" on a national stage. He led the charge to put basketball in the Olympics, and finally succeeded with the 1936 Games in Berlin. There were events called regional championships, national championships and world championships that had his stamp on them, even though most were organized simply to make money.

His story, though, actually begins years before his destiny to lead the coaching profession to prosperity, which was preordained by those who inspired and angered him.

Forrest Allen was born in 1887 in Jamesport, Missouri, and a short time later moved to the Kansas City suburb of Independence, Missouri, where he was raised. Arguably, Allen could be identified as the second most famous resident of the city after our 33rd President, Harry S. Truman. Allen often mentioned his friendship with President Truman, but most historians suggest that the age difference (Harry was four years older) would have identified the relationship as a passing awareness rather than a friendship.

Allen's parents, William T. Allen and Mary Elexzene Perry, were married in 1874 and moved to Missouri in 1875. Both came from a long line of military stock with family members fighting in the Revolutionary War and Civil War.

Forrest was the fourth of six sons who all relished competing in sports of all types. Homer, Elmer, Harry, Forrest, Hubert and Richard spanned a 15-year period, but youngest to oldest were usually a tight knit group. The Allen brood was very athletic with several of the brothers having acquired reputations as athletes prior to Forrest arriving on the sports scene. Harry Allen, always known as Pete, became a role model for his younger brother and was a major reason Forrest decided very early on, and against his parents' wishes, that athletics was where he wanted to earn his living.

As Blair Kerkhoff wrote in his biography of Allen: "Forrest was ten when he would watch his brother spend an afternoon winging a baseball for hours against a knothole on the side of the Allen barn. Later, Forrest couldn't be talked into catching Pete's fastballs, but his younger brother Hubert slipped on an oversized mitt and become a battery mate. Hubert went on to become an outstanding tennis player, winning many regional tournaments."

William Allen was constantly complaining about spending family income to buy new shoes for the competitive son, who played all sports. Individually, each Allen brother seemed to excel in a different sport, but Forrest played them all. Pete's basketball career began with being assigned the "checker" position, which meant he was called on to check opponents into concrete posts that were common in gymnasiums then.

Both Forrest and Pete had abbreviated careers under Naismith, but were never able to be teammates. The brothers did, however, play together on a touring team called the Amazing Allen Brothers, competing for years throughout the Midwest with remarkable success.

"We played for five years and lost only one game," Hubert Allen remembered in 1974. "Forrest was one of the best players I had ever seen play basketball. He was always the best all-around athlete of them all."

Forrest spent his grade-school years protecting himself from his older brothers and took these lessons to the court. He played for all-comers and against all-comers with his eyes firmly focused on the best in the business. With no distinct governing bodies controlling basketball, Forrest played for several area teams in the same seasons and was regularly traveling by train to meet commitments. In addition to creating a continual stir in Midwestern basketball circles, he was working two jobs to pay the bills. All of this travel and personal hardship paid off when Allen was selected as captain of the 1904 "Blue Diamonds" basketball team from the Kansas City Athletic Club, one of the most prestigious teams in the area.

Allen's legend and influence were remarkable already when he took the legend one stop further.

As the story goes, a group known as the Buffalo Germans, an AAU team from the Buffalo, New York, YMCA, had made a remarkable run with numerous championships. (The director of the Buffalo YMCA, Dr. Fred Burkhardt, learned the game of basketball at the International YMCA Training School from Dr. James Naismith.) The Germans made sports history from 1895 until they stopped competing in 1929. For three seasons, 1908-11, the Germans won 111 consecutive games. They were credited with being the "best team of the period" while winning games on grass wearing cleats, winning a game 134-0 and establishing an AAU Championship legacy during their existence. Let's put it this way: the Buffalo Germans were so good that they are one of five teams to be inducted into the Naismith Memorial Basketball Hall of Fame.

During the 1904 season, the Germans won the National AAU championship, the Pan-American Games and all of the games in a scheduled tournament that ran in conjunction with the Olympic Games—before basketball was introduced as an Olympic sport. At that same time, Allen was leading the KCAC team to a remarkable season that included a victory over the University of Kansas, 27-10. According to Allen's book, "My Basket-ball Bible," published in 1924, he was the captain of the Blue Diamonds and was picked as "All-American Guard."

Always the businessman, Allen challenged the Buffalo Germans to a three-game series in Kansas City and, consistent with his personality, guaranteed all of the team's expenses with the agreement to compete. He made these guarantees without KCAC permission or pre-arranged support. However, he proved his business and marketing acumen when the event succeeded in identifying Kansas City as a major event venue and raising enough to pay all of the expenses and clear a healthy profit. The match was scheduled for March of 1905, and billed as the "World's Championship of Basketball."

Not long after official documents were signed, the AAU provided sanction for the event, giving the winner claim to the title, AAU National Champions.

"The Convention Hall series will be among the most important ever played in the West," Naismith, never comfortable commenting on basketball in a competitive setting, told *The Kansas City Star* newspaper. "The tendency in the East is to play a more open game than in the West and the large size of the Convention half-court may give the Easterners an advantage. If Kansas City's teamwork is on par with its individual players I think the Olympic Champions will have their work cut out for them."

Indeed. The first two games of the series were split and the only topic of agreement was the poor quality of the officiating. The Buffalo Germans, dissatisfied with the calls in game two, requested that Naismith officiate the final and deciding match. He agreed only after assurances by both teams that the game would be officiated by the official YMCA rules of the game.

The final game went to the KCAC club by a final score of 45-14. Basketball was played at the time with a designated foul shooter. Records show that Allen hit 17 foul shots for the Blue Diamonds.

"I was much delighted with the interest shown in the game and personally I believe that the time is coming when basketball will compete successfully with football for popular flavor," Naismith told *The Kansas City Star* a few days after the contest. "In inventing the game, I worked on the following theory as the basis for the game: football is rough because the players are tackled; the players are tackled because they run with the ball. So with this idea always in mind that the players must not run with the ball, I worked out the details of the game. Certainly basketball has a great future before it, if it is played in the same manner that it was the other night."

Incidentally, remember how the Buffalo Germans requested Naismith referee the deciding third game? *The Star* newspaper reported after the game that "Referee Naismith was very strict and Buffaloes were penalized again and again."

After the series had ended, with Allen adding to his local hero status, Naismith approached him about attending the University of Kansas. Allen always intended to attend KU, but this discussion made the decision even easier.

Allen was a smash with the Jayhawks, but his playing days were short-lived. He spent one season as a player at the University of Kansas (1905-1906), and developed a relationship with the game's inventor. His playing career as a Jayhawk ended with a need to "find a job and pay the bills." During that one year at KU, Allen honed his considerable talent by playing for two other teams. He continued his relationship with the KCAC team and suited up for the Woodmen of Independence when time and schedules permitted. With Kansas finishing at 12 –7 for the season, Allen was voted captain for the next year, and Naismith was disappointed to learn of Allen's decision to leave. An extended stay would probably have gone a long way in improving Naismith's sub-par coaching record.

Allen often acted as the player-coach on his teams. In 1907, he ran into Naismith in one of the buildings at KU, and told his mentor that he'd like to make a living coaching basketball. According to Allen in his book "Coach 'Phog' Allen's Sport Stories," here's how the exchange happened:

"With a merry laugh as he met me in the hall, he said, 'I've got a good joke on you, you bloody beggar.' He set me back temporarily. I wondered what I had been doing. Then he laughed aloud again, continuing, 'They want you to coach basketball down at Baker.' With surprise, I said, 'What's so funny about that?'

He replied, 'Why, you can't coach basketball, you play it.'

"I countered with these words, 'Well, you certainly can teach free-throwing. You can teach the boys to pass at angles and run in curves.

"The inventor of basketball actually had no conception that the game could be coached."

Phog Allen took this as a challenge. He became coach at Baker University. Records of the time indicate this was the first contract agreeing to pay a basketball coach. This remains a great story, but there is no real proof to any of it, except that no one has come forward to refute the statement. Phog was actually assisting Baker during his playing days at KU, teaching the boys basketball a couple of nights a week.

During the next four years, Allen coached high school football and basketball, three college basketball teams, held two non-sports related jobs, continued to play basketball for several teams, and found time to marry Bessie Milton. A typical day for him would begin at one of his jobs, and then later in the day, he would be off to coach one of his high school teams, before finally boarding a train and heading to one of the colleges to finish the day. This work schedule, driven by an insatiable love of sports and need for money, would drive Phog Allen for the remainder of his life.

In 1907, James Naismith quit coaching at KU, completed building the finest physical education facility west of the Mississippi, and presided over the birth of the Missouri Valley Conference. Joining Missouri, Nebraska, Iowa and Washington University of St. Louis, KU was now entrenched in the world of major college athletics. This change was not to Naismith's liking and he knew he had to find the right coach to face the obvious challenges of the new conference. The best possible person happened to be the one he laughed at for wanting to coach: Phog Allen.

Unbelievably, Allen coached both the KU and Baker University basketball teams that year and had amazing success. Baker finished 13-6, while KU finished 18-6 overall and 6-0 in the Missouri Valley Conference, winning the first of many conference championships. During that first year at KU and Baker, he also coached the football and basketball teams at Independence High School to very respectable results. The following year he coached KU to a 25-3 record and a second Missouri Valley championship, while coaching Haskell Indian School to a record of 27-5, winning 19-of-24 road games and the Aboriginal National Championship.

During his brief coaching career, Allen found that he had an affinity for diagnosing and treating athletic injuries. At this point in his career, his entrepreneurial spirit kicked in and he often noted: "A coach who could treat player's injuries would have an advantage." So, after two very successful years at the helm of the program, Allen would once again leave Naismith and KU to pursue personal interests.

Allen enrolled in the Central College of Osteopathy in Kansas City. He graduated three years later with a degree and added the title Doctor to his name. While attending Central, Allen used his athletic reputation and his studies to assist high school athletes with athletic injuries. Dr. Allen had created the first sports medicine clinic established with the athlete specifically in mind. This was a time when hawkers were selling miracle elixirs to heal all ailments. "Doc" Allen was simply offering a different option. In Kansas City, his diagnosis and treatment were being performed on high school stars with recognized success. In 1910, he treated Kansas City's greatest athlete at the time, Casey Stengel, who would later become a major-league baseball player and one of the most successful managers in professional baseball history. Stengel, who was actually a dentist in Kansas City before winning seven World Series titles as a manager, recommended Dr. Allen whenever asked. At one point, Stengel even sent Mickey Mantle to Kansas City for a diagnosis of an undisclosed illness that was affecting his performance.

As Allen was completing his schooling in 1912, he was summoned to the University of Illinois, where a reporter for the *Champaign Daily News* wrote:

"Dr. F.C. Allen, miracle man. At least that's the way 35 athletes at the university, formerly, more or less injured, look at him. Dr. Allen comes from Warrensburg, MO, where he is athletic director at Missouri State Normal College, and his specialties are putting dislocated bones back in place, easing strained tendons and reducing sprains on the double quick. That in short is what he did for the 35 injured performers. 'I like to coach football and fix the fellows up,' said the miracle man. 'I believe that I could make money practicing in some big city, but I wouldn't leave my position in Warrensburg for anything.' "

Dr. Forrest "Phog" Allen may be the only physician who graduated from medical school without having graduated from high school or college. His high school attendance is well documented, with no record of a diploma, and his work at KU was far too short to achieve any academic results. This did not hurt his status as his national reputation as a "sports-injury healer" followed him for years. Many professional athletes suffering serious, career-threatening injuries arrived in Kansas seeking his diagnosis and treatment.

In 1950, Johnny Mize, Yankees first baseman who later was inducted into the Baseball Hall of Fame, was seemingly washed up and relegated to the minor leagues for the remainder of the season. After treatment from Dr. Allen, he made a complete recovery and hit 25 home runs and had 72 runs batted in.

"I sure wouldn't be here if I couldn't throw and I give Dr. Allen complete credit for enabling me to throw," Mize told the *Topeka Daily Capital*. "When I started going to Dr. Allen, I couldn't throw at all. I saw him several times. I don't know what it was in my shoulder that kept me from throwing and nobody else seemed to. But Dr. Allen did. Whatever it was, he found it. He's quite a swell guy. I think he's one of the finest men I ever knew."

Allen's treatment wasn't confined to pro athletes, though. He treated many of the Jayhawks—and even some of the Jayhawks' rivals.

The 1923 Kansas team photo, with Naismith and Allen in suits and just behind and to the left of the coaches is Adolph Rupp. This team won the Missouri Valley Conference (16-0) and the Helms Foundation Championship.

COACH PROFILE

RICK BARNES –
UNIVERSITY OF TEXAS
(NABC MEMBER 28 YEARS)

"Obviously we are extremely pleased with the effort of our guys in the classroom and on the court this past year, especially when you consider that our regular-season schedule affects both academic semesters and how much class time is missed during our team play in the Big 12 Conference and the NCAA Tournament." (Six Longhorns named to 2008 Big 12 All-Academic Team.)

It's always been easy to point to certain schools and identify them with certain sports. Texas, for instance, has been known as a football school. That is, until Rick Barnes became the Longhorns' basketball coach in 1998.

What makes Barnes so successful? Besides his on-court coaching, Barnes is an outstanding recruiter. Rick Barnes is one of the few who has maintained a consistent level of excellence, not only at Texas, but also across his career. When you evaluate the career of a coach, his true ability to recruit and retain his athletes will be evident in the missing roller coaster highs and lows evident in many programs.

Barnes focuses on both talent and character. In 2008, the Longhorns enjoyed academic success with six players selected for the Big 12 All-Academic team. The Longhorns boast a team GPA higher than 3.0.

Barnes, a native of Hickory, North Carolina, honed his coaching skills with assistant positions at North State Academy, Davidson College, George Mason University, Alabama, and Ohio State.

He got his first head coaching position in a return to George Mason in 1987-88. After one successful season there, Barnes took on the rebuilding of the Providence program. Barnes led the Friars to postseason play (NIT and NCAA) in all but one of his six years. Sensing his greatness, Clemson hired Barnes, and wouldn't regret it. Barnes took the Tigers to a school-first, three-straight NCAA Tournaments before Texas hired him away.

During his first decade, Barnes, the Big 12's Coach of the Year three times, led Texas to the NCAA Tournament 10 consecutive years, earning one Final Four and two Elite Eight appearances.

Thanks to Rick Barnes, the Texas Longhorns can be mentioned in the same conversation as basketball powerhouses such as Duke, Kansas, North Carolina, and UCLA. Thanks to Rick Barnes, Texas is no longer just a "football school."

"If I hadn't seen Phog after my sophomore season I may have been through as a player," said former Missouri quarterback Phil Snowden, who led the Tigers to the 1959 Orange Bowl, after being out of the game with severe shoulder problems. "No question Phog Allen saved my career as an athlete."

After finally graduating from an attended institution, Dr. Forrest Allen took his healing and coaching talents to Central Missouri State. For seven successful years, including winning every conference game in three sports in 1912, he honed his coaching skills. The story changed considerably in 1914 when the Missouri Intercollegiate Athletic Association (MIAA) voted Central Missouri State out of the conference. Some of the issues included Allen's 76-0 route of The Normal School of Kirksville and unsportsmanlike practices that included stealing signs and profanity-laced action on the field of play. Despite being surrounded by rumors of ineligible players and other unfounded allegations, Dr. Hawkins, Central Missouri's president, awarded Allen a new contract, partly based upon the institution's faculty passing a resolution of support.

Discontent and war interrupted Allen's career at CMS when he joined the war effort in 1918.

Upon his return from the war, Allen resumed his duties at CMS, but recognized quickly that too many things had changed during his time away. This unsettled environment, and a feeling that his time had passed, persuaded Allen to resign his position and return to his medical practice full-time. Rumors persisted that the CMS Regents, in conjunction with area physicians, strongly suggested that he should be an administrator and coach and discontinue his medical practice. As was usually the case, he chose the direction less traveled and opened his Warrensburg medical practice full-time.

In 1919, not long after resuming his medical duties, Allen became one of two candidates for the position of Athletic Director at the University of Kansas. The other candidate, Bert Kennedy, was a practicing dentist and KU football coach with the highest winning percentage in school history. It was widely reported that James Naismith was promoting Kennedy due to concerns with Allen's ability to stay for the long term. Similarly, there was a major push by KU alumni for a "football man," but Phog Allen was back on campus with an athletic council vote of 7-2 and complete support of the chancellor, Frank Strong.

Of no surprise to anyone close to the program, the KU basketball coach, Karl Schlademan, who also was the school's track coach, resigned after only one game into the 1919 season. Allen took the reins and, as they say, the rest is history. So much for thoughts of him exiting soon. Dr. F.C. "Phog" Allen coached the Jayhawks for 39 seasons (including 1907-09), compiling a record of 590-219. During that time, he won 24 conference championships, two Helms Foundation national championships (pre-NCAA Tournament), and one NCAA national title (1952).

A sidelight of some note occurred in 1920, when a football coach hired by Dr. Allen was not released from his contractual obligation and could not come to Lawrence and coach the team. In his final football coaching effort, Coach Allen may have provided the University of Kansas with one of the greatest football seasons in its 100-year football history. The final record of 5-2-1 was only part of the story. Stealing an idea from his dear friend Naismith, after having set many records and celebrating many inconceivable victories, Allen used his personality and the enthusiasm generated by the football success to raise the necessary funds to build a football stadium for the university.

"When I returned to Kansas in 1919 as director of athletics, there was but one motive in mind and that was to build a stadium in memory of Tommy Johnson, Kansas' greatest athlete," Allen wrote in 1943. "But the World War had just finished and there were 129 Kansas men and women who made the supreme sacrifice in the First World War and, naturally, the stadium was given the name of the World War Memorial in the name of these heroes and heroines. But if I had it to do of my own experiences and relationships, had the war not happened, there would have been only one name on that stadium, and that would have been 'Tommy Johnson Memorial Stadium.' He deserved the honor."

By the way, another interesting sidebar about KU's football stadium: one of the people who helped build the stadium, at least for a few weeks one summer, was a high school kid from Indiana named John Wooden. According to Wooden, Allen tried to convince him to attend KU. Of course, Wooden ended up playing at Purdue before eventually embarking on a remarkable coaching career at UCLA.

During Allen's second tenure as KU basketball coach, he took the role of coaching basketball to an entirely new level. Motivated by other successful coaches around the country, he used his famous work ethic to build a basketball legacy that is still relished in Lawrence.

Allen's coaching success provided many opportunities to teach basketball at coaching schools and clinics around the country. He would never fail to mention his knowledge of sports medicine, nutrition and other training ideas that were not necessarily staples of the sports world. Allen would often trade information with the likes of Knute Rockne, Amos Alonzo Stagg, and Pop Warner. His approach was always thought to be ahead of the times.

As the game's popularity spread, it seemed that the rules were in a constant state of instability. Coaches would get comfortable with a competition strategy and then the NCAA, AAU, or the YMCA would change something significant. In 1927, the above-mentioned governing bodies voted the "dribble" out of the game. The Joint Rules Committee voted to limit it to one bounce, according to NABC historian Ed Hickox.

This movement was led by legendary Wisconsin and Missouri coach, and Allen antagonist, Dr. Walter E. Meanwell, who believed that "the game moved better with

Deletion of the Dribble —

Back in April of 1929 the national Basket Ball Rules Committee eliminated the dribble from the game of Basket Ball.

Knute Rockne and I were speaking at the Drake University Field House to the National Educational Association. He spoke on the Pedagogy of Foot Ball and I upon the Pedagogy of Basket Ball.

The next morning after the fatal mistake of the Rules Committee, I lashed out at the "their autocratic and high handed action."

There was at that time no organization of Basket Ball Coaches.

I called a meeting of all College and University Coaches two weeks hence, at the date of the Annual Drake Relays in Des Moines Ia. The Coaches at their meeting forthright

Phog Allen shares his memory of beginning the NABC.

several short passes." While many were willing to accept the earlier changes as necessary, or important for the game's growth, this one hit a nerve. In a scheduled speech before the American Physical Education Association, Allen threw away his prepared remarks and confronted this abuse of power by the sport's self-proclaimed governing bodies. The intensity in the address was recognized by many of the journalists who knew Dr. Allen and attended the Drake University convention.

The basketball coaches around the country were still competing in regional organizations and had little knowledge of their counterparts across the United States. There had been little cross-region competition by college teams and the traveling AAU organizations were not embraced within the fraternity of college and university programs. This was the first attempt to bring basketball regions together to face a common problem. Rules issues had been a problem from the very beginning and 1927 was no different. Regional rules interpretations were rampant and the coaches' response was unique.

As the news of Allen's speech hit the wire service and word of the very specific attack spread, the response was unprecedented. In a short period of time, Allen received numerous telegrams, some accounts reporting as many as 200, from coaches around the country supporting his view of the governance and of the rule change.

Allen developed a plan of attack and invited all who could come, to a meeting at the Kansas Relays being held at Drake University. Several prominent coaches made the journey and the assembled group elected Phog Allen chairman of the basketball coaching fraternity. The intensity of the meeting was a reflection of the fact that this Joint Rules Committee was a self-appointed group, with only two of its 20 members actively coaching the game.

The coaches assembled at the Kansas Relays voted to schedule an additional emergency meeting for June 10, 1927, at the Auditorium Hotel in Chicago. This meeting would be the first-ever recorded by the National Association of Basketball Coaches of the United States.

"The National Association of Basketball Coaches was born out of necessity, sired by courage, and fostered by far-sighted confidence in the basic greatness of this game of basketball," NABC historian Hickox said. "We are fortunate today that forward-looking basketball coaches had the courage and willingness to take responsibility, the energy and interest to give it expression, the optimism and confidence to implement it, and the continued forcefulness to carry on in the face of the seeming indifference of some of their colleagues."

Many of the prominent coaches around the country made an appearance in Chicago. Surprisingly, so did many of the not so prominent coaches who loved the game and were concerned about the change. This emotional group of coaches built the structure of the NABC, providing a constitution and identifying the group's first slogan or motto: *"To further dignify the basketball coaching profession,"* which, for 80 years, has been the message that brings the NABC electorate back to the center, when occasionally drifting off the stated course. The officers elected at that meeting included vice presidents Craig Ruby of Illinois, Lew Andreas of Syracuse, and Nibs Price of California. President Phog Allen was re-elected for the following year, and his first order of business was to nominate his mentor and the game's inventor, Dr. James Naismith, as the NABC's honorary president.

Not long after defeating the rules authorities, the coaches arrived in Chicago to officially christen their organization. The official name selected was the National Association of Basketball Coaches of the United States, and Phog Allen was officially crowned president for the first two years.

The early NABC Constitution included: "The objects and purpose of this association shall be:

1. To foster and encourage the playing of the game of basketball in accordance with the finest traditions of intercollegiate competition;
2. To require adherence at all times to the Basketball Coaches Code;
3. To maintain at all times a membership group which shall be representative of the various sections of the United States and, as such, conducive to the establishment of friendly contacts and good understanding between coaches of the different sections;
4. To promote constructive discussion and the dissemination of information relative to the game of basketball or its general welfare, or such aspects or phases thereof as may be of general interest; and in general
5. To further at all times the best interests and well being of the game of basketball, and to maintain it in its proper plane in the scheme of education."

Phog Allen was basketball's lightening rod, and because of his reputation and antagonist attitudes, he was able to present the NABC to a national audience in 1927.

As a writer with the Associated Press penned in 1950: "We've known Phog since way back when, and like him and admire his ability. He's out to win, and isn't averse to seeing his name in print. You just can't be neutral around the fiery Kansan. You either like him or can't stand him, and that is all right with him, as there's nothing neutral about him, either. After all, you can't get anywhere in neutral, and Phog has gone a long way."

From that day forward, the NABC paid particular attention to the direction of the game. The dribble rule, attacked with alarming intensity, never happened and "The Guardians of the Game" had made their first save. This intimidating force, displayed by the coaches, was the first of many successful endeavors that the NABC has launched to attempt to put a stop to bureaucratic foolishness within the game of basketball.

Within seven years after the group formed, college basketball took off on a national stage. The emphasis on competition was increasing and the media was constantly attempting to determine the nation's best. The Helms Foundation was providing awards, All-American teams and even selected the "national champion," even though no games were being contested to secure that honor. Times changed considerably when New York City and Madison Square Garden became the center of the college game.

When 16,000 rabid basketball fans attended double-headers sponsored by the New York City Sports Writers, even the

Basketball shoes have always been a money maker.
NCBA Championship, March 20-21, 1959

most knowledgeable fans were astonished. Even with the games being contested by relatively local teams, having 16,000 paying customers for a college basketball event was simply unheard of.

As these games gained in popularity and teams like Kentucky, Notre Dame and other prominent university programs began to participate, discussions began to be held about moving the action to the spring and offering a representative field from across the country. What was once thought of as a New York City event with little national interest, this talk of post-season participation began to gain support across the country. Word of the plans for this event spread rapidly and the NABC members were once again shocked into action.

"The college administrators from around the rest of the country had hastily arranged a regional playoff system, one planned out and administrated by Ohio State head coach Harold Olsen," Peter Bjarkman wrote in his book, *The Biographical History of Basketball.*

Never to be outdone and especially wary of the big-city coaches in the East, Allen was seriously motivated by this "happening" and urged the NABC to get ahead of the wave.

"I think this would be a very interesting experiment," Allen wrote in a letter to Everett Morris of the *New York Herald Tribune.* "I believe the effort will go a long way toward nationalizing the game and doing away with provincialism and sectional play. (New York promoter) Ned Irish has done a great job of building up basketball as a national sport in the minds of eastern people. Of course, the western people have been conscious of this fact for years."

Historians report that the NABC was envious of the success and used that motivation to form a committee to prepare a plan for a national tournament and make a presentation to the NCAA. During the formal proceedings of the 1938 NABC convention in Chicago, a committee of four coaches, Harold Olsen of Ohio State as chairman, Phog Allen of Kansas, John Bunn of Stanford, and A. C. "Dutch" Lonborg of Northwestern were charged to: "Start a National Tournament in cooperation with the National Collegiate Athletic Association (NCAA)."

GUARDIAN

HAROLD OLSEN
(NATIONAL TOURNAMENT
ARCHITECT, ENFORCER)

"If Naismith is the founding father of basketball and Phog Allen is the spiritual father of basketball coaching, then it is longtime Ohio State University coach Harold "Ole" Olsen who merits designation as "father" of college basketball's greatest showpiece– the NCAA postseason tournament."

—Author, Peter Bjarkman

Harold Olsen was born in Wisconsin in 1895. Consistent with many of basketball's early "Guardians," Olsen was a star in three sports at Rice Lake High School and led his teams to championship results. Olsen took his wide array of athletic skills to the University of Wisconsin where he played basketball for four seasons, gaining Big 10 honors.

After graduating from Wisconsin in 1917, Olsen was unsure of a direction and didn't really begin a career for a couple of years. When he finally focused on coaching, he took his first job at Rippon College, where he coached for two years. Finding a passion for coaching and some success at Rippon, Olsen set off for Ohio State University (OSU) and the Big 10. He had experienced success as a player in that conference and was confident that he could do the same as a coach. His confidence was well founded as he built a very enviable basketball program. His Buckeye teams would win five Big 10 Championships and would finish runner-up to Oregon in the very first National Basketball Tournament. It should noted that he was also the architect and tournament director of that same tournament.

Olsen expanded his influence as his success was recognized. He took a turn as Chairman of the Rules Committee and was sitting when the 10-second rule was implemented. He led the NABC during the 1932-1933 season and chaired the NABC committee that was appointed to create a national championship proposal to the NCAA. The proposal was accepted and a national tournament was first introduced in 1939.

After eight years as the National Tournament chairman, Olsen joined the 1948 United States Olympic Committee and completed his coaching career as a professional coach, leading the Chicago Stags during 1946-1949. He was inducted into the Naismith Memorial Hall of Fame as a contributor in 1959.

Harold Olsen took his appointment to the national tournament exploratory committee very seriously. He was assigned this responsibility and he would strive to fulfill his obligations with very meticulous leadership. Olsen left no stone unturned and it was this pre-planning phobia that allowed the first event to take place only five months after the NCAA would give its approval.

Although some of the more prominent coaches were against the idea, and for the first time we heard faculty mention, *"maybe the athletes will miss too much class time,"* the committee moved forward. The one caveat that came with the approval required the NABC to maintain the responsibility for operation of the national tournament.

As the 1939 *Basketball Guide* pointed out: "It is entirely fitting that the 'prestige' of college basketball should be supported, and demonstrated to the nation, by the colleges themselves, rather than this to be left to private promotion and enterprise. It was also fitting that the suggestion for such a tournament, under collegiate auspices, should come from the National Association of Basketball Coaches, an organization of college basketball coaches, which cooperates with the N.C.A.A. in seeking to improve and develop the game in the colleges."

It was only because of Olsen's intense preparation and attention to detail that the tournament schedule was distributed and the eligibility and playoff plan announced. The NABC committee presented a scenario that offered equal representation to everyone. The country was divided into eight regions with four on each side of the Mississippi River. The Eastern playoffs were scheduled for The Palestra in Philadelphia

COACH PROFILE

JIM BOEHEIM –
SYRACUSE UNIVERSITY
(NABC MEMBER 36 YEARS)

"I have no interest in pursuing anything else after I stop coaching basketball unless it is coaching little league."

Jim Boeheim has never played a college game, walked a sideline, or raised a trophy when the dominating color was not orange. He began his fascination with Syracuse University as a high school player, and he continues to pursue national championships with the Orangemen today.

Boeheim is unique in that the only place he has ever coached is Syracuse. This says a great deal about the coach and the university. Today's quick-fingered ADs are not as likely to allow a coach to strive for the pinnacle of success without actually reaching it. Boeheim led Syracuse to that pinnacle in New Orleans in 1987, only to have it snatched away, giving the championship to Bob Knight.

Boeheim began this quest for college basketball's Holy Grail as a player for Syracuse. In his senior year, he was elected as team captain and along with All-American Dave Bing, led Syracuse to a 22-6 record and an NCAA Tournament berth, but the championship would not be realized. After graduation, Boeheim played professional basketball for two years in the Eastern League, winning two league championships, before returning to Syracuse as a coach.

The uniqueness of coaching at one institution and achieving a book's worth of accolades is bested only by his success beating cancer. As a cancer survivor, Boeheim works tirelessly to promote cancer awareness and raise funds for NABC-sponsored "Coaches vs. Cancer," which has raised more than $30 million for cancer research.

Boeheim is approaching the 800-win plateau. He lost twice in the NCAA Finals before winning the National Championship in 2003. He was enshrined in the Naismith Memorial Basketball Hall of Fame in 2005.

Boeheim has also been a regular participant in the USA Basketball program. He was a member of Mike Krzyzewski's staff for the 2008 Olympic Team. And, as one of the few coaches who relies on a 2-3 zone defense almost exclusively, he's a valuable strategist in international competition. This expertise and reliance almost exclusively on zone defense has made him a popular clinic speaker and important teaching member of the USA Basketball staff.

and the Western playoffs at Treasure Island in San Francisco. Originally, the plan called for the championship game to be played in the Chicago Stadium, but the stadium was slow to respond to the NABC request and the game went to Newman Gymnasium at Northwestern University in Evanston, Illinois. Never to take chances, Olsen was quick to adjust because he knew they could not hold a tournament without an appropriate facility.

Phog Allen worked very hard to bring the Western version of the playoffs to Kansas City's Municipal Auditorium, but the National Association of Intercollegiate Basketball (which is now the NAIA) had already secured the facility for its national event. So the first college basketball playoffs went west. When the Chicago Stadium finally responded in the affirmative, the NABC decided that the publicity had been purchased and distribution was well along, making a change of venue impossible.

The best plans always meander through a myriad of problems before success can be declared, don't they? A perfect example was the Region Five playoffs for the right to participate in the 1939 National Championship Tournament. Original plans called for a playoff system consisting of games between the Big Six winner and the Missouri Valley winner to determine a representative. First, both leagues ended the regular season with multiple teams tied for the league championship. Following that, the University of Missouri faculty committee voted to keep the team home, using missed class time as the reason for non-participation. This created a cumbersome three-team tournament. When the dust had cleared in Oklahoma City, Oklahoma won out over Oklahoma A&M and Drake University. This playoff format created enough energy and interest, though, to be the only regional playoff that ended with financial success.

The next event that resulted in a favorable position for eventual champion Oregon was the 1939 invitation to Madison Square Garden. Stanford and its great player, Frank Luisetti, were originally scheduled to participate, but changed its plans because the team already had made several trips across the country. Stanford coach John Bunn recommended the Oregon Ducks to the NIT Chairman, Ned Irish. Reluctant, due to Oregon's lack of national reputation, Irish hesitated. Coach Howard Hobson, a talent scout for the New York Yankees, was in New York and made it a point to visit Ned Irish. This meeting got Oregon an invitation and Hobson a lifetime friend.

"Luckily, I had been working as a 'resident scout' for the New York Yankees, and had been invited by the Yanks, all expenses paid, to the World Series in Chicago and on to New York for scout meetings as a reward for helping sign on Yankee Joe Gordon," Hobson said. "Since I was also scouting Fordham for the Oregon football team, I thought I'd go to the World Series, scout Fordham, and arrange for the basketball team's appearance in Madison Square, all on the free, Yankee-paid ticket, satisfying Oregon budget concerns and at the same time making a strong impression on Irish."

After a convoluted array of playoff formats and financial woes, the Oregon Ducks beat Olsen's Ohio State Buckeyes in a hot and oppressive environment that included 5,500 paying customers. The 1939 Oregon Ducks were an interesting champion.

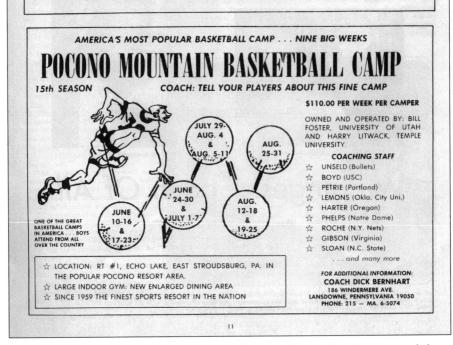

Basketball's Coaches' Creed

I BELIEVE that basketball has an important place in the general education scheme and pledge myself to cooperate with others in the field of education to so administer it that its value never will be questioned.

I BELIEVE that other coaches of this sport are as earnest in its protection as I am, and I will do all in my power to further their endeavors.

I BELIEVE that my own actions should be so regulated that at all times I will be a credit to my profession.

I BELIEVE that the members of the National Basketball Committee are capably expressing the rules of the game and will abide by these rules in both spirit and letter.

I BELIEVE in the exercise of the patience, tolerance, and diplomacy at my command in my relations with all players, co-workers, game officials and spectators.

I BELIEVE that the proper administration of this sport offers an effective laboratory method to develop in its adherents high ideals of sportsmanship; qualities of cooperation, courage, unselfishness and self control; desires for clean healthful living; and respect for wise discipline and authority.

I BELIEVE that those admirable characteristics, properly instilled by me through teaching and demonstration, will have a long carry-over and will aid each one connected with the sport to become a better citizen.

I BELIEVE in and will support all reasonable moves to improve athletic conditions, to provide for adequate equipment, and to promote the welfare of an increased number of participants.

(This creed was written by George Edwards, basketball coach at Missouri University, and was adopted by the National Association of Basketball Coaches during their 1932 convention and reaffirmed 1972 convention).

AMERICA'S MOST POPULAR BASKETBALL CAMP . . . NINE BIG WEEKS

POCONO MOUNTAIN BASKETBALL CAMP

15th SEASON   **COACH: TELL YOUR PLAYERS ABOUT THIS FINE CAMP**

$110.00 PER WEEK PER CAMPER

JULY 29-AUG. 4 & AUG. 5-11

AUG. 25-31

JUNE 24-30 & JULY 1-7

AUG. 12-18 & 19-25

JUNE 10-16 & 17-23

ONE OF THE GREAT BASKETBALL CAMPS IN AMERICA . . . BOYS ATTEND FROM ALL OVER THE COUNTRY

OWNED AND OPERATED BY: BILL FOSTER, UNIVERSITY OF UTAH AND HARRY LITWACK, TEMPLE UNIVERSITY.

COACHING STAFF
- ☆ UNSELD (Bullets)
- ☆ BOYD (USC)
- ☆ PETRIE (Portland)
- ☆ LEMONS (Okla. City Uni.)
- ☆ HARTER (Oregon)
- ☆ PHELPS (Notre Dame)
- ☆ ROCHE (N.Y. Nets)
- ☆ GIBSON (Virginia)
- ☆ SLOAN (N.C. State)
    . . . and many more

☆ LOCATION: RT #1, ECHO LAKE, EAST STROUDSBURG, PA. IN THE POPULAR POCONO RESORT AREA.

☆ LARGE INDOOR GYM: NEW ENLARGED DINING AREA

☆ SINCE 1959 THE FINEST SPORTS RESORT IN THE NATION

FOR ADDITIONAL INFORMATION:
COACH DICK BERNHART
186 WINDERMERE AVE.
LANSDOWNE, PENNSYLVANIA 19050
PHONE: 215 — MA. 6-5074

11

The National Association of Basketball Coaches of the United States has always worried about their national perception. 1971 NABC Coaches Clinic Program

Their unique style of play, including a continuous fast break, fatigued opponents and attracted talented players.

Many of the people attending the first championship game were coaches from around the country, supporting the NABC event. When the final books were approved, the event was a fiscal failure. The NABC was $2,531 in the red and had no internal funds to relieve this debt. After much discussion about the future of the event, the NCAA agreed to a loan to pay the debt in return for the NABC returning tournament responsibility to the NCAA for future championship events.

The NABC-sponsored national tournament of 1939 was the initial attempt by the coaches to provide a basketball rallying point for national pride. From that perspective it was successful. Although their hearts were in the right place, money, facilities, location, and publicity would be their undoing. Many of the 5,500 in attendance were members of the NABC and the ticket to the event was part of their membership dues. This fact alone demonstrates how stretched they were for capital, and with no sponsor or broadcast contract, the event was doomed for fiscal failure before it was even staged.

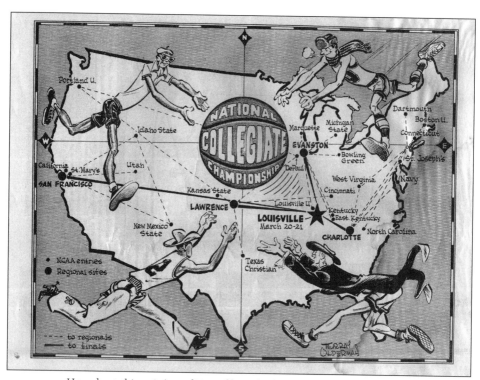

How about this artist's rendition of how the basketball fan might view the NCAA National Championship?
National Collegiate Basketball Championship, March 20-21, 1959

The concept of the national tournament, prepared by Harold Olsen and sold to the NCAA, was very sound. Everyone in attendance from the NABC and the NCAA recognized the quality of the event that Olsen had provided for the participants and the attending fans. The leadership was not lost on anyone and Coach Olsen would continue to lead the tournament for the first eight years of its existence. Many will attest to Olsen's intensity for saving the event and even scheduling the second for 1940. The NCAA was reluctant to sanction a tournament for 1940 and the members of the NABC Tournament Committee were reluctant to schedule an event for 1940, but with some prodding by its chairman, it was agreed to try again. Based on a guarantee of fiscal success by none other than Phog Allen, the motions were passed, in return for the NABC/NCAA identifying Kansas City as the host venue. This decision was actually made easier because of Phog's history of big-event success and the region's support and recorded profit after the 1939 playoffs in Oklahoma City.

Olsen and Allen proved a worthy partnership when the 1940 tournament turned out to be a great success. The NABC was able to erase the debt with the NCAA, provide operational cash for both organizations, and provide some travel cost assistance to the participating teams ($750 each). Olsen had proven his continued leadership was warranted and Allen had proven once again that his legend as a "big event master" was a true statement to his capabilities.

It was actually after this 1940 event that the NABC would make good on their word to hand the tournament back to the NCAA and would do so with few concessions. In hindsight, this is the most lopsided deal in the history of college athletics. The deal that was suggested between the two organizations included committee membership, tickets and a five-percent cut of the net profits for the lifetime of the tournament. The NCAA agreed to the first two, but would only commit to the *possibility* of profit sharing, requiring the NABC to write and request a percentage each year. The NABC agreed to the deal and would henceforth petition the NCAA for a percentage of the profits from the tournament. Incidentally, the latest television contract signed between the NCAA and CBS for the NCAA Tournament was for $6 billion!

NABC Presidents

1927-29 Forrest "Phog" Allen, Kansas
1929-30 Craig Ruby, Illinois
1930-31 Lew Andreas , Syracuse
1931-32 Arthur Schabinger, Creighton
1932-33 Harold Olsen, Ohio State
1933-34 Roy Mundorff, Georgia Tech
1934-35 Howard Ortner, Cornell
1935-36 Arthur "Dutch" Lonborg, Northwestern
1936-37 Henry "Doc" Carlson, Pittsburgh
1937-38 George Edwards, Missouri
1938-39 William Chandler, Marquette
1939-40 Brandon Grover, Ohio
1940-41 Nat Holman, CCNY
1941-42 Nelson Norgren, Chicago
1942-44 Edward Kelleher, Fordham
1944-46 Edward Hickox, Springfield
1946-47 Blair Gullion, Connecticut
1947-48 Howard Hobson, Oregon
1948-49 Herbert Read, Western Michigan
1949-50 John Bunn, Springfield
1950-51 Vadal Peterson, Utah
1951-52 Bruce Drake, Oklahoma
1952-53 Franklin Cappon, Princeton
1953-54 Edgar "Eddie" Hickey, St. Louis
1954-55 Paul "Tony" Hinkle, Butler
1955-56 Harold "Bud" Foster, Wisconsin
1956-57 Ray Oostering, Trinity
1957-58 Amory "Slats" Gill, Oregon State
1958-59 Clifford Wells, Tulane
1959-60 Everett Shelton, Sacramento State
1960-61 Bill Henderson, Baylor
1961-62 Wilbur Stalcup, Missouri
1962-63 Harold Anderso, Bowling Green
1963-64 Lee Williams, Colby
1964-65 Forrest Twogood, Southern California
1965-66 Ben Carnevale, Navy
1966-67 Alvin "Doggie" Julian, Dartmouth
1967-68 Henry Iba, Oklahoma State
1968-69 William Gardiner, Catholic
1969-70 Stan Watts, Brigham Young
1970-71 Adolph Rupp, Kentucky
1971-72 Bill Wall, MacMurray
1972-73 Fred Taylor, Ohio State
1973-74 Joe Vancisin, Yale
1974-75 Bob Polk, Rice
1975-76 Bill Foster, Duke
1976-77 Abe Lemons, Texas
1977-78 Barry Dowd, Texas
1978-79 Ned Wulk, Arizona State
1979-80 Wilber Renken, Albright
1980-81 Marv Harshman, Washington
1981-82 Dean Smith, North Carolina
1982-83 Fred "Tex" Winter, Long Beach State
1983-84 Joe O'Brien, Assumption
1984-85 Jack Hartman, Kansas State
1985-86 John Thompson, Georgetown
1986-87 Billy Key, Missouri-Rolla
1987-88 Eddie Sutton, Kentucky
1988-89 Jud Heathcote, Michigan State
1989-90 Clarence "Big House" Gaines, Winston-Salem State
1990-91 Gerald Meyers, Texas Tech
1991-92 Herb Kenny, Wesleyan
1992-93 Johnny Orr, Iowa State
1993-94 George Blaney, Holy Cross
1994-95 Bill Knapton, Beloit
1995-96 George Raveling, Retired
1996-97 Bob Hanson, Kansas State
1997-98 Mike Jarvis, George Washington
1998-99 Mike Krzyzewski, Duke
1999-00 Denny Crum, Louisville
2000-01 Gene Keady, Purdue
2001-02 Roy Williams, University of Kansas
2002-03 Ken Kaufman, Retired
2003-04 Kelvin Sampson, University of Oklahoma
2004-05 Pat Kennedy, Towson University
2005-06 Jim Burson, Muskingum College
2006-07 Oliver Purnell, Clemson University
2007-08 Jim Boeheim, Syracuse University
2008-09 Tubby Smith, University of Minnesota

BOOK TWO

THE RULES

THE RULES SHAPE THE GAME

The NABC, coaches, players, and officials from around the world have been far more than interested observers in the development of the rules of basketball.

As is often the case, coaches would conclude stellar careers with Hall of Fame induction and then lead the philosophy discussion and present the position of the NABC membership as it waded into the rules fray. They seldom agreed, but when the good of the game was in jeopardy, the "call to arms" was never ignored. The evolution of the rules follows an intriguing path, but those influential individuals who held sway over the rules decisions can be counted on one hand, and their time in service to the game would actually cover decades. Four years after the invention of the game, an unidentified group of people with YMCA credentials formed the first rules committee to "change" what Naismith had posted on the wall in 1891.

From there, groups popped up around the country with the changes that they felt would *really make the game great*. The situation was often so convoluted that when teams from different areas would play, each half was governed by a different set of rules and the halves would look nothing alike. Officials had to barter on what rules to use in every game they worked. The coaches never won a game on the road because officials were reluctant to anger the crowds or the local coaches. It was not until chaos reined supreme that coaches felt compelled to become more aggressively involved.

James Naismith rarely spoke of his invention, but the topic he would regularly agree to discuss was the rules. He never wavered from his commitment to the 13 Original and was outspoken and precise in his concern for where the game was headed.

As important as the influence of the game's inventor, basketball governance was a continuous concern. With some years more peaceful than others, the game was regularly being adjusted by someone who felt a need to change something, usually to his own benefit. Members of the coaching ranks were no different from the officials, the administrators, the promoters, or the fans. From the very beginning, Naismith was always in some level of disagreement with the people and groups claiming partial ownership of the game, and wanting to change it for the "better."

"The responsibility of the coaches is even greater than that of the officials, as many of the latter are influenced by the attitude of the coaches," Naismith said in 1913. "When the coach lacks the knowledge or ability to perfect a team in individual skill, he is willing to permit holding, in order that his men may keep the score down. He may even request that fouls be overlooked; thus roughness is introduced, for which the rules frequently got the blame. Thus the official, to retain his popularity, frequently officiates as the coaches ask. I have been asked by the members of the association if there was not some way to change the rules so that as to eliminate roughness. There is apparently only one way to meet the difficulty, namely, to have officials responsible to a Central Board, to get the information from impartial sources rather than from coaches and managers."

Basketball leaders were always politicking with suggestions for a change to better fit their facility or their image of the game. This barrage was often pitting inventor, director, coach, and administrator against one another on the topic of how the game should be played, taught, coached, officiated, and adapted. During the game's earliest development, the participants across the country adjusted rules and scoring, suited to their circumstances.

"Thirty years ago there were three published codes of basketball rules: The Collegiate, the A.A.U., and the Professional, to say nothing of the numerous unprinted codes," Oswald Tower, the U.S. Rules Interpreter, wrote in 1941. "This caused a

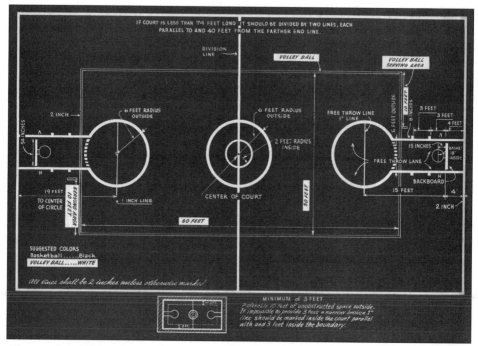

The game hasn't changed so much that we still have to worry about the volleyball lines on the court.
1940's Hillyard Scouting

chaotic condition, with many teams not knowing just what code they were following and others using a home brew, which would be a hodge-podge of various sets."

Rules adaptations that included such things as the use of pivot feet; how dribblers could not score; 20-foot foul lines; three-point, two-point, and one-point shots were actively being taught. There was actually a time when there was a designated shooter for all free throws, and in some scenarios around the nation, a free throw counted three points. (Some college teams probably wish that was the case today.) It was time for someone to undertake the challenges of supervising and refining the game across the country. It had become increasingly clear that the YMCA was incapable of managing basketball in an orderly fashion while continuing quality leadership for all of the charitable responsibilities around the globe.

Basketball was growing so quickly that something had to be done to legislate some control. The Amateur Athletic Union (AAU) accepted this responsibility and immediately prepared plans to shape the game into the AAU paradigm of how a sport should be organized and governed. The first unneeded change was the organization's "official set of rules," which differed enough from the YMCA that people playing the game from the time of Naismith now had to make a choice of which set of rules they were going to adapt for their organization's contests.

The next decision to set the basketball world on edge was the AAU's mandate that teams playing basketball in organized groups or leagues must register their team's players and gain sanction for their activities. This was the first attempt at tightening the regulations and restricting some of the player and team freedoms of the earlier years. As we learned from Phog Allen's career, an accomplished player could play on as many teams as he could; a coach could coach as many teams as he had time for and at whatever levels would have him; and games could be scheduled wherever, whenever and however the parties chose to do so.

There was some sound thinking on the part of the AAU and the YMCA as they started to tackle some of the more difficult problems. Still facing amateur basketball was how to control the issues of rules and fan abuse, identifying professional athletes, controlling the schedule, and participant and media influence in certain sections of the country.

Different organizations—YMCA, AAU, etc.—used different rules. So, there was considerable leeway in determining which set of playing rules were going to be used in any particular contest, tournament, or championship. The rules did include a great deal of detail on how each of the authority figures were to conduct themselves and manage the product at hand, but the specific rules that were assigned to the game of basketball were conspicuous in their absence. One would have to assume that an agreement would have to be reached before the first jump ball as to the set of rules being enjoyed that evening; YMCA, AAU, collegiate or professional.

Additional confusion arrived when President Theodore Roosevelt, identifying a national emergency of growing hostility in college football competition, created the Intercollegiate Athletic Association of the United States (IAAUS), which in 1910 would become the National Collegiate Athletic Association (NCAA) and govern sports competition among colleges and universities. So joining the YMCA and the AAU and further confusing the scene, the IAAUS's newly formed Collegiate Basket Ball Rules Committee of 1907 issued the basketball rules that governed all competition involving institutions of higher education in the game already bursting at the seams with rules variations.

Earlier that year, the University of Pennsylvania had been sanctioned by the AAU for playing against a team that was not properly registered and with players not properly approved for organized association competitions. Members of college basketball's elite decided then that they would not be dictated to by the AAU and would form their own organization to govern "college basket ball," forever separating it from "basket ball" for everyone else.

Never to be satisfied with simple policies and procedures already in place, the higher education authorities responded to a "questionable" need and, armed with the mandate from the President and with the injustice faced by the University of Pennsylvania, the Intercollegiate Athletic Association of the United States (IAAUS) came to the rescue of college basketball.

"It is believed that by this means the main evils of basket ball will be eliminated in the colleges. Then by strictly prohibiting collegians from playing on outside teams, by discouraging games between colleges and athletic clubs, and long barnstorming trips about the country it is expected that the whole situation will be cleaned up." New York Times, March 1907

After its first three years, the IAAUS begrudgingly realized that little work was done to solve the immediate problems facing the game. So, a new committee was appointed to move forward with the work of the first. There were a few continuing members, but the committee would become more focused on rules alignment with the addition of Dr. James Naismith and the first "Guardian" of the rules, Oswald Tower.

GUARDIAN
OSWALD TOWER
(RULES, RULES, RULES, RULES)

Photo courtesty: Phillips Academy Andover

"So the secret is out. Here is the man who has had the rules of the game in his hands for 34 years, and well has he met his trust. This is the fellow who has done so much to perpetuate and crystallize its finest traditions. Now we know who has been guiding the destiny of basketball through the period of its growth. The game was born in the mind of Dr. Naismith, nourished in the mind of Oswald Tower ... May your future be so bright, Mr. Tower, as your service has been great."
— Timothy Duncan, *Boston Sunday Post*, 1947

For anyone with a good knowledge of basketball coaching, it might seem odd that Oswald Tower is considered a "Guardian" of the game. After all, he was never a member of the NABC, and he coached only briefly right out of college. For 50 years, however, he was the gatekeeper of basketball's rules.

Tower was a member of the rules committee (IAAUS/NCAA) from 1910 until 1959. He was editor of the *Basketball Guide*, the official rulebook for 44 years; he was identified as the earliest IAAUS official rules interpreter; and he officiated at all levels. As a member of the Helms Hall of Fame and the Naismith Memorial Basketball Hall of Fame, his position in the game was secured before it was even up for debate.

Oswald Tower was born in North Adams, Massachusetts, on November 23, 1883. He spent his childhood there and was very competitive in football, basketball, and baseball. There is also some reference to his running "the distances" in high school track and field. His family was a hard-working group that always struggled to make ends meet. Upon his graduation from Drury High School, he was on his own and it was off to work in a local print shop. For two years, his weekly salary of $7.50 and an additional fee for playing some semi-pro basketball were stockpiled so that he could realize his dream of attending college.

Tower finally succeeded when Williams College offered a partial academic scholarship. He played four years of varsity basketball there including every minute of every game during the last three seasons. He was selected captain of the team as a senior and even coached Drury High School during his college playing career. Immediately after graduation, Tower had a short stint as basketball coach at both Wilbraham Academy and then Philips Academy of Andover. He stayed at Philips for

COACH PROFILE

JIM CALHOUN –
UNIVERSITY OF CONNECTICUT
(NABC MEMBER 35 YEARS)

"I'm proud to have the opportunity to not only get involved (Coaches vs. Cancer), but to be a role model for my players, that you can, and should, give back."

Jim Calhoun had a rougher beginning than most. After a stellar high school sports career and a college basketball scholarship, his father passed away and it fell on Jim to work and support his mom and five brothers and sisters. He worked as a stonecutter and gravedigger to support the group.

Maybe it was this early life-lesson and heavy responsibility that has brought this coach to the point of greatness. Maybe it was the 1-17 record in his first year of coaching that hardened his resolve. Maybe it was the 20-1 record with the same team shortly thereafter that built his confidence. Calhoun built his reputation at Northeastern University where he built a championship program and took the program and the athletic department to the NCAA Division I level of competition and then qualified for post-season play in four of his final five seasons.

The University of Connecticut coach is presently undefeated in games played in the NCAA Final Four. Two national championships, included with five Elite Eight appearances would be included in a career of post-season experience. Rapidly approaching the incredible feat of 800 wins would be reason enough to embrace and applaud Calhoun being inducted into the Naismith Memorial Basketball Hall of Fame and the College Basketball Hall of Fame, but there is a more important message.

Jim Calhoun is a cancer survivor and advocate for the Coaches vs. Cancer program through the NABC, but he is also a very active supporter of Autism Speaks, which is working very hard to find a cure for this quickly spreading national epidemic. Coach and his wife Pat are also named for their support of the UConn Cardiology Research Fund and work diligently to provide research dollars for Juvenile Diabetes. It is the stonecutter's toughness, the gravedigger's resolve, the coach's patience and the champion's confidence that drives him to make a difference and to encourage those around him to do the same.

the remainder of his professional career, but coaching was out and rules interpretation and officiating became his passion.

Tower officiated the game for 35 years, becoming the most respected basketball official in the northeastern part of the United States. Coaches knew they would get a consistent and appropriately interpreted game whenever he was in the gym. They also knew that they would be held to a high level regarding team decorum and sportsmanship.

As an article in the *Boston Herald* on December 9, 1945, read: "Old-timers, many young men and women, too—Tower tossed his whistle away only a dozen years ago—remember his entrance at a basketball game wherever it was played. Ramrod straight, his spare brown hair neatly plastered down on his head, Oswald Tower would blink like a man leaving a world of books for the bright glare of reality, upon entering a hall. His white, blue-striped silk shirt was always immaculate, and his pants were pressed, and his high, laced gym shoes were polished in a nice black. He looked like 'class.'

"In the real old days, of course, when the pros dribbled with two hands and slugged each other now and then, and spit in each other's eyes, and used elbows and knees to good effect, Tower was something of 'a showpiece.'

"'Here comes Oswald Tower,' the crowd would murmur. They were enamored of that name—Oswald Tower of Andover—and of his appearance. A gentleman, a scholar, a bookworm. Used to be quite an athlete in his day, at that."

Tower's talent was widely identified very early on and he was asked to become an original member of the national rules committee and to be the Editor of the *Basketball Guide*, including duties as the nation's "official" rules interpreter from 1915-1959.

It was difficult to pick up a book, magazine, or article about basketball at the time and not at least come across the name Oswald Tower. He would set the standard for John Bunn, Edward Steitz, Henry Nichols, and Ed Bilik, who followed in his shadow as commanders of the rules of the game. He appeared to never shy away from discussing the rules.

The rules committee, in an effort to face the game's problems head on, invited coaches, officials, and administrators to a meeting in the fall of 1914. The attitude was that the problems must be accurately identified and some priorities established before they began the process of eliminating the problems one at a time. It was the opinion of the chairman, Joseph E. Raycroft, basketball coach at the University of Chicago, that involving these groups would eventually bring all of the entities of basketball governance to the bargaining table.

The Tower/Raycroft wish would become a reality when the AAU rules officials agreed to meet in a session a month later, the results of which were reported to the media.

"For the first time in the history of basket ball the amateur and collegiate rules for the game will be similar this year," an article in the *New York Times* reported in December 1914. "During the winter the AAU officials held conferences and obtained a consensus of opinion from the different amateur basket ball authorities as to their attitude toward uniform rules for collegians and the amateur fives. Since that time, George T. Hepburn has discussed the matter with collegiate authorities, with the result that the basketball rules, when issued next month, will be alike for AAU teams and for the college fives."

In what would become the biggest change to date, a Joint Rules Committee was suggested and adopted. Selecting members of each regulating body presently in charge, the newest rules organization would begin the arduous task of bringing order to what were long-lasting levels of disagreement across the nation.

One of the first moves to stabilize the game by this new committee was the rule abolishing the scramble out of bounds to gain the next possession. In past games, when the ball was knocked out of the playing area, the players would charge after it and the first player to gain full control of the ball would gain possession for his team. Now the official would determine which team caused it to leave and the other team would be awarded the ball. This move would identify the game official as the party to determine which team knocked the ball out of bounds and then award the possession to the other.

The newest attempt at unified basketball governance actually began the process with a great deal of forethought and research. Although the arduous task was never-ending, some confidence could be taken from this *New York Times* article outlining a normal year's work that resulted in some uniformity across the country, while easing the responsibility on the officials managing the event.

Important rule changes made by the Intercollegiate Basketball league for the coming year were announced yesterday by officials of the league.....

1. *The most radical of the alterations to the rules will permit a player who has been taken from the game at any time to be sent back in the contest later, provided he has not committed four personal fouls; the new regulation, however, will not affect the banishment of a player exceeding the allowance for personal fouls.*
2. *The second change provides that after a held ball beneath the basket, the ball will be brought out to the 15-foot line, where it will be tossed up.*

Coaches across the country were as satisfied as coaches ever can be and the major priorities assigned to the Joint Rules Committee seemed to be taking hold.

Over time, there were other rules refinements, and the committee was maintaining a close watch on the smaller details as it worked to maintain the national consistency sought by so many for so many years. Then, in 1926, the peace accord ends and all hell breaks loose once again. One of the most successful and revered coaches in the country flexes his muscles on the Joint Rules Committee and basketball history is changed.

GUARDIAN

DR. WALTER E. MEANWELL
(DOCTOR, COACH,
INNOVATOR, AGITATOR)

Photo courtesty:
Wisconsin Athletic Communications

"There are critics who say that too many changes are made in basketball rules, but a careful analysis of the facts shows that fundamental changes have been very few; that the game of 1894 has been modified very little; that the changes, as they affect the playing of the game, have been relatively unimportant. There have been no changes as revolutionary as the forward pass in football or as radical as the foul-strike rule in baseball."

— Dr. Walter Meanwell

Maybe the most impressive coaching record described in this book, Dr. Walter E. Meanwell was 44-1 in his first three seasons as a coach. With no significant basketball pedigree, he became the first basketball coach at the University of Wisconsin and won the Western Conference Championship (Big 10) the first three years he was there. During that incredible stretch, his only loss was at the University of Chicago in the 1922 season's final game.

Meanwell's first club at Wisconsin was awarded the Helms' National Championship, so he became the first coach to win a national championship in his first season as a university basketball coach. He continued to build his coaching reputation by winning nine championships in his first 12 years on the sidelines. His career at Wisconsin was interrupted for two years when he was recruited to take the basketball coaching position with the University of Missouri. After two championship years in the Missouri Valley Conference, he returned to Wisconsin to complete his coaching career. A career highlight for Meanwell was never losing a game to Phog Allen at Kansas while winning those two championships. This humiliation by an archrival may have stoked the fires in Allen's belly when he learned of Meanwell's effort to eliminate the dribble.

Meanwell was the rules official who disregarded the wishes of Naismith, the coach at Missouri whom Allen could never beat, and the influential member of the rules committee who provided the impetus behind the successful vote to eliminate the dribble from the game in 1927. His outspoken demeanor and incredible success as a basketball coach were recognized with his induction into the Naismith Memorial Basketball Hall of Fame in 1959.

> ## Rules Changes
>
> A coach is not affected by the changes of the Basket Ball rules nearly as much as is the effect upon the players, the officials and the ~~fans~~ followers of the game - The spectators.
>
> The coach teaches fundamentals of the game, to his players ~~such~~ as shooting, passing, pivoting, dribbling and guarding. These fundamentals never change. So the coach is handicapped least of all. But the coach naturally wants the rules of the game simplified. They can be understood by all, if the rules are simplified. There is no need, or reason for this great confusion which exists at the present time.

Phog Allen explains how rules changes affect players and officials more than coaches.

COACH PROFILE

JOHN CALIPARI –
UNIVERSITY OF MEMPHIS
(NABC MEMBER 22 YEARS)

"A lot of what we do is crisis management."

Calipari has had reams written about his exploits over the years in his career and certainly, every step has been reviewed for appropriateness. Some people just gravitate to that kind of scrutiny. One would not have thought that as he began his career with Ted Owens at Kansas and Paul Evans at Pittsburgh, but when he became the out-spoken, gyrating sideline genius leading the University of Massachusetts out of basketball purgatory, it all changed.

Calipari is an enigma, known for supposedly grabbing the riches of the NBA and his post-game battle with John Chaney often shared by ESPN. Upon his arrival at the University of Memphis, he installed a program that encouraged past players from the Tiger's program to return and get their degrees. He works diligently to support his players' academic progress, and spends valuable time within the university academic hierarchy to better structure his program for academic success.

One cannot argue that "winning" is what he does, but is it possible that he does it the right way? There are a lot of coaches who can recruit, but he seems to open quickly and efficiently a pipeline to the nation's best. Might it just be possible that this pipeline is so heavily stocked because of an academic approach to championship building? Maybe ESPN should ask him that.

Calipari stumbled the first year with UMass, but then went on a run that included seven straight post-season opportunities, five straight Atlantic 10 Championships and one Final Four appearance. This success led to three years as the head coach of the New York Nets and one appearance in the NBA playoffs. He then assisted Larry Brown with the Philadelphia 76ers for one season before returning to college basketball at Memphis University. He led the Tigers to the 2008 National Championship game, where they lost to the Kansas Jayhawks. Late-game free throws failed the team, making one wonder about his theory: "The only thing I pay attention to with free-throw shooting is what a guy does in the last four minutes of a game. If you can improve a player's self-esteem and confidence, get them to relax, teach visualization and routine, they will shoot as well, or better, when the pressure is on."

Meanwell was born in Leeds, England, in January 1884. His family arrived in the United States about 10 years later and he grew up in Rochester, New York. During the era of his success, he directly competed with Allen in the areas of basketball development and endorsement, in basketball shoe development and endorsement, in coaching (Missouri vs. Kansas), in book publishing (both coaches were published in 1924), in emphasizing different aspects of sports medicine and, finally, in the development of the rules of the game.

With a medical degree and a Ph.D., Dr. Meanwell attacked the game of basketball with a visibly different approach. His teams were known for their physical play and very limited dribbling.

"Skill in catching and passing the ball is more necessary to success than almost any other element in basket ball," Meanwell wrote in 1924. "Ability with the ball breeds confidence and morale. Fast, accurate passing will bring the ball frequently to within such close distances that even an ordinary shooter can score. Therefore, the poorer a team is at shooting the more time and attention should be devoted to improving the handling of the ball and speeding up the pass."

The section of Meanwell's book that is specific to passing spans 21 pages, and the detail is incredible. The minutely detailed placement of the hands and feet and the use of each of the different passes available to the player in possession of the ball, are clearly displayed. In contrast, the section on dribbling is half that size.

As a coach, Meanwell's final record stood at 290-110. His expertise became legendary and he would claim many followers to his approach. He would travel the country sharing his ideas and innovations with all who would listen and could probably be identified as the instigator in the design and implementation of the "coaching clinic."

But Meanwell gained much notoriety very early in the development of the game. He was ahead of his time in recognizing the need for competent governance and a consistent set of rules. As many searched for their Holy Grail, he searched for the "perfect" set of rules. He was in constant disagreement with Naismith and others who felt that the game was designed to fill a need and was handling that responsibility nicely. Disregarding his opponents, he took his seat as a member of the Joint Rules Committee for several years.

During that time, Meanwell and the Joint Rules Committee enjoyed a few years of smooth sailing. This calm came to a crashing halt in 1926-27 with the rule to limit the dribble as a part of the game. Meanwell's decision to persuade the Joint Rules Committee to eliminate the dribble had wide-reaching effects on the game's governance. Allowing only one dribble per possession, the rule virtually eliminated this part of the offensive attack. In a move championed by the coaches embracing the Meanwell style, he was able to persuade the Joint Rules Committee to vote 9-8 to pass, and the rest is NABC history. When Allen and the other coaches had finished their attack, not only was the rule change never implemented, but the entire committee was evaluated and changed to increase the number of coaches in the group.

As Phog Allen wrote: *"Back in April of 1927, the National Basketball Rules Committee eliminated the dribble from the game of Basket Ball. Knute Rockne and I were speaking at the Drake University Field House to the National Education Association. He spoke on the Pedagogy of Football and I spoke on the Pedagogy of Basket Ball. The next morning after the fatal mistake of the Rules Committee, I lashed out at their autocratic and high-handed action.*

"There was at that time no organization of Basket Ball Coaches. I called a meeting of all college and university coaches two weeks hence, at the date of the annual Drake Relays in Des Moines, Iowa. The coaches at their meeting forthright deplored the action of the Rules Committee and went on record as overwhelmingly favoring the retention of the dribble.

"The National Coaches Association was born at that time. They saved the dribble from extinction because they felt that the dribble was a very necessary ingredient of the game."

This blatant attack by a few against the masses backfired in a big way. The Joint Rules Committee lost the confidence needed to lead and, again, there was a splintering of groups embracing the game as their own. At this point in history, the Joint Rules Committee was powerless, Walter E. Meanwell became less significant and would return to his role as a basketball coach. This very fluid mixture of personalities, groups, and philosophies would take a few years to once again sort themselves out and move forward.

GUARDIAN

EDWARD S. STEITZ
(COACH, ADMINISTRATOR,
RULES CZAR)

"As Editor, national interpreter, and guardian of rules for college basketball the past 21 years, the buck stops with me. It is my responsibility to compile all the data and conduct all the studies on proposed rules. We do not change rules without years of research and supporting data to justify a change."

— **Edward Steitz**

Photo courtesty: Springfield College

Following in the footsteps of a legend is never an easy task. Many have tried and many have fallen by the wayside after a valiant effort. In the case of Edward Steitz, he not only replaced one legend, he replaced three, and in each case showed a remarkable resiliency. Following Hall of Fame coach John Bunn at Springfield College, Steitz achieved a record of 160-86 before assuming the duties of athletic director on a full-time basis. Steitz replaced Oswald Tower and John Bunn as the nation's rules gurus and NCAA rules interpreters and would hold that position from 1965-1990.

Although the NBA takes credit for the 3-point shot, here in the 1940's the NABC was already experimenting. The line is where it stands today.

Leading into the 1970s, goaltending was clarified (Wilt Chamberlain rule) and the dunk outlawed (Lew Alcindor rule), but these had little impact on the competition levels of the game itself. The elimination of goaltending was an effort to bring the defensive side of the game more in line with the offense. When the dunk was eliminated, it was an effort to once again minimize the impact of the very tall player without raising the height of the basket.

The dunk was reinstated after Alcindor graduated and the excitement of the play overwhelmed the original reasons for the ban. It was an attempt to try to slow down or stop the massive advantage that UCLA had created over the rest of the Division-I schools across the country. When it was obvious that the dunk was not the reason Wooden was winning all of those championships, the committee gave back what had become one of the game's most exciting plays.

During Steitz's tenure, the game eliminated the jump ball during competition in 1981, introduced the 45-second shot clock in 1985, and unveiled the three-point field goal the following year. Finally, consistent with his Springfield College contemporaries, he would follow Hall of Fame coach Ed Hickox and act as Hall of Fame secretary for 17 years.

Edward Steitz was born in Brooklyn, New York, in 1920 and in the bustling diversity of the five boroughs developed an intense, detail-oriented personality. He was an outstanding high school student and was readily accepted into Cornell University of the Ivy League. He would go to college intent on being a veterinarian and serving animals for the remainder of his days. As many of his contemporaries, this dream was interrupted by a period serving his country in the military. It was during his military career that Steitz would do a major reevaluation and decide to serve humanity instead of the animal kingdom.

Not long after returning from his service obligations Steitz began his long and prosperous relationship with Springfield College. He filled many roles there as he traversed the challenges of a teaching position, a master's degree, a Ph.D., and the head basketball coaching position.

The Steitz footprint extended the already impressive Springfield influence beyond the rules committees and Naismith Memorial Basketball Hall of Fame. He recognized the major influence international basketball was going to have on the game and moved to ensure that the American influence was not relegated to the back of the room.

As a coach, sport administrator, officials' assigner and Olympic consultant, he traveled the world in an effort to maintain some order in the game's international development. As a Springfield alumnus and a basketball aficionado, he was well aware of the trouble with fixing something after the problem had already taken hold. Steitz was motivated to see the game's growth follow consistent and manageable guidelines.

COACH PROFILE
TOM CREAN –
INDIANA UNIVERSITY
(NABC MEMBER 22 YEARS)

"I cannot begin to tell you how excited I am to join the Indiana University family. This is one of the elite institutions and basketball programs in America and we take the responsibility of upholding that tradition very seriously."

Very often, coaches who are working the sideline of a less prominent program have to make a tough choice to gain access to an elite program. Coaches sometime return to the ranks of assistant coach at an elite program to gain needed exposure, or take on the responsibility of re-building a program damaged by some unusual source.

Tom Crean did just that when he brought his family and his expertise to Bloomington, Indiana. After an ugly NCAA rules revelation, mid-season coaching change and several players being dismissed or transferred, the program was in total disarray. The quote above shares his inner feelings, but more internal problems and external distractions have left the program on life-support.

Crean is a career-long assistant coach who finally got his chance to shine at Marquette University. He led the Warriors to the Big East Conference affiliation and even a Final Four appearance, last done by the legendary Al McGuire. One could argue that his program was on a high and thriving, so why the change?

Crean's coaching career began while he was an undergraduate at Central Michigan University. He worked as an assistant at Mount Pleasant while attending Central Michigan and then worked as an assistant at Alma College. A graduate assistantship with Jud Heathcote began a 10-year stint as an NCAA Division I assistant coach. After his graduate assistantship ended, he moved to Western Kentucky University for four years, then Pittsburgh for a year before returning to Michigan State as a full-time assistant. After 10 years, Crean finally got his first head coaching position at Marquette University. The program began a string of seven consecutive post-season appearances culminating with a Final Four appearance in 2003.

Although he tasted elite status at Michigan State, his career was littered with lesser-known programs. But the success of State and his run of success at Marquette helped him when Indiana offered Tom Crean an elite program—in disarray—but elite just the same. Will the same steps that he used to revitalize Marquette, do the same at Indiana? Only time will tell.

He held many influential board positions and was rewarded for his worldwide efforts with induction in March, 2007 into the FIBA Hall of Fame.

Edward Steitz maintained a high profile in the United States Olympic development program. He served the worldwide officiating needs with clinics offered in the farthest reaches of basketball competition. Steitz was involved with the official's selection process for Olympic Basketball competition and would serve in an official capacity throughout eight different Olympic competitions.

Finally, and certainly not least important, Steitz was the founder of what was then ABA/USA. This national organization has taken over the governance of amateur basketball and is now known as USA Basketball. The organization continues its original charge to improve opportunities for basketball competition outside of the college and university basketball seasons, with an emphasis on all age groups. An emphasis that originated with the organization's original charter, USA Basketball continues to develop strong international competition activities for all ages and skill levels of basketball competitors.

In spite of all those accolades, Edward Steitz is really known for his work in the rules business. He has authored more than 300 articles on basketball and the rules of the game.

The rules section of the book is not complete without involving the most modern of influences that ever has had an impact on the college game. One of the increasing influences that Steitz had to understand was media reproduction and reporting. With sporting events becoming a growing fascination with the nation, media outlets were competing for an edge. Originally, fans watched replays of games and even had local television covering some games live. Radio sports were a youthful addiction that spread the excitement across the populace, and then television captured us completely. College basketball gradually followed football as a profitable opportunity for network television as those young radio listeners became adults. Schools were setting attendance records and the NCAA was gaining increasing revenue from selling broadcasting rights. However, when a nationally televised basketball game of some importance was deemed to be boring and fans actually began changing the channel during the game, something had to be done.

"Five basketball seasons ago on a March afternoon in Greensboro, NC, two superb basketball teams met to decide the Atlantic Coast Conference tournament championship. Virginia had Ralph Sampson and Othell Wilson; North Carolina had James Worthy, Sam Perkins and Michael Jordan," John Feinstein wrote in 1986 *New York Post*. With 12 minutes left, Tar Heels coach Dean Smith decided to hold the ball. Cavaliers coach Terry Holland decided not to chase. So, while the crowd agonized, all those talented players stood around and looked at each other. Smith blamed Holland,

and Holland blamed Smith, but that wasn't the point. What could have been a superb game became a boring one."

The Atlantic Coast Conference game between North Carolina (No. 1 in the nation) and Virginia (No. 3 in the nation) became the event people would point to and comment how the game had become too controlled and over-coached. Something had to be done before college basketball lost the support of television executives. Preserving the excitement of the game for the television fans during high-impact games and tournament play had to become a priority.

After five-plus years of debating, experimenting, and deciding, the NCAA Basketball Rules Committee finally introduced the 45-second clock in 1985. (It has since been lowered to 35 seconds.)

But Steitz's gang and television's influence was not yet complete. Just one year later, the same rules committee that had reacted to the deliberate style that the game had embraced now introduced the three-point field goal, instantly. There weren't years of trying it out, as was the case with the shot clock.

Regardless of the overwhelming opposition by the "big time" coaches, Bob Knight—who still calls the change, "the Steitz Rule"—and Mike Krzyzewski, the NCAA selected a shot made at a distance of 19'9" from the center of the rim to be awarded three points. The distance is exactly the same one that had been so overwhelmingly rejected years before in a national survey of the NABC coaches.

Here are some coaching opinions published in the *USA Today*, on April 3, 1986. (It's funny to look back now and realize that a few of the coaches who opposed the three-pointer have benefited from it greatly.)

Eddie Sutton, Kentucky – *"It caught me by surprise. I thought the general feeling among the coaches was that the game was enjoying an all-time peak in popularity and we should leave it alone."*

Lute Olson, Arizona – *"We used the three-point goal my last year in the Big Ten and I was one of the people in favor of it."*

Mike Krzyzewski, Duke – *"We've just had a year of no chaos and now we are introducing chaos. I don't think that is good for the game. There are a lot of major coaches shocked by this."*

Dean Smith, North Carolina – *"Using the shot clock, I think we do need a three-point goal. When we used a 19-foot three-point goal in the ACC in 1983, we had great games. The fans and the players loved it and that is who the game is for."*

Don Monson, Oregon – *"The last thing I want is the three-point goal. We had it one year when I coached in the Big Sky Conference, it does nothing but promote poor shots."*

Digger Phelps, Notre Dame – *"I'm very surprised to see it pass. I didn't realize it was under serious consideration, based on the recommendation by major conferences, which generally seemed to be negative."*

Jim Boeheim, Syracuse – *"I'm not in favor of it. You don't have a chance to prepare for it. You can't just go out now and get someone. I guess I go back to this, that if you have a good game, why mess around with it anymore."*

Larry Brown, Kansas – *"I think the three-pointer has merit, I'm a little confused about the distance. I don't want it to be such an easy shot that it becomes more important than anything, because I don't think that is the purpose."*

Steitz and the NCAA rules committee took an entirely different view of the rules change. The group knew the coaches didn't favor it, but Steitz was quick to point out that the game isn't played for the coaches. This was a great example of when the NABC was unable to change minds, when a governing body had made a change in basketball in direct opposition to the majority of those employed in the profession.

Of course, the controversy faded into the sunset and the game has never been more popular. Once again, the insight and courage of the game's "official" rules interpreters got it right.

Frankly, the financial figures clearly display the success of the changes regardless of the sentiment of the coaches. According to NCAA documents, in 1970 the NCAA received $511,000 from NBC for the rights to televise the 1971 NCAA Basketball Championship, and after all income and expenses were tallied the NCAA had enjoyed a net profit of $399,222.56.

Now, fast forward to 1987, after the implementation of the shot clock and the three-point field goal. The NCAA is paid more than $33 million to televise the tournament. The NCAA enjoys a net profit of nearly $15 million. Even though 16 years had passed, that's quite a revenue boost.

Now, fast forward again, to 2008. The contract between CBS and the NCAA to televise the Men's Division I National Basketball Tournament reads $6 billion (that's right BILLION) for a period of 11 years. That is the TV rights only. That is not the ticket receipts, sponsorship cash, or the income from the NCAA licensed apparel. (Remember, the NABC used to own this thing.)

As we sit, flush with cash, and selling 80,000 tickets to the Final Four in Detroit in 2009, there is a storm brewing on the horizon. Already there is going to be a different three-point line in 2009 and Steitz will tell us that is not the only change. He firmly believes that we have outgrown our basketball boundaries and should look at many different ways to expand the barriers that are presently restricting college basketball. Steitz actually has been known to agree with our founder, Phog Allen, and contemplate the changing of the basket.

"The first thing you've got to talk about are widening the courts, widening the lane and raising the baskets. Now we can't widen 99 percent of the courts in this country, so that's not really an option. The other two are possible, but you'll have a hard time getting the coaches to approve them. Changes like that are considered too radical, but we need to consider a trapezoidal lane like that used in international competition and raising the baskets two feet," Steitz told the *Boston Globe* in 1987.

"I think it was about 20 years ago that we had the Big Ten Conferences coaches talked into raising the baskets to 12 feet for their conference games. We thought it was a done deal. Then the coaches had a summer picnic and golf affair and they all got to talking and decided it would hurt the conference champion when they went to the NCAA tournament. And, of course, every coach thought he was going to be the champion so they decided against it."

Oswald Tower, Walter Meanwell, John Bunn and Edward Steitz have protected the game through rules legislation for a century or more. They have provided us with great pleasure and saved us from considerable pain.

With Edward Steitz passing away in 1990, the rules committee was briefly in the hands of Henry Nichols. Nichols was a veteran basketball official with years of experience at the highest levels. He had been the chair of the NCAA Officials Committee for several years and would take on this dual role. NCAA administrators felt that this might make for a more comfortable exchange of ideas. Whether it was a case of paranoia, or some specific issues, no one would comment except to say that a change was made to separate the committees again. The rules committee returned to where it all began, Ed Bilik, coach and administrator at Springfield College.

Ed Bilik, during an interview for this book in 2008, was guarded in his comments regarding the future of the rules of the game. He had not seen the quote from Steitz, but did not feel that enlarging the court was on anyone's list for discussion. He did discuss the issue of moving the basket from 10 feet and what he said was rather obvious, but is never really mentioned as part of the discussion:

"There is always talk about changing the height of the basket, but the girls are adamant about keeping the height where it is, "he said." We do not presently have the time or the technology to change the basket dimensions between games so there is no real logic in discussing changing the height."

On the morning of the interview for this book, the international rules people announced that they were getting rid of the trapezoid lane in favor of the NBA style. Bilik, speaking only his personal opinion, shared that this was where college basketball was headed. He could not be specific to time frame or width, but of all the things that Steitz had suggested, that was the one that he felt would come to pass at some point.

The only other topic discussed was that of consistent officiating. He felt that there were some things that had to be adjusted. Like Naismith, Wooden and others interviewed for this book, Bilik felt that basketball needs change to return to officiating the game as it was intended. He agreed with the assessment that traveling and palming had trickled down into the college game and it needed to be sent back to the NBA.

NCAA CHAMPIONS

1939	University of Oregon, Howard Hobson
1940	Indiana University, Branch McCracken
1941	University of Wisconsin, Harold Foster
1942	Stanford University, Everett Dean
1943	University of Wyoming, Everett Shelton
1944	University of Utah, Vadal Peterson
1945	Oklahoma State University, Henry Iba
1946	Oklahoma State University, Henry Iba
1947	Holy Cross University, Alvin Julian
1948	University of Kentucky, Adolph Rupp
1949	University of Kentucky, Adolph Rupp
1950	City College of New York, Nat Holman
1951	University of Kentucky, Adolph Rupp
1952	University of Kansas, Forrest "Phog" Allen
1953	Indiana University, Branch McCracken
1954	La Salle College, Kenneth Loeffler
1955	University of San Francisco, Phil Woolpert
1956	University of San Francisco, Phil Woolpert
1957	University of North Carolina, Frank McGuire
1958	University of Kentucky, Adolph Rupp
1959	University of California, Pete Newell
1960	Ohio State University, Fred Taylor
1961	University of Cincinnati, Edwin Jucker
1962	University of Cincinnati, Edwin Jucker
1963	Loyola of Illinois, George Ireland
1964	UCLA, John Wooden
1965	UCLA, John Wooden
1966	Texas Western University, Don Haskins
1967	UCLA, John Wooden
1968	UCLA, John Wooden
1969	UCLA, John Wooden
1970	UCLA, John Wooden
1971	UCLA, John Wooden
1972	UCLA, John Wooden
1973	UCLA, John Wooden
1974	North Carolina State University, Norm Sloan
1975	UCLA, John Wooden
1976	Indiana University, Bob Knight
1977	Marquette University, Al McGuire
1978	University of Kentucky, Joe B. Hall
1979	Michigan State University, Jud Heathcote
1980	University of Louisville, Denny Crum
1981	Indiana University, Bob Knight
1982	University of North Carolina, Dean Smith
1983	North Carolina State University, Jim Valvano
1984	Georgetown University, John Thompson Jr.
1985	Villanova University, Rollie Massimino
1986	University of Louisville, Denny Crum
1987	Indiana University, Bob Knight
1988	University of Kansas, Larry Brown
1989	University of Michigan, Steve Fisher
1990	University of Nevada-Las Vegas, Jerry Tarkanian
1991	Duke University, Mike Krzyzewski
1992	Duke University, Mike Krzyzewski
1993	University of North Carolina, Dean Smith
1994	University of Arkansas, Nolan Richardson
1995	UCLA, Jim Harrick
1996	University of Kentucky, Rick Pitino
1997	University of Arizona, Lute Olson
1998	University of Kentucky, Tubby Smith
1999	University of Connecticut, Jim Calhoun
2000	Michigan State University, Tom Izzo
2001	Duke University, Mike Krzyzewski
2002	University of Maryland, Gary Williams
2003	Syracuse University, Jim Boeheim
2004	University of Connecticut, Jim Calhoun
2005	University of North Carolina, Roy Williams
2006	University of Florida, Billy Donovan
2007	University of Florida, Billy Donovan
2008	University of Kansas, Bill Self

Presented by year, winning school and head coach.

BOOK THREE

THE PARALLEL UNIVERSE

Within normal guidelines, and without historical significance, the introduction of the African-American influence in basketball would be an easy segue. After all, coaches such as George Raveling, John Thompson Jr., and John Chaney can be picked readily out of a crowd. But it was not always that way. Segregation would influence the game and white basketball and black basketball would stay separated until players, coaches, and fans refused to allow that standard any longer.

Researching the African-American influence in basketball, and more specifically, in basketball coaching, doesn't provide a plethora of names to investigate. Reading and interviewing personalities with knowledge of the subject seemed always to provide the same group of coaches as the founding fathers or the mentors for what we enjoy today. There was never a great deal of agreement about what each meant to the movement, but the same names continued to be addressed. More interesting, finding a connection between members of the group was very difficult. Each coach would give speeches, provide biographical information and be displayed in various halls of fame, but rarely was there a mention of other minority coaches as mentors.

In every case, the individual coach would identify his mentors as coaches with strong resumes in major college basketball. Completely aware that the times would dictate that African-American coaches would have had to work in a world that was only recently integrated, and in some cases continued to be segregated, it was very interesting that they did not at least reference those who had bull-dozed the barriers interfering with professional advancement.

"In our community (African-American) there are two different groups of people, those that want to improve the black community and those that want to make it into white society," coach Ben Jobe said in 2008 when asked about this obvious contradiction. "Both groups recognized each other's goals, but they would never work together."

The story once again begins in the days of basketball's origins but follows a very separate—albeit parallel—universe. Believe it or not, James Naismith and Phog Allen provided unpopular, integrated influence in a very segregated world of sports. These two, with unending influence, would touch one young man, and he would influence the African-American basketball community at many levels in a multitude of ways.

Certainly, there was basketball being played by black players and led by black coaches from the very beginning. One of the great teams of the earliest days was the New York Renaissance (Rens). A team that was started in 1922 by Robert L. Douglas, the Rens would finish their reign after 27 years with a record of 473-49. This great team would travel the country taking on the best teams of their time. Regarded as the best basketball team in the United States from 1933-1936, the Rens won a record of 88 games in a row during the 1933-34 season. Inducted into the Naismith Memorial Basketball Hall of Fame as a team, the Rens were easily the black equivalent of the Buffalo Germans or the Original Celtics. Groups like the Rens influenced other groups to compete. The Harlem Globetrotters, who would become the ambassadors of basketball around the world, were one of those groups.

However, there seems to be a disconnect between the African-American coaches from different generations. Clarence Gaines and Ben Jobe had direct connections to John B. McLendon Jr. But the others, though aware of Coach McLendon, denied any motivation or support from the man whose basketball lineage goes back to Naismith.

"Our community was split between those that wanted to improve the HBCU (Historically Black Colleges and Universities) and those that wanted to find jobs in the colleges and universities outside the HBCU," Jobe said. "We didn't agree and we didn't mix together much."

GUARDIAN

JOHN B. MCLENDON JR.
(SEGREGATION, INTEGRATION, CHAMPION)

"Here was a man that was never whistled for a technical foul during his entire career. According to many of his players he never used profanity and never raised his voice."
— Dr. Milton S. Katz, author of
"Breaking Through"

During John B. McLendon Jr.'s career, he won three consecutive NAIA National Championships, became the first African-American coach elected into the Hall of Fame, broke the color barrier in professional basketball coaching, and worked as a scout for the United States Olympic movement. But that only scratches the surface of his significance to the sport.

McLendon, a highly successful basketball coach, was a pioneer who paved some rocky roads for many of the coaching and playing stars of our time. His ability

COACH PROFILE

BILLY DONOVAN –
UNIVERSITY OF FLORIDA
(NABC MEMBER 17 YEARS)

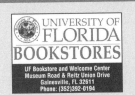

UF Bookstore and Welcome Center
Museum Road & Reitz Union Drive
Gainesville, FL 32611
Phone: (352)392-0194

"We want this night to last forever! You have to live in the moment. There will be adversity and challenges. That is what has brought us close together as a team… Live in the moment, cherish each moment, and go out there and play as a team." (Second consecutive national championship game)

It is a rare occurrence to find an elite player with street creds and a Final Four appearance walking the sidelines after his playing career is over. Most modern coaches played some basketball, but Billy Donovan was a high school (St. Agnes of Long Island) and college star (Providence College). Upon the arrival of Rick Pitino, Donovan and the Friars rode his shooting touch to a Final Four appearance, and he won the Southeast Regional MVP award during that run. The Utah Jazz drafted Donovan, and he finished his career two years later on the bench of Pitino's New York Knicks.

"Billy the Kid" took his fearless approach to scoring to Wall Street, but the lure of the game was too strong. As Pitino's assistant, he was able to use the success of the University of Kentucky to begin his own successful coaching career.

He had instant success at Marshall with a Southern Conference North championship his first season and, after two terrific years, the University of Florida hired him as head coach. Florida did not qualify for the post-season his first year, but then the program took off. Donovan's Gators lived his approach to coaching: "Systems win! Believe in your system, and then sell it to your players." The Gators qualified for the post-season ever since, losing in the National Championship game in 2000, but winning consecutive National Championships in 2006 and 2007.

After that first National Championship in 2006, the players made a pact to return to the Gators to try to win again. The country was captivated by this rare story, and followed the team as they stormed through the season and the NCAA Tournament to fulfill the promise they had made a year earlier. Donovan lost his entire line-up after the second championship and saw four of those young men become wealthy members of the NBA.

After being courted to coach in the NBA himself, Billy Donovan returned the keys to the Orlando Magic and remains coach of the Florida Gators, where he is recruiting another group of stars to extend his record as winningest coach in school history.

to look beyond daily disrespect and discouragement to change anger into energy and to identify possibility in rejection, provided the African-American community with a model for achieving success.

McLendon was born in Hiawatha, Kansas, in 1915. He graduated from Sumner High School in Kansas City. After one year at Kansas City Junior College, he enrolled at the University of Kansas because his dad told him that going there would give him a chance to study basketball from the game's inventor. He simply ignored the fact that segregation would not allow him to play basketball at Kansas.

"Dr. Naismith taught us more than just basketball, but we were always jumping on him to talk more about basketball," McLendon said. "He just didn't want to do it. He's the reason I went to Kansas."

McLendon's groundbreaking career started almost immediately, becoming only one of the 60 non-white students in the recently integrated university. More specifically, he was the only non-white student in Naismith's first class of students to major in the physical education program.

With Allen and Naismith teaching all of the courses required for a degree in physical education, the students had clear access to the two sports legends, warts and all.

"They had interesting arguments all the time," McLendon said. "They were not bitter. They were always friends as far as I could see. I think I learned from them that you can remain friends even when you disagree about things that are important to you."

Long before John B. McLendon was breaking down barriers in the basketball world, he was breaking down barriers at KU. Apparently, the university had integrated the student body, but it had not integrated the swimming pool. One of the academic requirements for a degree in physical education was to pass a swimming test. Officials of the institution were willing to make an exception and allow McLendon to skip the swimming test, but he would have none of that. He was adamant that he would leave the university with the same degree as his fellow majors.

McLendon, Naismith, and Allen discussed options for solving the problem without incident. McLendon convinced his mentors to leave the pool open for two weeks for everyone's use and if there were no reported incidents, he would be permitted to train for and take the swimming exam. Unbeknownst to his esteemed faculty, McLendon asked all black classmates to avoid the pool for two weeks, thus eliminating the chance for trouble. With no reported problems during the agreed upon time limit, Naismith opened the pool without restriction. There were some reports that the pool was drained and refilled after McLendon's test was passed, but no records of that having occurred were ever preserved. But there is record of a successful swimming test included in McLendon's academic record.

After a season coaching basketball at Lawrence Memorial High School, an assignment for graduation, Naismith encouraged McLendon to pursue the profession.

McLendon and Naismith shared many adventures in the classroom and in life, but the depth of the relationship was revealed when McLendon let it slip that he would "mow the good doctor's lawn for 50 cents a week." You can judge for yourself the level of respect between the two when McLendon added, "Basketball finally got to the Olympics in 1936, and there was a campaign to raise funds to send Dr. Naismith to Berlin. I was living on 35 cents a day, but I contributed my 50 cents."

John B. McLendon graduated from Kansas with a B.S. in physical education and moved on to the University of Iowa, completing a Masters Degree in health, physical education, and recreation. McLendon learned a great deal from his relationship with Dr. Naismith during his years at Kansas. The teaching and learning was more than just basketball.

With a league championship won at Lawrence Memorial High School and two college degrees, he was off to begin his college coaching career as an assistant coach at North Carolina College (NCC). The assistant title was short lived as he assumed the duties of the head coach after only two years of being an apprentice.

He became the head coach at NCC in 1940 and remained in that position for 12 years. The program immediately changed its focus and sense of urgency as the new coach attacked his first college opportunity. McLendon's original contract called for a room, some meals, and a cash allotment of $50 dollars a month.

He recruited many players from the Midwest and would have his players work on campus to offset the cost of the education. He had many players who would be considered Division I caliber if they were playing today. In fact, one of his recruits, Sam Jones, eventually played professionally for the Boston Celtics and was chosen as one of the NBA's 50 greatest players of all-time.

Coach McLendon was ahead of his time in a number of areas. On the court, he emphasized a faster style of play. In addition, the focus of his program was on an intense conditioning program that was unprecedented at the time. His players would run miles prior to the season beginning, and would win games simply due to superior conditioning. More importantly, off the court he demanded class attendance and academic responsibility for all of his players. There was also a focused hatred for the segregationist policies in sport. He would risk everything to attempt to change that atmosphere.

McLendon was never shy in his opinions about segregation and the ability of his players to compete against anyone. NCC was involved in what has been named the "secret game," where McLendon and his players risked death or imprisonment to play a basketball game against a team from Duke University.

According to author Milton Katz: "The Ku Klux Klan had held a public meeting in Durham just one week before. And earlier in the year when a black GI failed to move quickly to the back of the bus, the bus driver shot and killed him. An all-white jury took just twenty minutes to exonerate the driver for his action."

During some playground banter, a challenge was made between NCC players and some guys just back from the war. A group of white medical students, that year's intramural champions at Duke, was challenged to a game by some of McLendon's guys. Originally laughed off, McLendon devised a plan to bring the team from Duke to NCC on a Sunday morning when the community would be busy in church. Piled into a couple of cars, the Duke kids arrived at NCC and slipped into the gymnasium through the back door. McLendon had arranged for a clock operator and an official, and the teams squared off in a basketball game.

NCC won handily, 88-44, and the color line was officially broken. Only a select few people knew it happened. Some of the NCC students had heard rumblings about the game and watched through the gym windows, but the game was able to remain a secret for 50 years. The players gathered in the NCC dorm after the game, unaware of what they had done. It was McLendon's view that true integration would not happen until the black players around the country understood that they could compete with the white players in head-to-head battle.

In 1952, after 13 successful seasons at NCC, an event occurred that sent McLendon on the road. The state of North Carolina voted that *"no state funds could be spent on college athletics."* Although the bigger schools might have had some contingency funds or fund-raising opportunities, most small schools didn't. New NCC President, Alfonso Elder, had to make a tough decision and reduce the emphasis on athletics at his college. Although the decision was unpopular, little could be done.

McLendon saw no alternative but to resign and take his fast-break style to another institution. There were student and community protests, but they weren't enough to change the decision. At one point McLendon did submit a list of demands that would have to be met by the institution if he were to consider staying at NCC. Although the administration loved him and what he had accomplished, there was no response to the list.

McLendon accepted an offer from Hampton Institute, where he rebuilt a tired program and provided the best record in the program's 26-year history. The difficulty facing Hampton was the requirement that students would pay for their education. With no tuition incentive for recruiting, McLendon chose after two seasons to pursue an opportunity to lead the Tigers of Tennessee A&I State University in Nashville.

It was in this portion of his career that John B. McLendon hit center stage. While winning numerous championships and breaking numerous records, sports people outside of the African-American community were noticing McLendon and his program. His high-scoring teams were fan favorites, but that was only the beginning of the story.

McLendon knew that for his programs to gain the respect they deserved, they would need to find a way to garner national attention. He set out to encourage national sports organizations to evaluate and embrace the Historically Black Colleges and Universities (HBCU) so that African-American athletes and coaches could be recognized. Although there were vestiges of integration popping up around the nation, the deep South remained firmly segregated. In 1950, along with other charter members Henry Jefferson and Eddie Jackson, McLendon began the National Athletic Steering Committee. This group was determined to plan and initiate the integration of the HBCU membership into national championship organizations.

Making every effort to follow acceptable rules and protocols, McLendon approached the NABC to see if the organization would sponsor legislation to include African-American schools and coaches into the organizations that govern national competitions. The NABC would discuss and table such a measure, but the NCAA would emphatically shut the door. Tug Wilson, a member of the NCAA administrative staff, refused to consider the idea and responded with some directives of his own.

"It would be impractical to recommend your request to the Executive Committee of the NCAA," he said. "With district representation governing the selection process, this would mean that if a colored team was selected from a district, there would be no other representation. It was the feeling judged from the records of one of your good teams playing on the coast, that the quality of competition is not equal to tournament caliber."

McLendon was frustrated because in the South competition between black schools and white schools was forbidden so that moving through any sort of district qualifying was impossible. In a very heated and uncharacteristic tirade to a reporter, McLendon identified the NCAA as No Colored Athletes Allowed. The NCAA then offered the Steering Committee an opportunity to present the case at the next convention, but it was conveniently held in a segregated hotel in Dallas. Not long after, the NCAA Executive Committee officially denied the proposal to restructure the tournament, squashing any attempt for integration.

"You may rest assured that our selection committee will watch the performance of teams of the four major colored conferences," Walter Byers announced on behalf of the NCAA. "When one of your schools has an outstanding basketball team, it will be considered for a member-at-large berth in the tournament field on the same basis as the other member schools of this association."

McLendon and the National Athletic Steering Committee made no headway with the NCAA, but they did find the National Association of Intercollegiate Basketball (NAIB) more willing to listen to the committee's proposals. The NAIB tournament had been unofficially segregated to that point, but it had no written rules prohibiting teams of color from participation. In 1952, the NAIB officially opened their organization and their tournaments for all teams that met their standards.

The Steering Committee had worked diligently to gain basketball recognition for the HBCU and the work became a reality in 1953 when McLendon's Tennessee A&I Tigers won the NAIA District Championship and, without fanfare, fully integrated the first national basketball championship tournament. The championship was not to be had this time, but the Tigers would eventually win three consecutive NAIA National Championships in 1957, '58 and '59, making McLendon the first and only African-American basketball coach to do that. In addition, he was the first black coach selected as the NAIA Coach of the Year.

John B. McLendon was not finished trailblazing, though. George Steinbrenner (yes, that one) made McLendon the first black coach in professional basketball when he hired McLendon to coach the Cleveland Pipers in the American Basketball League. He would also be the first black coach to be assigned a position on the United States Olympic team staff, albeit as a scout. Then in 1966, McLendon became the first black basketball coach at a traditionally white university when Cleveland State hired him to run their program. Today, McLendon is represented at the school with his name being forever associated with their basketball facility.

John B. McLendon, who died in October 1999, touched thousands of players, coaches, administrators, and officials—black and white—connected to this great game. He was honored with induction into the Naismith Memorial Basketball Hall of Fame in 1979. He insisted at the time that his career was a success because of the teachings of James Naismith.

"It's sort of like being back in the classroom," McLendon said. "I had no idea we'd (he and Naismith) wind up together in a place like this. Especially me. When he was teaching me there in Kansas, I couldn't even get into the pool … It took time and patience, but things did change."

GUARDIAN

BEN JOBE
(HBCU, RE-BUILDER,
GENTLEMAN, COMPETITOR)

Photo courtesy: Ben Jobe

"He is one of two legendary pioneering African-American coaches– John McLendon, his mentor, being the other– who spent time in Denver and helped change a game that becomes an American sports obsession each March. Their contribution went far beyond wins and losses. They inspired, innovated, and helped break down barriers to enable blacks to have the impact they have today, as players and coaches."

— **Chris Dempsey,** *Denver Post*

Growing up in Nashville, Tennessee, Ben Jobe was sure that he'd get to play for John B. McLendon Jr. at North Carolina Central. After all, Jobe was an outstanding player at Pearl High School, where he was an All-State selection in 1950 and then All-Nation pick in 1951. But when high school graduation happened, McLendon was coaching at Hampton University and they were non-scholarship, which eliminated Hampton as an option. Instead, Jobe would go on to star at Nashville's Fisk University, where he earned All-Conference honors his final two seasons.

During the latter stages of Jobe's career at Fisk, McLendon took the head coaching position at Tennessee State and the two renewed their relationship.

"Often after my practice at Fisk, I would hitch a ride to State to watch McLendon practice," Jobe said. "I would sometimes stay at his home and return the next morning. He lived in a barracks left over from the war and we would go there and talk about the game."

When Jobe took the coaching job at Cameron High School in Nashville, McLendon would come to the school after his practice and help Jobe run the team.

Jobe took his mentor's words to heart and Cameron had a masterful season, winning 24 games and qualifying for the state tournament. He was so sure that the winning would continue throughout the tournament that when Cameron lost, he immediately resigned his position. Jobe had not considered defeat and he simply reacted.

Jobe left for California shortly after that crushing loss and started playing again while making a living in the insurance business. He was just so personally scarred by that loss and too far from his mentor to understand that losing was a part of coaching.

COACH PROFILE

PAUL HEWITT –
GEORGIA TECH UNIVERSITY
(NABC MEMBER 19 YEARS)

"I was more nervous than excited. The first thing I had to do was a press conference. While they're great for the media and fans, it's just like a wedding. Everyone likes going to the wedding and having the honeymoon, but after that you have to be married. That's when the real work starts."

Paul Hewitt is the only foreign-born member of the profiled coaches. He led the Georgia Tech Yellow Jackets to the Final Four in 2004. What an exciting and career changing event that must have been, in only his second position as a head coach. Growing up in Kingston, Jamaica, and then Westbury, New York, one can't help but wonder if he ever dreamed of taking a team to the Final Four. Hewitt's high school career in Westbury was followed by a four-year college playing career at St. John Fisher College in Rochester, New York.

Paul Hewitt began his coaching career as an assistant coach at C.W. Post on Long Island. That opportunity would lead to a series of assistant positions at elite basketball programs around the country. He would hone his skills with stops at USC, Fordham, and Villanova before he would get his first opportunity to lead a program.

Siena University, in upstate New York hired him as their head coach in 1997 and he led Siena to post-season competition in the NIT the second season and the NCAA in the third season. Coaches leading little-known programs to the national stage often lead to greater opportunities and so it was for Hewitt. Georgia Tech would take note of Siena's appearance and hire Hewitt in 2000. He would lead the Yellow Jackets to five post-season appearances in eight years.

Hewitt distinguished himself by earning Coach of the Year honors in his final season at Siena and then again in his first season at Georgia Tech. The Jackets would enjoy the finest season under Hewitt when they qualified for the Final Four in 2004, earned a spot in the championship game, only to lose to Jim Calhoun and the University of Connecticut.

Many will say that it is easier to get to the top than it is to stay there. The Hewitt led Yellow Jackets have not returned to the pinnacle of college basketball since that incredible run, but "experts" like Dick Vitale and Digger Phelps insist that it is only a matter of time before Hewitt will lead them back to a spot in the Final Four and an NCAA National Championship.

Things in the insurance industry didn't come easy. Jobe tried to look forward and relieved his stress playing basketball as often as he could. He didn't realize his next opportunity was in front of him.

"I was playing in a game and afterwards, I ran into a guy I knew from college," Jobe said. "He gave me his card from something called the African American Institute. The insurance job was a struggle and I soon found myself on the way to Washington, D.C. They sent me to school in London and Paris to learn the African language and culture and then off to Sierra Leone as a 'Games Master.' That is what I really was; I was supposed to know about every game there was. I taught soccer and cricket, but really I just asked the oldest kids to be in charge of those games and then I introduced basketball."

The African kids were familiar with a game called "net ball," actually a game invented by Phog Allen for schools that did not have the facilities for basketball. In Africa, this game was thought to be for girls, so in the beginning, it was a tough sell, but Jobe broke through the barriers.

Ben Jobe returned to the States, took the head coaching position at Tuskegee Institute and renewed his friendship with McLendon, who by that time was creating quite a stir in coaching circles. This would be the first of many stops for Jobe in the world of Historically Black Colleges and Universities (HBCU) that included stints at Talladega College, Alabama State University, South Carolina State, Alabama A&M University and Southern University.

This does not mean that Jobe never ventured out, but he was committed to a similar position as McLendon: *"Let's use our efforts to improve the HBCU member schools."*

At one point in his career, he would take an assistant's position with Hall of Fame coach Frank McGuire at the University of South Carolina. McGuire favored a slow game, but was interested in the faster style favored by McLendon and Jobe. During this stop, Jobe joined Bobby Cremins as South Carolina assistants.

"Ben had a great deal of class, always well-spoken and well-dressed, a real professional," Cremins wrote in an e-mail for this book. "He was ahead of his time or else everybody would know about Ben Jobe."

Cremins and Jobe remain friends today, even though it was Cremins' Georgia Tech University team that would provide Jobe with

The McGuire Boys! Frank of South Carolina and Al of Marquette discussing hoops.

a career highlight: the Southern University victory over Georgia Tech in the NCAA Championship Tournament in front of a national television audience.

That high point definitely helps even out the low point, which happened when Jobe was an assistant at South Carolina.

"Frank McGuire asked me to write to a high school coach in D.C. named John Thompson [Jr.], who had a great black player, about that player coming to South Carolina," Jobe said. "I will never forget that Thompson called me on the phone and cussed me out for recruiting a black player, from a black coach, for a white coach and white school. He basically called me an 'Uncle Tom' and I realized that as far as we had come, it was not far enough."

Jobe ventured away from the HBCU programs for a stint at the University of Denver and in the NBA with the Nuggets, but took those experiences, returned, and worked to improve HBCU programs throughout his career. Ben Jobe would complete his career with a record of 524-333 and four NCAA Tournament appearances and one NIT appearance. When asked to offer advice to young coaches who are just entering coaching, he got a huge smile on his face and said, "Stay ahead of the posse. When you are walking across the campus and you see the university president and you wave and he does not wave back, it is time to clean out your office."

GUARDIAN

CLARENCE "BIG HOUSE" GAINES (NCAA COLLEGE DIVISION PIONEER)

"Our role as mentors, monitors and managers should have a humbling effect on us. We're expected to win, while molding young people into model citizens. Perhaps expectations are a little unreasonable, but we continue to accept the challenges. We routinely face obstacles that, though formidable, are not insurmountable. While the problems are not ours alone, we can influence many of the circumstances from which they arise. Thus, we are in uniquely influential positions to make a difference."

— Letter to NABC membership, 1989

Photo courtesty:
Winston Salem State University

Clarence Gaines was born in Paducah, Kentucky, in 1923. After he and his family survived the Great Depression, he became a two-sport star at Lincoln High School in Paducah. Not unusual for the time, he then had a two-sport career in college at Morgan

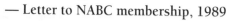

State in Maryland, playing football and basketball for four years. His nickname "Big House" originated when he arrived at Morgan State and his dorm director was startled at his enormous size and commented, "I've never seen anything bigger than you but a house." The name never left him. So, with a degree in chemistry, an All-American award, and a nickname, "Big House" left for Winston-Salem, North Carolina, and his first coaching job.

Gaines was going to be a dentist, but he couldn't afford dental school. He decided to earn some money coaching football, basketball and track & field at Winston-Salem State. He was sure that in only a few years he would be able to save enough to go off the dental school. His contract listed him as an assistant in all three sports, but that was short-lived. In 1947, he became the head coach of all three and gradually the dream of becoming a dentist faded away.

"I don't think I was meant to be a dentist," he said. "Coaching is what the Lord called me to do."

While Gaines is recognized as a great coach, he is also mentioned when people talk about coaches who are truly great people. He touched thousands of lives and everyone who met Big House remembers the place and the time. Billy Packer will often comment that after he made a rude comment about a coach on television, he got a phone call from Gaines, reminding him that coaching was an honorable profession, and they should be respected. Packer said that the call is something that he remembers every time he is asked to do an interview.

A Glance At ...
Clarence "Big House" Gaines

- 1948 CIAA Football Coach of the Year
- CIAA Tournament Outstanding Coach '53, '57, '60, '61, '63, '66, '70, '77
- CIAA Coach of the Year '57, '61, '63, '70, '75, '80
- 1968 Helms Foundation Hall of Fame
- 1976 NAIA District #26 Outstanding Coach Award
- 1976 CIAA Sports Hall of Fame
- 1980 Winston-Salem State Hall of Fame
- 1982 Naismith Memorial Basketball Hall of Fame
- 1989 NABC President

One of the earliest black members of the NABC board, Gaines was often called upon to be the conscience of the organization. He frequently reminded the membership of their responsibilities beyond basketball.

"Dick Schultz, in his remarks about the NCAA and a possible restructuring, leaves each of us with a great responsibility," Gaines wrote in a letter to the NABC members in 1989. "He continues to remind us that the organization (NABC) can only function as you want it to function. The membership makes and changes all the rules. We, the coaches, can render a greater service to basketball by thoroughly comprehending the legislative practices."

Gaines won an NCAA Division II National Championship in 1967 after his team went 31-1. It was the first time an HBCU institution won an NCAA national championship. For his efforts, Gaines was honored as the National Coach of the Year. That great team was led by one of the great players of all-time, Earl "The Pearl" Monroe, a New York City star who came to Winston-Salem to play.

And boy, did Monroe ever play! He averaged 26.7 points a game during 110 games played. His senior year—the year of the national championship—he averaged an astonishing 41.5 points and was selected as the NCAA College Division (Division II) Player of the Year. Gaines had taken a playground star from the big city and coached him to collegiate stardom and NBA stardom—including induction into the Basketball Hall of Fame.

Clarence "Big House" Gaines retired after coaching for 47 years at Winston-Salem State University. His retirement was recognized with national regret, but without a shortage of rewards.

Coach Gaines was recognized for his coaching prowess, his community service, and his never-ending spirit across North Carolina, the United States and wherever basketball was played.

He finished his career second in wins (828), ahead of everyone except Adolph Rupp at that time. He will always be remembered in Winston-Salem with his name adorning the Arena, C.E. GAINES CENTER.

GUARDIAN

JOHN CHANEY
(FATHER FIGURE, FIGHTER,
MATCH-UP ZONE)

"As a coach, I've had plenty of players go to the NBA, but that's not important to me. I'm just happy we were able to give them a chance to improve their lives. Now they can go out and help others who didn't have the same opportunity they did."

— John Chaney

Can a coach be successful recruiting unknown kids, and then make them practice at 6 a.m. every day? Can a coach be successful harping on every single misstep and error on the court? Can a coach be successful when he has a stable full of athletes itching to fly and play a style of basketball that emphasizes defense and rebounding,

COACH PROFILE
BEN HOWLAND – UCLA
(NABC MEMBER 18 YEARS)

"My recommendation and one of the things I told Kevin (Love), and I will tell both the Westbrooks and the Collisons, when I meet with them over the next few days, is that they definitely should not sign with an agent, even if they put their names in, and to keep going to school."

Ben Howland has a streak of three Final Four appearances in three years and the comparisons to John Wooden are on everyone's lips. Let's hope that the version that ends with "when he wins the big one" will stay away for a while. Coach Wooden persevered through the naysayers and so will Howland. This Southern California native was two-time All-California player at Cerritos High School leading to a college career at Santa Barbara City College and Weber State University. This defensive specialist would even be able to play for pay in Uruguay.

One of the more unusual challenges he faced as an assistant coach was to be responsible for guarding Dream Team guard John Stockton every day while playing at Gonzaga University. Howland carried his mantra for defense through several stops as an assistant before Northern Arizona University hired him as its head coach.

Howland developed his taste for the limelight assisting Jerry Pimm at the University of California-Santa Barbara and gaining five consecutive post-season appearances. He won the Big Sky Conference two consecutive years at Northern Arizona and qualified for post-season play. Coach refined his defensive philosophy coaching Pittsburgh in the rugged Big East Conference, winning the title twice and led Pitt to an appearance in the Sweet Sixteen. Howland would return to California as the UCLA head coach in 2003.

Ben Howland has a record that few could match. He has coached in three NCAA Division-I conferences, has been Coach of the Year in each, and was selected Naismith National Coach of the Year. He introduced toughness and defense to the Bruins program and to the Pac 10 Conference, and is single-handedly removing the Pac 10 perception as a finesse conference. Howland joined Tom Izzo and Mike Krzyzewski as the only three coaches who earned three consecutive trips to the Final Four since the tournament was expanded to 64 teams.

Maybe John Wooden said it best when asked about the state of Bruin basketball. "We are in a good place with Ben (Howland)," he said.

and wins with scores in the 50s? Apparently, the answer to all those questions is a resounding YES. At least that is what John Chaney did at Temple University.

Between 1983 and 1988, he won at least 25 games a year and was awarded five National Coach of the Year awards.

"The most bothersome and misunderstood aspect of this business," Chaney said, "is that people who win are looked at as people who are good coaches."

John Chaney was born in Jacksonville, Florida, in 1932. His family would move to Philadelphia and he would become one of the famous personalities of that great city, but not before he paid the dues necessary of all black athletes and coaches. He would become a major source of influence for those hoping to compete as a professional athlete or a basketball coach of some visibility.

As a player, Chaney was a tenacious competitor who was picked as Philadelphia Public League Most Valuable Player at Ben Franklin High in 1951, his senior year. He agreed to attend historically black Bethune-Cookman College and then had a brief stint with the Harlem Globetrotters. Chaney also spent a few years in professional basketball in the Eastern League, where he won an MVP award. Chaney finished his playing career in the Eastern League after a car he was riding in was involved in a head-on crash. The accident left him in the hospital for a month with phlebitis. But he wanted to stay in basketball somehow.

With few opportunities available

A Glance At … John Chaney

- Temple record 499-238
- Atlantic 10 record 327-108
- 18 NCAA Division I Tournament appearances
- NCAA Regional Finalist '88, '91, '93, '99, '01
- NIT appearances '89, '02, '03, '04, '05
- Atlantic 10 Season Championships '85, '87, '88, '90, '98, '99, '00, '02
- Atlantic 10 Tournament Championships '85, '87, '88, '90, '00, '01
- Temple– 15 20-win seasons
- USBWA National Coach of the Year 1987, 1988
- National Coach of the Year, AP Coach of the Year 1988
- Eastern Basketball Coach of the Year 1993

in coaching, Chaney took the reins of a junior high school team and worked with older players on the playground. He was mentoring kids on life, while teaching them about the game of basketball. Chaney got his first real chance to coach at Simon Gratz High School in Philadelphia. Then, after successful years leading high school teams to a 63-23 record, Chaney got his first taste of college coaching at HBCU Cheyney State University.

Cheyney State was a NCAA Division II institution playing in the highly competitive Pennsylvania State Athletic Conference and was competing without the advantage of scholarships. Always seeming to be behind the eight-ball, Chaney built a program that few could match. In a decade, he achieved a record of 225-56 and won the NCAA Division II National Championship in 1978.

This success led to a 1982 appointment, at the age of 50, to lead the Temple University Owls and try his hand at competing with the likes of Bob Knight and Dean Smith. He succeeded.

Chaney's career was not without issues. He worked his way through the segregated years, finding whatever opportunity came along. He refused to be assigned to a life of poverty and restriction and battled for everything he achieved. When he finally arrived at Temple, those battle scars were so ingrained that he was unable to soften his approach and any slight that seemed to be directed at him or his players was answered with a significant response.

There were problems with officials, administrators and peers during his tenure at Temple, but he would always serve his punishments with dignity.

Always emotional and repentant, he would support and defend his players with the same furor. There was never a question of his loyalty to his players, his university, or his profession.

"For me, clearly, he's a pioneer for a lot of us young African-American coaches," George Washington University coach Karl Hobbs told *The Washington Post* in 2005, "because of the stance that he took back in the early '90s when there was a big push for hiring more African-American coaches, and he led the charge for that. And so to a large degree, he's responsible for me being in the position that I'm in now."

John Chaney retired in 2006 as his Temple Owls were about to enter NIT competition in March. His wife was ill and it was time to use what energy and fight he had left for her.

There were nicer people in the profession; there were better-dressed people in the profession; there were better-educated people in the profession, but there has never been a more passionate, harder working, student-athlete advocating coach in the profession.

While John Chaney was stalking the sidelines on the East Coast, a similar occurrence was taking place out West. There was a dynamic individual working his way through the maze of segregation and winning basketball games. Although the results could be compared, certainly the styles and the route to the big time were entirely different.

GUARDIAN

NOLAN RICHARDSON
(ATHLETE, CHAMPION, 40-MINUTES OF HELL)

"I'm very fortunate, I'm very lucky and I'm very appreciative. I think the good Lord really blessed me for having the opportunity. See, I don't think I would've been here if I had to pass the SAT back then."

— Nolan Richardson

When discussing Nolan Richardson, one can never be sure of the motivation behind the man. He faced all of the challenges growing up and won more than he lost. He was a great athlete, but used his talents to serve others. He won championships at several levels, but when apparently reaching the pinnacle of college basketball success, he seemed to slowly tear down everything he had worked so hard to build.

Nolan Richardson was born and raised in El Paso, Texas. After his birth in 1941, he had little contact with his father. After his mother passed away, he was raised by his grandmother, Rose Richardson. Rose, who was the daughter of a slave, was never far from Nolan's thoughts.

As Richardson says, "She taught me to battle for stuff."

Richardson was a four-sport star in high school. He really made a name for himself at Bowie High, but his memory of those times is of the split city and a curfew that required all to be off the streets at night. Rose would always be on the porch awaiting her grandson's arrival, doing all she could to protect her boy from the ugliness of the neighborhood. Daily, he said her message was, *"You are special"*, and he took that to heart.

Richardson learned to focus his anger and his passion during a sports-related incident in high school. He was the only black player on the baseball team and when the team qualified for the playoffs, he was not permitted to stay at the team hotel. While his teammates were swimming and eating hotel meals, he had to stay *"across the tracks."* This snub brought on such hostility that he responded with an incredible tournament and realized the depth of his internal strength.

"You gotta keep going berserk," Rose told Nolan. "That's the only way you're going to make it, either with your bat or with the ball, which means that if you're good enough, you're going to get your scholarship and you can keep going. If you're good enough in the classroom and get enough education behind you, you keep fighting.

Eventually, somebody's going to open the door. You just keep knocking. It'll open. And when it does, you knock that damn door down."

That door opened in the form of a scholarship at Texas Western from legendary coach Don Haskins. Similar to Bowie High School, Richardson was one of the first black athletes donning the Texas Western uniforms. He didn't get away from the segregated attitudes when he went to college, and this time he was left home from a game at Centenary because they remained a segregated campus at that time. He listened on the radio, disgusted when the team lost, while the best player was left home.

While Richardson was playing at Texas Western, he was sure that Haskins worked at team chemistry by "having the team bond together by making sure we all hated him." Years after leaving college, he realized what lessons he had learned from the hall of fame coach: "discipline, hard work and to attack at both ends."

With Rose Richardson forever in his heart, Nolan began a coaching career that would constantly tear down racial barriers. Not specifically stated, but one can get the feeling that there was a method to this madness. He returned to Bowie High School as the first black coach, and followed that as the first black coach at Western Texas Junior College. In 1980, Richardson led Western Texas to a 37-0 record and won the NJCAA National Championship. He then moved to Tulsa and became the first black head coach at UT. Each stop a barrier removed; each stop a successful program; each stop a *damn door knocked down.*

When asked directly about the barrier smashing, he responded, "I was first because no one else got a chance."

Ben Jobe remembers seeing Richardson's junior college team play.

"(John) McLendon and I were in Hutchinson (Kansas) watching the junior college national championship," Jobe said, "when this team with a black coach came on the court and pressed and ran the competition out of the gym. I looked at John and asked who that was, and he responded, 'I don't know, but I sure love his style.' That was the first we heard about Richardson."

Nolan Richardson followed Eddie Sutton at Arkansas and became the first black coach at the southern university. There was a very mixed reaction to his arrival, even though the program was in shambles. Trying to get the slow Razorbacks to play the game at the frenetic pace that Richardson favored was like trying to get a 2-year-old to stop running around a room full of people. A 12-16 record was the final indication that recruiting would have to change. Richardson focused the next three years on athleticism and it showed with a record of 89-16.

Richardson took the Razorbacks to the Final Four three times during this period and in coaching circles his defense became know as "40 Minutes of Hell." Arkansas lost to Duke in the 1990 NCAA Tournament and then returned the favor in the 1994 national title game in Charlotte, North Carolina. Richardson was crowned with the honor of National Basketball Coach of the Year.

Arkansas returned to the Final Four in 1995, where the Razorbacks lost in the national championship to UCLA. The program seemed to struggle for a time after that loss and Richardson became more and more frustrated with what he identified as a double standard for coaches at the university.

After seventeen years and a coaching record of 389-169, Richardson decided to take on the institution and Director of Athletics Frank Broyles in a very public and very ugly exchange of words.

The embattled coach was fired after claims of racial discrimination were found to be unsubstantiated. Richardson sued the university and several external parts of the athletic department based on his discrimination claims. The lawsuit was dismissed.

Richardson, like McLendon, never pursued any type of leadership role in the NABC. Although he could (and would) be a coach with some tremendous influence, that type of leadership doesn't appeal to him.

· "The NABC was a way to get tickets to the Final Four," he said in December 2007. "I belonged for 29 years, but I can't identify any particular significance they might have held."

Richardson was selected in 2008 for the National Collegiate Basketball Hall of Fame.

GUARDIAN

GEORGE RAVELING
(COACH, RECRUITER,
SHOE ENTREPRENEUR)

"There wasn't a parent out there who wasn't at ease with George Raveling. ... (He) was the sole reason I came to Washington State from Sacramento. He immediately became a father figure to me."
— **Former Raveling player James Donaldson, who went on to a 14-year NBA career**

George Raveling, a former president of the NABC, was born in Washington, D.C., on June 27, 1937, and prepped at St. Michaels in Hoban Heights, Pennsylvania. He was an honor student and even tried his hand in politics, winning the vice-presidency of his senior class.

COACH PROFILE

BOB HUGGINS –
UNIVERSITY OF WEST VIRGINIA
(NABC MEMBER 24 YEARS)

"I'm excited that we (WVU) can go full steam ahead into the future. As I've said before, we want to win a national championship. We want to go play in the Final Four. We want to be one of the teams that year-in and year-out, when they talk about people having a chance to win a national championship, we want to be in that conversation."

Now here is a tough profile to write. We have to weave together winning championships, graduation difficulties, a unique coaching style, heart attacks, screams and hugs, and a hero returning home. Bob Huggins has never shied away from confrontation or competition, and he has returned to Morgantown to lead the Mountaineers to the pinnacle of college basketball.

Huggins used a series of assistant positions to prepare for his head coaching career. After assisting university programs at West Virginia, Ohio State, and Central Florida, Huggins got his first chance as a head coach at Walsh University. He would compile an impressive record of 71-26 with a season-best 34-1, the loss occurring in the NAIA National Tournament.

After a five-year tenure as the head coach at Akron University, he moved to the University of Cincinnati and the fireworks began. Cincinnati was now back among the elite programs in the country. That is attributed directly to Huggins and his ability to recruit and coach talent. After 14 consecutive NCAA bids, two Elite Eight appearances, and one Final Four, a very low graduation rate and a philosophical difference with school administration sent him to the sidelines.

After a well-publicized heart attack and recovery, Kansas State embraced the coach. He would last only one season, but in that season he would bring two future first-round draft choices and a post-season appearance to Manhattan. Even under a new coach, it was Huggins' players who led K-State to the NCAA Tournament in 2007-08.

For those who say, "You can never go home," Huggins expanded the envelope. Huggins led the Mountaineers to a Sweet Sixteen berth in his first season, and with a new contract in hand, the fans are looking for more of the same and better.

After a solid prep basketball career, he took his formidable talents to Villanova University, where he was voted "senior student of the year" in 1960 by the school newspaper and was an All-American on the basketball court before the NBA's Philadelphia Warriors drafted him. (He ended up playing in the Eastern League for several years.)

Raveling began his coaching career as an assistant at his alma mater (Villanova), where he began a masterful run recruiting prep players for major universities. He would be recognized for recruiting the major pieces of the Villanova team that reached the Final Four in 1971. He did not have the opportunity to share the victories, however, because he had moved on to Maryland to assist Lefty Driesell. It was here that he became the first African-American coach in the Atlantic Coast Conference (ACC). After three years with Driesell, Raveling was ready for a leadership position of his own. He had been coaching the Terrapins' freshmen team and posted an undefeated 1971 season (freshman were not eligible for varsity competition). Now he needed a university president to have the courage to hire a black head coach to lead a major college program.

A Glance At ... George Raveling

- 1975 Pac-10 Coach of the Year
- 1977 National Black Sports Foundation Coach of the Year
- 1983 NABC District Coach of the Year
- 1992 BCA Coach of the Year
- 1992 Pac-10 Coach of the Year
- 1992 Basketball Weekly Coach of the Year
- 1992 Kodak National Coach of the Year
- 1994 Inducted Pac-10 Basketball Hall of Fame

Raveling found his chance at Washington State University (WSU) in 1973. He accepted the position and became the first black head coach in Pac-10 history. He would lead the Cougars for 11 years, recording a record of 167-136. In his final eight years at WSU, he trailed only John Wooden (UCLA) and Ralph Miller (Oregon State) in winning percentage. In 1980, he led the Cougars to their first NCAA Tournament appearance since 1941. (They went again under Raveling in 1983.)

The nomadic lifestyle of a basketball coach continued for Raveling as he left WSU for the University of Iowa for three years and then returned to the Pac-10 as head coach at the University of Southern California (USC).

"I view this as coming home," he said. "I felt there were only four or five jobs in the country that I would leave Iowa for and USC is one of them. I think Los Angeles is one of the great cities in the world. My aspirations and my comfort zone are much more compatible to an urban area and this area has the intangibles to build a successful program."

Raveling said in 2007 that looking back, the only career move that he considered a mistake was leaving Iowa when he did. His last two Hawkeye teams reached 20 wins and received tournament berths. He felt the program was on the edge of greatness, and would have liked to have ridden that opportunity to the end of the string.

Always with the personality of a recruiter (or politician, depending on how you see it), Raveling parlayed successful coaching stops and coach of the year awards into unique opportunities. He was selected to coach the West team at the 1979 Olympic Festival; to coach on Dave Gavitt's 1980 Olympic Trials staff; to coach Amateur Basketball Association of the United States of America (ABAUSA) teams in China and Korea; and then to assist Bob Knight on the Olympic staff in 1984.

Always a visionary and always exploring avenues to influence young people and coaches, Raveling wrote two books for coaches and produced a videotape titled, "If It Is To Be, It's Up To Me."

In 1994, George Raveling left the world of basketball coaching on a full-time basis. He contributed for a few years in international and Olympic levels of competition, before entering the high-dollar world of sports apparel. Now as an executive with Nike, he moves among coaches and athletes negotiating those arrangements that make coaches very wealthy and turn some athletes into millionaires. He continues to represent the company in all corners of the world.

GUARDIAN
JOHN THOMPSON JR.
(PLAYER, COACH, CHAMPION, ADVOCATE)

"I want to be a winner. I want my players to graduate and I want to get rich ... The biggest con in education is kids saying they were exploited. If the kid doesn't get an education, it's his fault. Put yourself in a position of power where you create a need for yourself that has an economic effect on somebody. The world is not black or white as much as it is green."

— John Thompson

John Thompson Jr. is retired now. He can be found sitting in the gym at Georgetown University watching practice, sitting in the stands for Georgetown games and on radio stations around the country voicing his opinions on today's game. He is as impressive a figure today as he was when he was playing for the

Boston Celtics as the understudy to Bill Russell for two world championship seasons.

Thompson, who was born in 1941 in Washington, D.C., was not necessarily interested in school and actually was rejected from his Catholic school for reading below his grade level. His mother refused to accept the school's position and, with a good dose of reading and being read to at home, he was able to make progress in junior high school. There was a re-start in the seventh grade, but from there he did OK. As he grew taller, he became interested in playing basketball and started hanging out at the Police Boys Club in the neighborhood. He learned the game from many playground legends and it was in junior high school that he learned what basketball could mean to him.

"Coach Kermit Tigg taught us that athletics is supposed to be more than recreation or recognition," Thompson said. "It was a form of security I needed."

Thompson's Archbishop John Carroll High School teams were setting records almost every time they took the court. Thompson accepted a basketball scholarship at Providence College, where he led the Friars to an NIT Championship and was selected New England College Player of the Year in 1964.

The Boston Celtics thought so much of Thompson that they drafted him out of Providence. According to the Celtics media guide in 1960:

"At John Carroll High, John fared so well that he twice made the All D.C. schoolboy team. After entering Providence College, he improved so much that he was named to the All-NIT club in his junior year and the All-New England club in his last two seasons. In addition to excelling as a rebounder, he also starred for the Friars as a scorer. He established three all-time campus marks—for the most points in a game (43), most points for one season (681), and most points over a four-year period (1520)."

After several years and two championships with the Celtics, mainly as Bill Russell's backup, Thompson returned to Washington. He left a lucrative deal to remain in the NBA on the table and accepted the position to coach the St. Anthony's High School team. He had great success at the high school level, finishing with a record of 122-28.

During all of this basketball playing and coaching, Thompson found time to complete a Master's Degree in guidance and counseling. In the next several years, he received honorary doctorates awarded for reasons far exceeding his accomplishments on the basketball court.

Relying on the lessons learned from Celtics' coach Red Auerbach, Bill Russell and his days coaching St. Anthony's, Thompson took on the challenge of coaching the Georgetown University Hoyas. Thompson took a 3-23 team and quickly turned the Hoyas into a college basketball powerhouse.

Thompson created some controversy when he appointed a woman to be an assistant coach. His first hire was Mary Fenlon, a former nun, who would strive to maintain order in all things non-basketball related.

"I'm a basketball coach, and if it were up to me, I'd spend all of our time on basketball," Thompson said. "Mary would not allow me to do that, she will shoo the kids out of the gym if she has to."

After getting Georgetown into the NCAA Tournament in 1975, Thompson's teams qualified for post-season play 24 consecutive years. Mixing in four NIT appearances and three Final Four appearances, he achieved a combined record of 596-239.

With a career winning percentage hovering above 73 percent in 1984, Thompson became the first African-American coach to win a Division I NCAA National Championship.

That incredible coaching record at Georgetown University was equaled by his players succeeding in the classroom. Everyone has heard the story about the flat basketball on his desk and his question, *what are you going to do when basketball is over?* The message was clear throughout the program that education was THE priority.

"I want my players to graduate," Thompson said, "but I'm not responsible for them getting an education. If they understand that they are responsible, they'll get it. The product we are trying to produce is not necessarily love and affection. It's education."

Center stage in the Georgetown success in basketball was a one-man boycott of a Big East game to emphasize the discrimination taking place with NCAA regulations tying scholarships and freshman eligibility. As the Georgetown-Providence game was about to tip-off, Thompson walked from the gym to a standing ovation.

"I don't think there is another coach in the country who could have taken the stand he did on proposition 42," said Richard Lapchick of the Center for Sports and Society. "He was powerful enough that he couldn't be fired and he raised an issue that a lot of white coaches supported him on. He was a lightening rod."

Most of the legislation that the NCAA wanted in, got in. There were other threats of sorts, but the only coach who used the game to make his point was Thompson.

Ironically, Thompson took the most criticism after something happened —or, rather, didn't happen—on an international stage. After serving as Dean Smith's assistant with the 1976 Olympic Team that won the gold medal, Thompson became the head coach for the 1988 U.S. Olympic Team. As it turned out, his was the first team that did not reach the final game. Thompson took the brunt of the criticism. The relatively unspoken perception of racism throughout his career came crashing to the forefront and he was soundly criticized for his selections to fill out the squad.

Analysts will point to the three international competitions, the 1987 Pan American Games, the 1988 Olympics and the 1990 World Championships—all American

COACH PROFILE

TOM IZZO –
MICHIGAN STATE UNIVERSITY
(NABC MEMBER 28 YEARS)

"I am so sick of people saying he's a defensive coach, he's a rebounding coach, a great running game coach, a great offensive execution coach, a great special-teams-sidelines-out-of-bounds-coach. I want utopia. I want my players to want utopia."

Who says you cannot replace a legend? This Iron Mountain native did just that and Tom Izzo says, "I am fine thank you." Tom Izzo was fortunate or unfortunate in having the opportunity to replace legendary basketball coach (and stand-up comedian) Jud Heathcote on the Michigan State bench. He got his chance to lead an elite program, or any program for that matter, when Heathcote decided to retire. He has won more than 300 games, made an appearance in four Final Fours, and won a National Championship.

It is actually unfair to say that Michigan State was his first head coaching position because he did have that role at Ishpeming High School. He then began the nomad trek through the assistant coaching ranks bouncing between Northern Michigan, Michigan State, Tulsa, and a return to Michigan State. This resume building resulted in Heathcote picking Izzo as the associate head coach for a time.

Izzo and the Spartans are regular attendees in post-season circles and have a string of NCAA Tournament appearances that do not look like they will be ending anytime soon. This continued success has allowed him to enjoy coaching in the USA Basketball program with a 2003 position in the Pan American Games. This Big 10 Coach of the Year, AP Coach of the Year and Henry Iba Award winner joins Ben Howland and Mike Krzyzewski as the only coaches to earn spots in three consecutive Final Fours since the tournament expanded to 64 teams.

losses—as a trend of building disinterest among the college stars. Each of those teams was coached by a Hall of Fame coach, but some players avoided the competitions and others took a more "me" focused approach. This trend was started a few years earlier when players such as Lew Alcindor, Elvin Hayes, and Bill Walton opted out of Olympic competition for a variety of reasons. There was considerable speculation that the addition of NBA players took the focus from those important international competitions.

It should be noted here that the common perception that Thompson was the reason NBA players and coaches became the participants in future Olympics is simply not true. The rule to allow professional players had already been made, but ratification came after the 1988 Games. Professional players were already allowed in the Olympics, but NBA players were not. The new rule changed all of that. The United States voted against the measure, but when it passed, it just seemed natural to coach NBA professionals with NBA coaches. This practice remained in place until Mike Krzyzewski was selected for the 2008 Games in China.

John Thompson's proudest moment was his selection to the Naismith Memorial Basketball Hall of Fame. He was unsure if he would ever get in. However, after three ballots, he made it.

"I'm not sure why (it means so much to me)," he said. "It is the period that ends all sentences. It's something that takes a lot of time and a lot of work. There are a lot of people I've always admired and respected who are in the Hall."

McLendon, Jobe, Gaines, Chaney, Richardson, Raveling, and Thompson all had one thing in common. They were the trailblazers. Everything that came after their careers was a blessing for the coaches wanting quality positions. As Billy Packer says, "some people say that if Gaines was that good, why didn't he coach in the ACC? People just don't have any understanding that he was never given the opportunity." These seven gentlemen broke down the barriers of segregation in the deep South, called attention to unsavory practices, promoted the HBCU schools, fought the NCAA over restriction focused on inner-city students, established a wide swath of successful coaching, and won national championships. Packer interviewed John Thompson many times and through those interviews, Thompson gave us a peek into his heart when he reacted to a question about being the first black person to win a national championship, "it's only because those that were far better than I, were never given the opportunity."

Originally, the Black Coaches Association was to have a significant role in this story. For whatever reason, this topic is a difficult one to pin down. The information was more scattered and disconnected than even the information going back to Naismith and Allen. People who participated in the very earliest meetings could not remember who led the discussions or even who the elected officials were. For sure, Thompson, Raveling, Chaney, and Richardson were the official BCA Advisory Board, even if no one would attest to it. They were listed on the stationary. It does not appear that the BCA should want their existence to be forgotten. This group should receive the lion's share of credit for the progress and improvements for African-American coaches. They are still active within the NABC and the NCAA, and contributions should be noted for the generations that follow. Only the original group can explain the effort to remain anonymous.

BOOK FOUR

THE MORAL COMPASS

The National Association of Basketball Coaches ran relatively smoothly from 1927-1967. The reining NABC President and NABC Board of Directors ran the operation on a part-time basis because each continued to be a college or university coach. With most coaches being strong-willed leaders, the NABC continued to influence the college basketball environment whenever necessary. There were rules issue, equipment issues, governance issues, but nothing really rankled the beast like the ruling that started the whole thing in 1927.

The biggest problem facing the organization was the public perception of a rudderless ship because the face and voice of the organization changed at the convention every year. The organization lacked consistency and unless something particularly sensitive came along that could be handled in the course of a year, every situation concerning the NABC would have to adapt a strategy with the yearly changing of the guard.

The membership provided an answer with the appointment of an executive secretary from within the ranks. This was the first position that could serve the organization for a period of unspecified length, but originally was a part-time position held by a coach. Edward Hickox was tabbed part-time Executive Secretary of the NABC. He would maintain his duties in the same position with the Naismith Memorial Basketball Hall of Fame.

This solved some of the inconsistency problems and offered another layer of management that would serve to present a recognizable face and personality to the organization and the nation. Each president wanted to be the most memorable and productive, so the task for the new Executive Secretary could become a major distraction as the likes of Iba and Rupp imposed their wills on the group.

The NABC decided that full-time representation was needed. Attendance at NCAA Rules, Officiating, Tournament, and Selection meetings were imperative. With the NABC continuing to be run on a part-time basis and especially quiet during the basketball season, its voice diminished and so its influence diminished. The game had gotten so big and the rewards so great that it was time to return to the days of being proactive and regain some of the lost control. The NABC had to maintain the small grip they continued to hold and look to expand the organization's dialogue on the affairs of the game. To continue with the present course and choose to be less than diligent could have had disastrous results.

GUARDIAN
CLIFFORD "CLIFF" WELLS
(THE ARCHITECT)

"Hank Luisetti, at Stanford, is credited with being the first to use a one-hander, and I can remember seeing it for the first time when I was coaching in high school. I told my players, 'the first guy who tries that sits on the bench.' Pretty soon, teams began to beat me with the one-handed shot. Well you know what they say, if you can't lick 'em, join 'em. That's what I did. I began to teach and encourage the one-hander."
— **Cliff Wells**

Cliff Wells was not the first coach who held the title of Executive Secretary for the National Association of Basketball Coaches. It was decided when he was picked for the full-time position in 1960 that he would work closely with the coach selected as incoming president each year, and certainly take policy and direction from the NABC Board, but his face and voice would become consistent in the representation.

Wells was born in Indianapolis, Indiana, and would have no contact or knowledge of basketball until his family bought a motel and restaurant in Bloomington. It was during a trip across town where he observed some children playing on an outside court, that his interest began. His parents put a hoop on the outside of the motel and when not in school or working, he just *"shot and shot."*

As a middle school student, he recruited the school principal to help him establish a basketball team at the school. He and others built an outside court at the school, and the Bloomington Central Grade School team was born. This may have been Wells' first venture into the business of architecture, but it was not his last. Wells began an architectural business on a small scale, but the basketball lessons were remembered.

Wells was an accomplished high school player and set some early shooting records at the school. He once made 9-10 of his team's free throws and won a big game 13-12. During his high school career, he would work with the Indiana State Government as a page, making a nice living at $5.00 a day. This job encouraged him to focus on getting a college degree and it took him 12 years, but he graduated from Indiana University (IU).

It was during this time of working and attending college that Cliff Wells started coaching high school basketball. This job suited him very well and he would remain as a high school basketball coach in Indiana for 29 years. As the dean of the basketball coaching ranks in Indiana, Wells won 617 games, including more than 50 post-season and invitational victories, and two state championships.

As the Well's children got older, the necessity of paying for an education became an obstacle of some concern. When reviewing an opportunity to coach at Tulane University, Cliff was able to provide a free education for his children as part of the compensation package for coaching and his career as a high school basketball coach ended and his career as a college basketball began. The motivation behind the move designed to remove that formidable obstacle, opened doors for leadership opportunities with the NABC.

He stayed at Tulane for the remainder of his career. His coaching record included 885 wins in high school and at Tulane. He has been recognized with several awards and induction into the Helms Foundation Hall of Fame and the Naismith Memorial Basketball Hall of Fame.

Cliff Wells retired from coaching in 1963 and moved the NABC office to Springfield College to take on the position of Executive Director of the Naismith Memorial Basketball Hall of Fame. The Naismith operation had become a responsibility of the NABC and it was a natural fit when Ed Hickox retired in 1963. Wells maintained this double duty until handing the reins of the NABC over to Bill Wall.

Cliff Wells and William Gardiner exchanging NABC hardware.

During the time of Wells' leadership, the NABC began to put down some roots of permanency. These roots were not planted in a central location, but they were anchored in a level of organization unknown to the group. Finally, the NABC would have policy and procedure manuals that provided job descriptions for committee positions, board positions, and president. Reviewing these early manuals provided a real clear blueprint to the plan of attack that Wells had chosen.

Included in the Wells papers were directives to other members of the NABC to begin to gather and organize the history of the organization and

COACH PROFILE

MIKE JARVIS –
FLORIDA ATLANTIC UNIVERSITY
(NABC MEMBER 22 YEARS)

"We are going to be playing in the dance. I don't know when. I'm not making those promises, but I am promising you that before very long, we're going to have a party here." (Florida Atlantic News Conference)

Mike Jarvis knew something we didn't know. When asked during the 2008 Final Four about his life, Jarvis said: "The Lord has blessed me with some time away and I know that there is a plan for my life." Basketball coaching can be a cruel profession and so it was for Mike Jarvis. After working the high school sidelines earning a spot on the college sidelines, this consistent winner had the opportunity to coach in the Big East at St. Johns University. After a marvelous run of success at St. John's, things got ugly with the NCAA.

Jarvis would leave St. John's during the season when the university refused to support his continuing. It was during this time of trial that he would rekindle his FAITH and recognize that there is a reason for everything. He would later be cleared of any wrongdoing by the NCAA and happily returned to coaching at Florida Atlantic University.

Cambridge Rindge & Latin High School in Boston, Massachusetts, is where he got his start as a player, where he got his start as a coach, and where he was fortunate to coach Patrick Ewing, great Georgetown and New York Knicks center. His lesson for life was always, "The more things we can get kids to do correctly off the court, the more they will do correctly on the court."

Mike Jarvis has always been, and continues to be, a very active participant in the National Association of Basketball Coaches. He was president of the organization and continues to lend his expertise to the NABC Foundation, which operates the College Basketball Experience and provides leadership for the Coaches vs. Cancer initiative.

Coaching stops at Boston University, George Washington and St. John's, coupled with an NIT Championship and an Elite Eight appearance, groomed Jarvis to re-create that success and enthusiasm again at Florida Atlantic. It will not be long before we are reading about FAU among those programs being selected for post-season participation and their charismatic leader, Mike Jarvis, thanking everyone else for that success.

specifically the events leading up to the Bulletin, the Hall of Fame and the original history of the NABC as an organization. When the original efforts were submitted, Wells would always include the historical documents in all of his operational manuals and meeting programs that were provided with a great degree of detail. It seemed he was committed to NEVER allowing the membership to forget the roots of the organization.

Then there was the disappearing suitcase and the combined efforts of Wells and Wall to (once again) save the organization from extinction. At that time, the NABC was run out of a series of boxes and 3x5 cards to keep an orderly file system. With the membership arriving in one place at one time only once yearly, Wells would pack up the NABC and move it to the site of the national convention. During one such occasion, the NABC disappeared. The suitcase that held the entire organizational documents, including all membership information, was lost at Los Angeles International Airport.

Wells took out an ad in the 1965 *Bulletin*.

LOST LUGGAGE; *Last March, on my trip from Portland, Oregon to Lexington, Kentucky, my luggage was lost by the airlines by which I traveled. It has not yet been found, consequently all of my N.A.B.C. registration records are lost. I would appreciate it very much if each person who registered for the convention would send me the number of his membership card as an active, associate, or allied member.*

This case and all of the pertinent information was gone and it was necessary for the leadership to piece together the NABC. Even today, when the older coaches check in at the yearly convention, they will comment that their years of service are actually incorrect because of this unfortunate event. It was only because Wells and Wall were so organized and refused to throw anything away that the NABC recovered from this unfortunate incident.

Cliff Wells giving a plaque to Joe Vancisin for a job well done!

The NABC's policies and procedures manuals, historical documents, and intense level of organization are the results of the work of Wells. Most of what he designed, prepared, and took to the board for implementation is still in place. Bill Wall used this structure to expand the influence and Joe Vancisin used his structure to support expansion. In both cases, the construction was found to be secure.

GUARDIAN
WILLIAM "BILL" WALL
(THE POLITICIAN)

"I do not believe that anyone ever in (NABC) history has contributed more to it than you have always done. You not only made an outstanding president for about five or six years, because you actually ran the show, but your work as secretary was so outstanding ... I think I would be derelict as a former president not to write and tell you. I feel that way or I would not. I am not one to give out too many compliments, but when a man does an outstanding job, such as you have, it is going to be hard for Joe (Vancisin) to replace you."
— **Letter from legendary coach Adolph Rupp to Bill Wall, November 1975**

Bill Wall was one of the earliest small-college coaches to get actively involved with the NABC on the national level. He accepted committee responsibilities within the organization and became a vital cog in the machine that was working to find its place on the national sports stage.

Wall took on the role of Assistant to the Executive Secretary as the leadership role that Cliff Wells was wrestling with became more unruly. The Naismith Hall of Fame work was becoming more aggressive as the Springfield organization, which was funded by the NABC membership, struggled with the continued delay of groundbreaking for the memorial. Funding was becoming more and more difficult and the building was actually a hole in the ground and a foundation after funding shortfalls halted construction.

While Wall toiled in some obscurity as Cliff Wells' right-hand man and basketball coach at tiny MacMurray College, he was building a network of contacts and responsibilities across the basketball world. It would be Wall who would extend the influence of the NABC beyond college basketball coaching and spread the wealth of the organization around the country and around the world.

Bill Wall began his college playing career at Colorado College. After one year, though, he transferred back to his home state of Ohio to attend Ohio State University.

After graduation, Wall accepted his first coaching position at Summit Station High School coaching multiple sports. He earned his reputation, however, at MacMurray College, where, from 1957 until 1975, he held the positions of Physical Education faculty and department chair, director of athletics, and coach in basketball, baseball, tennis, golf, softball and lacrosse. Although he achieved success, small-college athletics were exactly that: small. It would be his outside efforts and interests that would provide the greatest opportunities.

Bill Wall spent two years at the helm of the NABC. Although that might seem brief, it was an important period. The NABC and the NCAA were struggling with the rapid expansion of college basketball. More and more fans and sports writers were taking an avid interest in the game. This led to some problems requiring a team effort to devise a plan to stop these troubles.

A Glance At … Bill Wall

Positions held:
1. Executive Director ABAUSA, 1975-1992
2. U.S. Olympic Basketball Committee, 1967-1972
3. FIBA
4. Executive Director, National Collegiate Baseball Foundation
5. Trustee, Naismith Memorial Basketball Hall of Fame
6. COPABA
7. NABC Board of Directors
8. NABC President
9. NABC Executive Director
10. MAC Conference Commissioner
11. Board of Directors, Women's Basketball Hall of Fame
12. International Basketball Board of the United States
13. United States Collegiate Sports Council
14. Olympic, Pan American, World Championship and Olympic Trials Staff

Awards Bestowed:
1. Illinois Basketball Hall of Fame
2. NABC Award of Merit
3. NABC Cliff Wells Award
4. MacMurray Hall of Fame– Gymnasium named after him
5. USA Baseball Federation Achievement Award
6. Fred Taylor Award at Ohio State
7. NCAA Appreciation Award
8. USA Basketball– Ed Steitz Award
9. NJCAA– Reed K. Swenson Award
10. John Bunn Award– Naismith Memorial Hall of Fame
11. FIBA– Order of Merit
12. NABC Metropolitan Award
13. Atlanta Tip-Off Club– Naismith Award

"…And there are other ills; the threat of gambling scandals, crowd-provoking bench behavior by coaches, a lack of real concern for the education of the athletes and the rupture of ties between honest educational and athletic programs," he told *Sports Illustrated* in 1972. "But the most serious of all is the matter of cheating in recruiting. Cheating is the end result of a vicious cycle that begins with a win-at-all-cost philosophy."

Bill Wall actually had the difficult assignment of representing the NABC during a Congressional hearing evaluating the impact that a merger of the National Basketball Association (NBA) and the rival American Basketball Association (ABA) might have on college basketball. He delivered a prepared statement and fielded questions about what impact the ABA's raiding of college basketball had and how this might be controlled by the merger. Dean Smith and Fred Taylor attended also, but Wall made the presentation:

"Our stated position indicates that a merger of the two professional leagues might result in a positive atmosphere for basketball at the collegiate level if certain considerations are provided for…

1. *That no professional game telecasts be permitted on Tuesday, Friday or Saturday.*
2. *That once a student-athlete enrolls in an academic institution that he not be tampered with or signed to a professional contract until that academic year is complete.*
3. *We would hope that a hardship player would have written into his contract a separate 'college fund in escrow' clause to that he may complete his education in the future.*
4. *We are deeply concerned … in a number of rumored relationships between professional teams and athletes who are still playing college basketball.*
5. *We request cooperation … especially during an Olympic year to insure that the finest eligible U.S. players be available to represent our country.*
6. *That consideration be given to the interests of our former athletes who are currently professional players … and to those who choose professional basketball in the future.*

It is not part of public record whether the NBA has supported the above suggestions in support of college basketball in the 30-plus years since the delivery, but at the time, the meeting seemed to be successful.

During the Wells-Wall partnership, the problem of illegal recruiting practices was starting to boom. Coaches had begun to be fired for not recruiting successfully or not winning enough games, and those teams that were taking the championship banners were sometimes cheating to get the players and then reaping the rewards of their transgressions. The NCAA was employing one national investigator to attempt to research a litany of charges being heaped upon them by coaches, writers, and fans

Coach Profile

Ernie Kent –
University of Oregon
(NABC Member 20 Years)

"I want to build on the momentum that has been generated from our recent success ... and take this program to the next level." (After signing a contract extension, 2008.)

Before Ernie Kent was a coach, he was a gang member. He was a member of the Kamikaze Kids and they wreaked havoc up and down the west coast of the United States. Dick Harter, head coach of the Oregon Ducks, led the Kamikaze Kids, and along with Greg Ballard and Ronnie Lee, Kent threatened the grip that the UCLA Bruins had on the Pac 10. The defensive philosophy employed by that group has helped Kent develop as a player and as a coach.

Different from almost all of the other coaches, Ernie Kent began his coaching career overseas. In Saudi Arabia, he had the arduous task of blending foreign players with the far more talented Americans who were allowed to play singly or in pairs. Dealing successfully with unusual circumstances can often lead to later success and so it was for Kent.

After returning stateside to assist the programs at Colorado State University and Stanford University, he would garner a reputation as an excellent recruiter. Kent's recruiting success with these two programs and a strong knowledge of the San Francisco Bay area got him an interview at St. Mary's. He became their head coach in 1991. After five years of building the program, he led St. Mary's to a 23-8 record and an NCAA Tournament appearance and the Pac 10 coaching opportunity at his alma mater in 1997. Eleven years at the University of Oregon has produced seven post-season tournament berths and NCAA Elite Eight appearances in 2002 and 2007, and Kent a Pac 10 Coach of the Year award.

Oregon is building a new arena, which will end the availability of one of the greatest home-court advantages in college basketball. "The Pit," Oregon basketball's home since the 1920s and the arena where the first ever NCAA National Champions (1939 Ducks) practiced and played will be gone forever. There is always a cost when change and growth occurs.

across the country. The NABC was particularly incensed because it had members who were losing jobs and other members who were the cause of those firings.

"A flagrant instance brought to my attention involved a major-college coach who is reported to have awarded the usual NCAA scholarship plus $250 a month and a new Camaro automobile to a star player," Wall also told *Sports Illustrated* in '72. "An option was added that if the player's parents moved to the city ... they would be housed in a free, furnished apartment."

In an effort to encourage the NCAA to spend some additional funds in the enforcement area, the NABC Board proposed that if the NCAA would begin the process of hiring one enforcement investigator for each of the eight competitive districts in the country, the NABC would put in place a "self reporting" process where the NABC would actually turn in incriminating documents against members who were actively cheating in the recruiting process.

The NCAA took the proposal under advisement and actually moved forward with a larger and more aggressive enforcement staff and the NABC provided incriminating documentation on several coaches.

Although Bill Wall would not name names or schools in discussing this process, he did provide details of how the operation worked.

This Past-Presidents photo shown sitting (L to R): Ev Shelton, Lee Williams, Bruce Drake, Adolph Rupp, Ben Carnevale and Bill Gardiner. Standing: Joe Vancisin, Bud Foster, Fred Taylor and Bill Wall.

"In those days it was very important to keep the sources of the incriminating information secret," he said. "The only member of the NABC authorized to see the documents to be sent to the NCAA was the Executive Secretary, and he alone would determine whether to forward or not. The coaches were instructed to gather as much information as they could and then mail it with no return address and from a post office that would not allow for identification from a post mark."

Several very prominent coaches were reprimanded by the NCAA during the process of self-reporting cheaters. The NCAA was pleased with the NABC's cooperation and would follow through with the hiring of a full-time investigator for each of the eight districts as originally proposed.

In 1975, Bill Wall left MacMurray College to become the Executive Director with ABAUSA. He offered to continue his dual roles with the NABC and ABAUSA. Contrary to the expected ruling, the NABC Board of Directors voted to make the NABC leadership position full-time and Wall had to make a choice. With opportunities to be involved with international basketball development, the Olympic program, and other national proposals for the positive expansion of basketball, he chose the ABAUSA position.

In 1975, Wall handed the boxes that made up the NABC office and approximately $100,000—an NABC certificate of deposit—to Joe Vancisin and the NABC was off to Connecticut.

GUARDIAN
JOSEPH "JOE" VANCISIN (THE CRAFTSMAN)

"It has been a perfect fit for the NABC to have had Joe Vancisin as Executive Director for the past 17 years. He has nurtured the growth of the entire association to encompass so many levels of basketball coaching and he has established a solid organization with financial stability."

—Then-NABC President Herb Kenny on Joe Vancisin's retirement, July 1992

It's somewhat impressive to note that Joe Vancisin's basketball career can be traced back to the latter part of James Naismith's life. In fact, he actually had contact with Dr. Naismith while a school-boy player in Connecticut. During a New England Championship game between Vancisin's Bassick High School of Bridgeport and Central High School of Hartford, Naismith was on hand to address the participating teams and toss up the first ball. Following the toss, the players, coaches, and fans in attendance honored the game's inventor. Joe Vancisin had the thrill of meeting Dr. Naismith and listening to what was one of his very last public appearances. Joe remembers Naismith commenting, *"That is the way I envisioned the game should be played."* Naismith died not long after that event in 1939 and Vancisin remembers that last opportunity very fondly.

Joe Vancisin New NABC President

Basketball at Yale dates to 1895 and for the past 16 years the head coach — and winningest coach in Yale's history — has been Joe Vancisin, the in-coming president of the National Association of Basketball Coaches.

Joe, who was elected to the NABC Board of Directors in 1967, succeeds in office his close friend Fred Taylor, Ohio State.

Vancisin, born just south of Yale in Bridgeport, Connecticut, captained the Dartmouth basketball team prior to his graduation in 1944. He received his basketball coaching baptism the following season at Dartmouth, guiding the freshmen five.

After doing a military stint, where he also had an opportunity to coach basketball, Joe, along with his college mentor Ozzie Cowles, moved on to Michigan where Cowles became head coach and Joe an assistant. Later Cowles and Vancisin went to Minnesota as head coach and assistant respectively. While at Minnesota Joe obtained his Master's Degree in Physical Education.

When the Yale coaching job became available Vancisin was selected and it has been a happy arrangement for both Yale and Joe. Joe also coaches the Yale Freshman golf team and in the 14 years he's been on the assignment he's had three undefeated teams.

Joe, a tireless worker on NABC committees, has conducted basketball clinics in various parts of the world. He is a great believer in their value in advancing the game of basketball.

"The NABC Clinics are extremely beneficial," Vancisin said recently, "to both the new and the more experienced coaches in our profession. The advancement of the techniques, strategies, and knowledge in basketball has always been one of our prime concerns. The regional NABC Clinics afford us a media through which coaches can keep abreast of the most current developments in the game."

In 1970 Joe was elected to the Board of Directors of the Naismith Basketball Hall of Fame in Springfield, Massachusetts and is a frequent contributor of basketball articles to a number of publications.

Last spring the veteran Yale coach was honored with the Alvin "Doggie" Julian Award given by the New England Association of Basketball Coaches to a member exemplifying "the highest overall standards and contributions to college basketball."

Vancisin is married and is the father of a son, at Williams College and a 17-year-old daughter. ∎

2

Joe Vancisin before he became the NABC's humble leader.

Vancisin played the game at a very high level in both high school and at Dartmouth College. His high school team was Connecticut State runner-up and won the New England Championship. During his junior year at Dartmouth, 1944, he lost in the NCAA Championship Finals to Utah. It was during these days that the Ivy League would excel in academics and athletics. The eight-team league was one of the first collegiate basketball leagues ever formed and was known as the Eastern League at that time. Yale, Princeton, Cornell, Harvard, Dartmouth, Pennsylvania, Columbia, and Brown were eastern powerhouses in many of the sports conducting intercollegiate competitions.

Upon graduation from Dartmouth, Vancisin went directly into the coaching profession. He led the Dartmouth freshmen for one season and then coached a military team to the First Service Command Championship. His former coach and mentor, Oswald "Ozzie" Cowles, asked him to come on board as his assistant with the Michigan Wolverines in 1947 and they won the Big 10 Championship. Unfortunately, the Wolverines were struggling with the worst basketball facility in the Big Ten.

"We were playing in an agriculture barn with the lighting so high that it didn't always make it to the court," Vancisin said. "Ozzie was convinced by the selection committee that there were plans for a new facility and he agreed to become the new basketball coach. Surrounding the court was a dirt floor and the seats were so far away the fans had little effect on the games. Basketball was such a low priority that the floor was often moved away during basketball season so the baseball team could practice indoors."

When it became apparent to the pair that the University of Michigan was a long way from building a new building for basketball, they were off to the University of Minnesota. The two coached the Golden Gophers for eight years before Vancisin felt the need to run his own program.

His first opportunity came when Howard Hobson left Yale University. By this time, Vancisin had wife Elizabeth at his side and plans for a family, and this move to his home state would prove to support the family growth and would end up being the last of a lifetime. Vancisin would become Yale's winningest coach, completing 19 seasons at the helm.

Vancisin became a board member for the NABC and then was elected NABC president for 1973-74. Vancisin was a member of the Olympic staff for Dean Smith of North Carolina (1976) and Dave Gavitt of Providence (1980).

Upon his retirement from Yale in 1975, Vancisin was hired as the Executive Secretary for the National Association of Basketball Coaches.

When Vancisin took over from Bill Wall in the summer of 1975, he had only nine months until the convention was scheduled for the 1976 Final Four.

The NABC had no office, no amenities, no communication services, and about 1,400 members who were anxious to receive their quarterly Bulletin and information on the convention. In the fall, it would be time for renewing the membership and collecting the next wave of membership dues. In addition, the coaches would be sending in their ticket requests for the convention and the games, immune to the fact that there was a new leader. Leadership was fine as long as everything continued to be the same.

Vancisin prepared the organization as a basketball coach would prepare for a season. He evaluated everything and everybody and made some determinations. He knew that revenue had to be increased and this would require a larger membership, but other revenue streams would need to be introduced. He also had a vision of how the convention could be improved to increase attendance and improve the national perception of the NABC.

Before any of this could begin, the NCAA dropped a bomb on the NABC. In 1940, in exchange for control of the national tournament, the NABC was guaranteed free tickets to the tournament for the NABC members.

But, in 1975, Walter Byers of the NCAA informed Joe that the tickets would no longer be given at no charge. The tickets would still be available to the group, but they would have to be purchased. To clarify the NCAA position on tickets, Tom Jernstedt was quick to point out that "this was not a change directed at the NABC. The NCAA

Joe Vancisin and Tex Winter posing while trying to enjoy the fabulous banquet fare.

governing board determined it was appropriate at that time to eliminate ALL free tickets to ALL NCAA Championship events, and the NABC was affected by the fall out from that legislation."

This decision, and an upholding of the decision after efforts to have it retracted, was the beginning of a period of a strained relationship between the NABC and the NCAA.

Late in Vancisin's leadership, there was talk of a coaches' boycott with discussions about forming a coaching union. This was all the by-product of the NCAA flexing its muscles in the areas of academics, income and cutting coaching opportunities.

Vancisin held the group steady as both the boycott and the union threats subsided. The NCAA embraced a new committee focused on minority concerns and although the relationship remained strained, the union talk tabled some of the proposed changes.

Joe Vancisin made many significant contributions to the NABC. The first external office, the first full-time secretary, the first African-American Board member and the list goes on. What rarely gets recognized are his changes that gave the organization a public personae and a national perception. First he grew the NABC exposition, or retail fair, to mega proportions. It was such a huge success that the NCAA felt obligated to restrict size and access as the influence of this event grew among basketball fans. The branding of basketball and the retail influence of basketball apparel and equipment really took on a national flavor through this operation and the expo moving city to city every year. Like the Fan Jam that followed years later, this event was deemed as competition for the NCAA's grip on college basketball external income streams.

The real significant change to the convention came with the arrival of the "formal" banquet that would attract attendees in the hundreds and sometimes exceeding one thousand participants. Joe brought in nationally renowned journalist Curt Gowdy to MC and the media to record the events and the awards of the college basketball world became part of the national media reporting schedule. The great coaches of the different eras would speak and the banquet would reflect the attitude and the strength attributed to the coaches group. Sadly, this great yearly gathering has been discontinued and there is no longer an event that brings all facets of the NABC together to pontificate on the "state of the game."

It needs to be noted here that Joe and Elizabeth Vancisin ran the NABC themselves. There was a small storefront at one time and then the organization was moved back into the Vancisin home. Joe was granted some clerical help and he hired Joyce St. John to assist with the organization. Rick Leddy, NABC journalist, commented, "They were 100 percent focused on the membership. Joe and Joyce always treated all of the coaches the same, regardless of their level."

Joe and Elizabeth Vancisin and Joyce St. John would accomplish all objectives stated above. And remember that $100,000 that Wall handed over when Vancisin

COACH PROFILE

JIM LARRANAGA –
GEORGE MASON UNIVERSITY
(NABC MEMBER 33 YEARS)

"I've made it clear over the years that my family and I loved it here at George Mason. I feel very fortunate to work under the great leadership...I've said it before that I hope to retire here at George Mason and this contract extension allows me to do that."

Here we have the best coach no one knows. Jim Larranaga was born in the Bronx, New York, and was a terrific player at Archbishop Molloy High School in the city. He earned a scholarship to Providence College and ended as one of the leading scorers in the college's basketball history. He was a captain, NIT participant and drafted by the Detroit Pistons of the NBA, but he chose coaching over a chance to play in the NBA.

Davidson College hired Larranaga as an assistant coach right out of college. He worked for Terry Holland there and, after some other stops, rejoined Holland at the University of Virginia. After a year as a player-coach in Belgium, he took his first head coaching opportunity at American University. After two seasons, he rejoined Holland and was on the Virginia staff that rode the career of Ralph Sampson to an NIT and two Final Four appearances. Larranaga would become the head coach at Bowling Green and then move to his present position at George Mason University. In each one of his coaching stops, he won more than he lost, but nothing eyebrow rising, until that day...

George Mason University and a coach named James Larranaga reached the second round of the NCAA Tournament...and then the third round...and then they were fitted for Cinderella's slipper. George Mason was going to the NCAA Final Four. Although George Mason would not win the championship, they won the hearts of millions of adoring fans. Americans love to cheer for the underdog and so they did during that great run. A coach named Larranaga, who coached at American, Bowling Green, and George Mason was not supposed to be able to do this, but he did!

George Mason has the luxury of recruiting players that are not on the one-and-done list. Those kids mature, graduate, and as the television says, "go into careers other than sports." What happens sometimes, though, is those recruits get better, gain experience, and end as seniors who accomplished unimaginable things. Coach Larranaga had such a bunch and lived a dream that we all have imagined a thousand times in our own fantasy worlds.

took over? Well, upon his retirement in 1992, Vancisin handed over $1.3 million to Jim Haney.

Joe Vancisin had doubled the membership numbers, raised the profile, and increased the bankroll ten-fold during his tenure as Executive Director of the National Association of Basketball Coaches.

GUARDIAN
JAMES "JIM" HANEY
(THE VISIONARY)

"NCAA men's basketball is in desperate need of an oversight committee that can protect the quality of the game, the student-athletes that compete and the men who coach the game."

— **Jim Haney**

With Joe Vancisin's exit, the NABC needed a leader who could help it keep its momentum. Long-time coach George Raveling considered taking over before choosing to stay in coaching. So, who would lead the organization?

The NABC had never been led by someone who was not a basketball coach. David Berst, Director of Enforcement for the NCAA, was interested and seriously considered. He said, "That was the only job that interested me enough to send a resume and interview. I could have helped."

Berst had been a player and assistant coach for Bill Wall at one time, but he didn't get the job. Jud Heathcote may have the best explanation.

"I think when it came right down to it, the Board could not pull the trigger on an NCAA guy to lead the organization," he said. "It was nothing against Dave personally, it was just the NCAA."

Ah, the bad blood remained.

So, Jim Haney, former assistant and head coach at the University of Oregon, was offered the position of Executive Director of the NABC in 1992. Living in Southern California at the time, Haney was elated about the opportunity until he received a curveball.

"Johnny Orr of the NABC called and offered me the job," Haney said. "I was excited to receive the offer, but there was an unexpected caveat to the offer. The NABC wanted the office to be close to the NCAA, so a move to Kansas was required. That was going to require some discussion with my wife, Carol."

Haney finally agreed to the terms and he and Carol made the move to Kansas and established the office in Overland Park, about three miles from the NCAA.

Jim Haney was a native of Pittsburgh and was a basketball star at Mount Lebanon High School. After gathering some state honors in Pennsylvania, he elected to play for Dick Harter at the University of Pennsylvania. He described his Ivy League career as "bench warmer," but he graduated with a degree in chemical engineering.

Harter had moved on to the University of Oregon and offered Haney a graduate assistantship with the Ducks. He took it. Making the normal coaching progression, he moved to full-time assistant and then became head coach when Harter left.

After several unspectacular years at the helm, Haney spent a brief time working with Gil Brandt and the Dallas Cowboys, and then a very brief time with Larry Brown at Kansas before settling in as the Assistant Commissioner of the Metro Conference. Stops as Commissioner of the Missouri Valley Conference and the Big West Conference preceded his acceptance as the newest leader of the NABC.

The NABC had succeeded in identifying the best candidate. Haney was a basketball player and coach at the highest levels, and he was different in that he was working in conference administration, plus he had a comfortable working relationship with the NCAA. It did not hurt that he had worked closely with Tom Jernstedt, NCAA executive vice president, while both were at Oregon.

Things had not changed a great deal since the Wall-Vancisin exchange in 1975. Haney had all of these changes mandated by the board, but he still had a convention to put on in New Orleans in 1993. The workload had to commit to two separate fronts, never an easy task. Building an office, finding competent staff and creating a revenue stream to support that staff, were a constant focus. In addition, the membership needed encouragment because change is never a well-received proposition.

Jim Haney established a vision for the NABC from Day 1. On the first day of work there was virtually no furniture in the corporate offices. For more than a few days, staff members sat on the floor brainstorming with Haney about the future, potential and possibilities for the NABC. Haney was a visionary in every sense and proved excellent at building a consensus among groups with different agendas.

The first staff member hired was Tom Ford, NABC assistant executive director, who had been the Director of Athletics at the University of Houston during the 1980s and the "Phi Slamma Jamma" days. With the NABC, Ford would be responsible for revenue, corporate relations, and communication with external organizations such as the Hall of Fame.

Carol Haney would take on the massive assignment of organizing membership and preparing the new organization for the very first convention, only months away. Other staff members included Andy Geerken, director of communications, who also established the *Time Out* newspaper and served as All-Star game administrator; Anne

Little, assistant to the executive director and convention coordinator; Debbie Page, accounting; and Kevin Henderson, director or public relations & special events, who also served as the director of the NABC Expo and Fan Jam. Troy Hilton, who began as an intern in 1992, now is an integral part of the association's affairs, working diligently in the convention housing operations, all-star game development and over-all success of the annual convention.

Jim Haney could now focus on the real reason he was hired, fixing the problems with the NCAA. It should never be assumed that anything was possible without a forward thinking Board of Directors. The NABC transformation was created and supported by these coaches who elected to become "agents of change."

NABC Board of Directors (1992 – 2008)

Cy Alexander, Tennessee State	Ernie Kent, Oregon
David Berst, NCAA	Bill Knapton, Beloit
George Blaney, Holy Cross	Lon Kruger, UNLV
Jim Boeheim, Syracuse	Mike Krzyzewski, Duke
Charlie Brock, Springfield	Phil Martelli, St. Joseph's
Jim Burson, Muskingum	Reggie Minton, Air Force
P.J. Carlesimo, Seton Hall	Page Moir, Roanoke
Dale Clayton, Carson-Newman	Mike Montgomery, California
Dennis Coleman, General Counsel (Ropes & Gray)	Gerald Myers, Texas Tech
	Dave Odom, South Carolina
Barry Collier, Butler	Johnny Orr, Iowa State
Denny Crum,Louisville	Oliver Purnell, Clemson
Dick Davey, Santa Clara	George Raveling, USC
Larry Gipson, Northeastern State	Lorenzo Romar, Washington
Bob Hanson, Kansas State	Bo Ryan, Wisconsin
Paul Hewitt, Georgia Tech	Kelvin Sampson, Oklahoma
Ron Hunter, IUPUI	Bill Self, Kansas
Tom Izzo, Michigan State	Jim Seward, Central Oklahoma
Mike Jarvis, Florida Atlantic	Greg Shaheen, NCAA
Jeff Jones, American	Tubby Smith, Minnesota
Ken Kaufman, WPI	Joe Tydlaska, CPA (Tydlaska & Co.)
Gene Keady, Purdue	Roy Williams, North Carolina
Pat Kennedy, Towson	Willis Wilson, Rice
Herb Kenny, Wesleyan	Rick Leddy, NABC Staff

The NABC Agents of Change, 1992–2008

Changes in attitude on both sides bought some time for negotiation. While both sides were sharing ideas, both stayed close to the vest waiting for that inevitable argument to reappear. As the sores healed, the frustration engulfing the NABC was not getting any better.

Mike Krzyzewski, board member and president during the early transition period, expressed the difficulty this way: "No single entity is running college basketball today. One of the failings with the NCAA is all decisions are made by committee."

"We worked hard as coaches to come to some mutual decisions," he added, "then we could never find the people who were going to do the voting. It was terribly frustrating."

Haney's biggest job was going to be bridging the communication gap between the two groups. Even now, Tom Jernstedt, the NCAA's Executive Vice President, reports that he has no memory of a problem, even though Haney and Krzyzewski say the opposite. With the board working through these trials, Haney went after income.

There had been discussion within the NCAA to develop some kind of basketball fan entertainment that would encourage family attendance at the Final Four. One of the issues was alcohol consumption during the weekend. The board thought that by encouraging families to attend it might curtail consumption to some degree. With the help of Regency Productions by Hyatt, a special event company, the NABC developed what became known as Fan Jam (Hoop City today). This interactive experience was a huge success, both as an attraction and as a moneymaker. As has been the case in the past, the NABC's success would mobilize the NCAA to take over the project. So, it was sold (without much choice) and Fan Jam and then the purchase price kept the NABC solvent for several years.

Fan Jam was the second fan festival for a major sporting event of this large scale. Major League Baseball was the first to create an event of this magnitude during

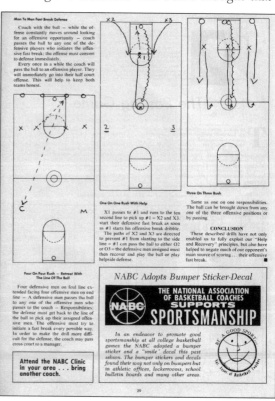

The NABC has always been a advocate of
SPORTSMANSHIP.

the MLB All-Star game and this is where Haney came up with the idea of doing the same for collegiate basketball. Later, Kevin Henderson, associate executive director of the NABC, was tapped to lead the production and operational side of Fan Jam and did so for five years. Henderson would later lead a team through the design and construction phase in the establishment of the College Basketball Experience (CBE) facility. Henderson currently serves as the CEO of the CBE and National Collegiate Basketball Hall of Fame.

Improving the public perception of basketball coaches across the country was another of Haney's stated goals. In 1989, four years before Haney took over the NABC, doctors diagnosed Missouri coach Norm Stewart with colon cancer. During his treatment, he teamed with the American Cancer Society to shoot three pointers for donations. At the same time, it became public knowledge that North Carolina State coach Jim Valvano was suffering from terminal bone cancer. Mike Krzyzewski, who was close to Valvano, championed an effort to use the plight of these two courageous coaches to create a program to support cancer research. The program was introduced in 1993 at the convention in New Orleans with a formal benefit to raise the necessary start-up funds and bring the effort to the attention of the national media. The NABC

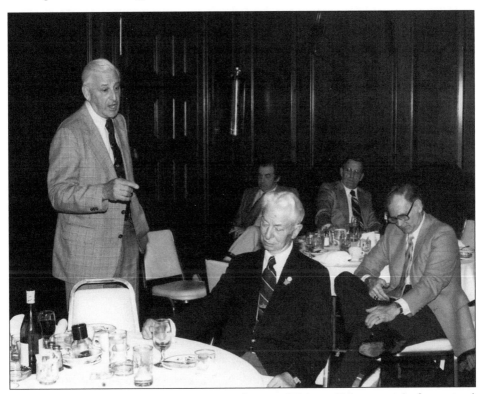

NABC President Ben Carnevale argues a point with Howard Hobson. Hobson won the first national championship in 1939. Abe Lemons, Fred Taylor and Joe Vancisin listen in.

has been running Coaches vs. Cancer and has raised more than $30 million for the American Cancer Society. Coaches vs. Cancer is now a staple of many campus programs to support local charities. What started as a three-point shot sponsor became a can-passing campaign at one game a season, provided game proceeds for one non-conference a season, and is now a full-throttle national program with high-powered events including pre-season tournaments.

The NABC is now enjoying a healthy yearly income from corporate sponsors, membership dues, NABC Expo, the CBE and NABC Classic. Coaches from all levels attend the conventions religiously and programs have expanded to share ideas on sound business practices, family support services, financial planning, and personal faith initiatives. What was a yearly male retreat has been transformed into a family event celebrating college basketball's finest hour.

Haney would point to the hiring of Reggie Minton as a turning point in the development of the new NABC. A long-time Division I basketball coach at the U.S. Air Force Academy with a great reputation and rapport among other coaches, Minton took the reigns of many of the external, basketball-focused issues and events. Minton was a board member and had been the recording secretary of the Black Coaches Association in conjunction with his years at the Air Force Academy. This addition would add a national coaching voice and give Haney time to refocus on the NCAA and the internal re-shaping.

As noted earlier, there were established goals and change had been swift. The NABC had now moved, restructured, altered vision, taken action and was facing the confrontations necessary in these changes.

"Human rights were being violated," Krzyzewski said. "We were advocates for kids and we had no voice. Access to our programs were diminished and there was a huge gap in the trust between coaches, athletic administrators and university presidents. The basketball coach was the most recognized guy on campus and jealousy was interfering with communication."

Under Haney's guidance, the NABC now has a solid relationship with the NCAA. And, the NABC Foundation was created to house the College Basketball Experience, Hall of Fame and Ticket to Reading Rewards, which gives the organization a tool for raising funds and funding great charitable work while offering donors a tax deduction and the confidence in the structure of the foundation.

In 2004, the NABC moved its offices from Overland Park, Kansas, to downtown Kansas City, Missouri. The offices are just blocks from the new Sprint Center arena as well as the College Basketball Experience (CBE), a state-of-the-art experiential facility opened by the NABC Foundation in the fall of 2007. The CBE is also the home of the National Collegiate Basketball Hall of Fame.

At just the right time for the NABC, the game of basketball exploded. The media embraced everything college basketball-related and when the NCAA scoffed at issues raised by the coaches, the media would get a hold of it and force the NCAA to discuss the circumstances in a public forum.

"Haney was as an important guy in the history of our organization as you could have," Krzyzewski said. "He was a great, great choice. Jim took Joe's spirit and ran with it. I have a lifetime of respect for all those guys on the board. Raveling, Thompson, they were all great. The basketball gods were good to us."

Jim Haney and the NABC Board have established numerous programs to promote the image of college basketball across America. They have accentuated the organization's mission to preserve and protect the game of basketball. The NABC has championed programs for opportunity development for minority candidates, fought for consistency in coaching positions and fought diligently for reasonable changes in the NCAA legislative process. The NABC footprint now includes initiatives in academics, community service, education, faith and charitable giving.

NABC NATIONAL INITIATIVES

Guardians of the Game

Developed a "Guardians of the Game" program, where coaches have a responsibility to protect and preserve the integrity of student-athletes, coaches and the game of basketball.

One Nation, One Flag, One People

Established following the terrorist attacks on September 11, 2001, to encourage the college basketball community, their fans and others to acknowledge the heroic efforts of our nations' servicemen and women, firefighters, emergency response personnel, police officers and health care workers.

NABC Reading and Math Program

This was established to encourage college coaches and players' visits to elementary school classrooms to work with students in both disciplines. Tools and programs for reading and math skills are provided.

Academic Honors Court

This program recognizes the talents and gifts that men's college basketball players possess off the court, and the hard work they exhibit in the classroom. In order to be named to the Honors Court, an athlete must meet a high standard of academic criteria, including a cumulative grade-point average of 3.2 as a junior and/or senior.

Partnership with the NCAA

The NABC has established a partnership with the NCAA for the promotion, sponsorship, marketing and overall betterment of men's college basketball. The two organizations work jointly in support of programs with special emphasis on the NCAA Final Four® and the NABC Convention.

Special Committee on Recruiting and Access (SCRA)

This committee was formed in conjunction with the NCAA to examine and redefine the areas of recruiting and access for men's college basketball. Among its primary functions, the SCRA reviews and recommends proposals for the NCAA legislative cycle relative to the recruiting calendar, contacts and evaluations and coaches' access to team members and prospective student-athletes.

Partnership with the Princeton Review Foundation

The NABC has partnered with the Princeton Review Foundation in an effort to lobby on legislative issues involving "Civil Rights Initiatives" in several states.

Alliance with High School Coaches Associations

The NABC formed an alliance with the National High School Basketball Coaches Directors (NHSBCD), an organization of the leaders of State Basketball Coaches Associations, to enhance participation and benefits in the NABC for high school coaches. Included among the actions and activities established was the formation of a high school coaches' congress to act as the voice of the high school basketball coaches within the NABC.

Professional Development Series for Coaches

A Professional Development Series of clinics and lectures is offered to NABC members at the annual NABC Convention. This effort was developed to enhance the knowledge and awareness of college basketball coaches in a variety of areas.

NABC Congress and Student-Athlete Council

The development of congresses for the three NCAA divisions of coaches provide greater input, representation and inclusion on all matters related to college basketball, including the image of coaches, basketball rules and NCAA legislation. A student-athlete council provides a new perspective and enabled input from men's basketball student-athletes.

The NABC created their own foundation so that supporters and donors could receive tax relief for support of the many programs relying on the NABC Foundation for support.

CREATION OF THE NABC FOUNDATION

Organized exclusively for charitable and educational purposes, the NABC Foundation is the founder and chief sponsor of Ticket to Reading Rewards, a national literacy program targeting middle school aged youth. In addition, the Foundation operates the College Basketball Experience (CBE), a state-of-the-art experiential facility which also includes the National Collegiate Basketball Hall of Fame in downtown Kansas City, Mo.

Coaches vs. Cancer

The NABC established this as a collaboration with the American Cancer Society as an initiative which leverages the personal experiences, community leadership, and professional excellence of basketball coaches nationwide to increase cancer awareness and promote healthy living through year-round awareness efforts, fundraising activities, and advocacy programs. Coaches vs. Cancer provides critical mission outreach, while raising funds in support of the Society's lifesaving cancer research, education, advocacy, and community service efforts. Since its inception, the program has raised in excess of $30 million.

2K Sports Classic to Benefit Coaches vs. Cancer

Held in November beginning on campus sites with the semifinals and championship played at New York City's Madison Square Garden.

The College Basketball Experience (CBE)

Opened in October, 2007, the College Basketball Experience is adjacent to the Sprint Center in downtown Kansas City, Mo. Included among the many venues at the state-of-the-art experiential facility are various interactive tests of basketball skills, all simulating the sights and sounds of a real college basketball game. The rich history and traditions of men's college basketball are portrayed throughout the facility, which is also the home of the National Collegiate Basketball Hall of Fame. Each year the CBE conducts the National Champions luncheon to honor the coach of the NCAA Division I national championship team.

The National Collegiate Basketball Hall of Fame

The inaugural induction ceremonies for the National Collegiate Basketball Hall of Fame were held in Kansas City, Mo., in November of 2006. Four founding members inducted during that ceremony included two legendary coaches - John Wooden of UCLA, also inducted for his playing career at Purdue; and Dean Smith, the outstanding former coach at the University of North Carolina. They were joined by two of the greatest collegiate players ever - Bill Russell, who led his University of San Francisco Dons to a pair of NCAA championships; and the University of Cincinnati's Oscar Robertson, arguably the finest player in college basketball history. The induction ceremonies are held every November in Kansas City at the College Basketball Experience and the Sprint Center.

O'Reilly's CBE Classic

A 16-team tournament held in November beginning on four campus sites. The four regional champions advance to the semifinals and finals at the Sprint Center in Kansas City on the Monday and Tuesday before Thanksgiving. The annual induction ceremonies for the National Collegiate Basketball Hall of Fame kick off the week on the eve of the tournament in Kansas City.

Consistent with the efforts of the past administration, the present NABC hierarchy continues to focus on the basketball coach as an important part of the total community of higher education and the communities where those institutions reside. Always fighting any negative perception that might weaken the product, the NABC works to protect the image of the coach.

ENHANCED PROGRAMS FOR PERSONAL AND PROFESSIONAL DEVELOPMENT

Guardians of the Game Awards Show

This gala event, transformed into an Emmy/Oscar-type presentation, is held annually at the annual NABC Convention during the NCAA Final Four® to honor the most outstanding coaches, student-athletes and others involved in college basketball. This night features the presentation of player and coach of the year honors in all divisions of basketball; the defensive player and big man of the year; and numerous awards to luminaries from men's college basketball, past and present.

Court of Honor Gala

Each year, the NABC honors an outstanding national figure from business and/or education at a Court of Honor Gala. The event is a celebration of dedication, leadership and commitment by an individual to college basketball.

NABC.com

The official website of the NABC was completely redesigned in 2008. The site offers a comprehensive view of the NABC, its various programs, news, feature stories and links to many associated organizations. NABC.com also provides information on membership and registration for the annual convention.

The Basketball Bulletin Monthly Newsletter

In an effort to keep its membership informed on a more regular basis, the NABC provides The Basketball Bulletin, a monthly email newsletter to its members and constituent groups.

Alumni Advisory Committee

The NABC established an alumni meeting at its annual convention to utilize the overwhelming knowledge and talents of its former coaches who have contributed so much to the game of college basketball and the coaching profession through the years.

Final Four® Coaches Club

All coaches whose teams have reached the NCAA Final Four® are honored annually at an exclusive event during the Final Four® and the NCAA Convention. The coaches receive custom blue blazers with team information on an inside panel.

Champions Luncheon

Coaches from all NCAA and NAIA divisions whose teams have won regular season conference championships are honored annually at the NABC Convention. The luncheon is a tribute to the sustained season-long success of the coaches and their teams.

Playbook for Life

In conjunction with The Hartford, the "Playbook for Life" was established to assist student-athletes with preparations for their futures. The program offers guidance and information in several areas including finance, health care and insurance.

Pursuing Victory with Honor

This program is conducted in conjunction with the Josephson Institute of Ethics and its *Character Counts* program. There is great emphasis on the six pillars of character – trustworthiness, respect, responsibility, fairness, caring and citizenship. The NABC has partnered with the Josephson Institute with the establishment of the *Gold Medal Standards* to set ground rules of sportsmanship and equip teacher-coaches with strategies to build life skills and character. These standards were established at an Ethics Summit in August of 2001.

Although sometimes complex and sometimes difficult, the NABC has continued to pursue areas that have caused coaches and families to struggle in the profession. A readily available support system has been provided at the convention and during the year to allow membership to embrace their faith and commit to being both coaches and family leaders.

FAITH and FAMILY BASED INITIATIVES

NABC Chaplain

Brett Fuller, pastor of Grace Covenant Church in Chantilly, Va., serves as the NABC chaplain, offering spiritual guidance to the membership. He contributes a regular column to the Time-Out magazine and works with the NABC Ministry team, the Fellowship of Christian Athletes, Athletes in Action and select coaches to address the needs of the NABC membership.

Jewish Ministry Outreach

Jewish ministry team is available to the NABC membership to assist those members of the Jewish faith.

Samaritan's Feet

The NABC has partnered with Samaritan's Feet, a humanitarian non-profit organization dedicated to taking a life-changing message of hope to people and equipping the feet of impoverished children in the U.S. and around the world with shoes. Ron Hunter, the head coach at IUPUI and an NABC board member, kicked off the program by coaching his team in a game against Oakland University with bare feet while seeking charitable donations of new shoes. Hunter and his IUPUI contingent later traveled to an impoverished region of Peru to distribute some 150,000 pairs of shoes.

National Center for Fathering

The NABC has partnered with the National Center for Fathering in its efforts to improve the well-being of children by inspiring and equipping men to be more effectively involved in the lives of children. In response to a dramatic trend towards fatherlessness in America, the Center was founded in 1990 to conduct research on fathers and fathering, and to develop practical resources to prepare dads for nearly every fathering situation. The National Center for Fathering is featured in the Time-Out magazine, a quarterly publication of the NABC.

America's Family Coaches

The NABC has partnered with Dr. Gary and Barb Rosberg in offering an extensive menu of family and marriage resources to its membership. The "Marriage Coaches" are regular contributors to the Time-Out magazine, a quarterly publication of the NABC.

Significant Charitable Efforts

The NABC has contributed to a number of humanitarian efforts including donating $100,000 to assist in gaining freedom for slaves being held in Sudan. In the aftermath of Hurricane Katrina in New Orleans, contributions were also made to the Red Cross and the NABC assisted with former Notre Dame coach Richard "Digger" Phelps' campaign to build homes for residents returning to their neighborhoods.

Operation Hardwood and Wounded Warriors

These programs are conducted with the USO as NABC members work with members of the United States' Armed Forces. Operation Hardwood sends several NABC coaches to work and interact with armed forces members abroad in basketball skills, discussion and base tournaments. Wounded Warriors connects veterans who have been wounded in the service of our country with college coaches and teams around the country.

METROPOLITAN AWARD WINNERS

1941	Nat Holman, CCNY	1977	Jack Friel, Washington State
1942	Ned Irish, Madison Square Garden	1978	John Nucatola, National Basketball
1943	George Keogan, Notre Dame		Association
1944	Oswald Tower, Rules Editor	1979	Clarence Gaines, Winston-Salem
1945	Harold Olsen, Ohio State	1980	John Wooden, UCLA
1946	Ed Kelleher, Fordham	1981	Frank McGuire, South Carolina
	James St. Clair, Southern Methodist	1982	Bruce Drake, Oklahoma
1947	Hank Iba, Oklahoma A&M	1983	Harry Litwack, Temple
1948	Doc Carlson, Pittsburg	1984	Curt Gowdy, Broadcaster
1949	Ed Hickox, Springfield	1985	Joel Eaves, Auburn/ Georgia
1950	Phog Allen, Kansas	1986	Ray Meyer, DePaul
1951	Sam Berry, Southern California	1987	Marv Harshman, Washington
1952	George Edwards, Missouri	1988	Ben Carevale, Navy
1953	Doc Meanwell, Wisconsin	1989	Pete Carlesimo, National Invitational
1954	Piggie Lambert, Purdue		Tournament
1955	A.A. Schabinger, Creighton	1990	Jack Gardner, Utah
1956	Lou Andreas, Syracuse	1991	Dave Gavitt, Big East Conference
1957	Frank Keaney, Rhode Island	1992	Vic Bubas, Sun Belt Conference
1958	Everett Dean, Indiana/Stanford	1993	Joe Vancisin, NABC
1959	Clarence Edmondson, Washigton		Ozzie Cowles, Michigan
1960	Vadal Peterson, Utah	1994	Lou Carneseca, St. John's
1961	John Bunn, Colorado State	1995	C.M. Newton, Kentucky
1962	Tony Hinkle, Butler	1996	Joe O'Brien, Naismith Memorial
1963	Cliff Wells, Tulane		Basketball Hall of Fame
1964	Bud Foster, Wisconsin	1997	Tom Jernstedt, NCAA
1965	Joe Lapchick, St. John's (N.Y.)	1998	Dean Smith, North Carolina
1966	Adolph Rupp, Kentucky	1999	Bill Wall, NABC/USA Basketball
1967	Doggie Julian, Dartmouth	2000	John Thompson, Georgetown
1968	Pete Newell, California	2001	Don Haskins, UTEP
1969	Ev Shelton, Sacramento State	2002	Mike Tranghese, Big East Conference
1970	Eddie Hickey, Marquette/St. Louis	2003	Jim Calhoun, Connecticut
1971	Stan Watts, Brigham Young	2004	Gerald Myers, Texas Tech
1972	Forrest Twogood, Southern California	2005	Norm Stewart, Missouri
1973	Howard Hobson, Oregon	2006	John J. "Jack" Powers, National
1974	Ed Steitz, Springfield		Invitation Tournament
1975	Clair Bee, Long Island	2007	Jim O'Connell, Associated Press
1976	John McClendon, Cleveland State	2008	Bob Knight, Army, Indiana, Texas Tech

BOOK FIVE

THE CONNECTORS

There are many firsts attributed to the National Association of Basketball Coaches. The pioneers in these groundbreaking areas were mega-stars of their time. In almost every case, the responsible party is a college or university basketball coach who was later enshrined in the Naismith Memorial Basketball Hall of Fame and, in some cases, other halls of significance. Most importantly, they were members of the NABC.

GUARDIAN
DR. H.C. CARLSON
(INNOVATOR, TEACHER, ACTOR, PUBLISHER)

"Start out in the morning with the winning spirit and bring it home, enhanced at night with advances physically, materially, morally and intellectually. Figure you are going ahead today, and that it may be your day of destiny. Act as if snapshots of your daily activities are to form your record, rather than the unnatural poses of rare occasions."

— Dr. H.C. Carlson

Henry Clifford Carlson, better know as H.C. or "Doc," was a football star turned basketball coach. Born in the heart of mining country in 1894, this Murray City, Ohio, native felt the wrath of the mines very early. Losing his father and his stepfather to mining accidents convinced H.C. to find employment elsewhere. He was a three-sport star at Fayette City (Pennsylvania) High School and he was able to use that talent to gain a scholarship to the University of Pittsburgh. He would continue his superlative three-sport career there, but make his mark in football. As captain and honored as an All-American, Carlson would lose only one game in his college football career.

Continuing at the Pittsburgh Medical School was paid for by playing professional football.

With the pressure of life and death an internal burden, Carlson searched for ways to ease that stress. He found some relief in coaching the basketball team at Pitt and would create a wonderful program. He would coach at Pittsburgh for 31 years and never stopped practicing medicine during that stretch. He finished with a record of 369-247, winning two Helms Foundation National Championships.

Even with all of this success, he is best known for inventing the first-ever continuity offense. This offense, which began with three players moving and two remaining still, eventually included four in motion and then five. It was so successful that some will claim Doc Carlson would hold the first actual coaching clinics, sharing his offensive system with coaches from around the area every summer.

H.C. Carlson maintained his association with the Pittsburgh Panthers for 50 years but would be remembered fondly for so many different things. His greatest legacy was his commitment to the human body. Carlson was the NABC president in 1936-1937 and was inducted into the Naismith Memorial Basketball Hall of Fame in 1961.

During the 1933-34 season, Carlson prepared and distributed a trial magazine that included the Pittsburgh offensive system, rules changes edited by Oswald Tower, and a motivational piece encouraging coaches to attend the 1934 NABC Convention. The product was received so enthusiastically that the coaches took time at the general meeting to pass unanimously a motion to have the Secretary-Treasurer provide a regular mailing to the membership. Since Carlson was the newly elected Secretary-Treasurer, he had just enlarged his own job description. This trial magazine became the *NABC Bulletin*, the official source of all things related to coaching basketball.

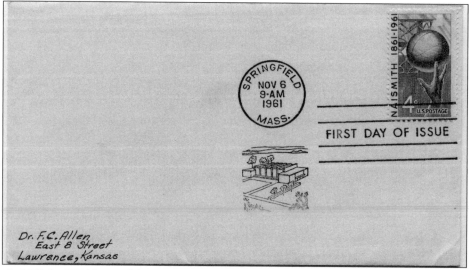

In 1961 the USPS honored the Naismith Memorial Hall of Fame with this commemorative stamp which was purchased by Phog Allen.

GUARDIAN
JOHN BUNN
(INNOVATOR, TEACHER, ADMINISTRATOR, AMBASSADOR)

"While there are many theories about basketball and many techniques practiced, the principles of dynamics, which govern the actions of the body, are invariable. Therefore, whatever the theory may be, it should be in harmony with these principles."

— John Bunn

As was often the case, the early coaches were educated in something other than education and would take on responsibilities far outside their job descriptions. John Bunn was no different. He was a coach, teacher, administrator, rules editor, and executive secretary. His degree was in Engineering and he began his career with Phog Allen and ended it looking after Springfield College and the Naismith Legacy, but had lots to do in between.

Bunn was born in Wellston, Ohio, in 1898 and the family moved to Kansas not long after. He was educated in Kansas, completing high school at Humboldt High School. He was a sensational athlete, lettering three years in football, basketball, baseball, and track. The University of Kansas was next where he was the first ever to gain 12 varsity letters at KU. He graduated in 1921 and immediately became an assistant basketball coach for Phog Allen. He held various positions in the athletic department over time and was an assistant professor in Industrial Engineering.

International Basketball
BY: BILL WALL

The National Association of Basketball Coaches (NABC) began its Foreign Fellowship program in 1970 during the Presidency of Henry Iba of Oklahoma State University to assist the development of basketball around the world. An NABC International Committee was established with Bill Wall, of MacMurray College, as chairman, charged with the responsibility of bringing an overseas coach to the United States during the month of March each year to observe basketball, and to set up subsequent summer clinics for U.S. coaches travelling abroad. The NABC Bulletin was mailed to all world basketball federations.

Three criteria were developed for the Fellowship: (1) Must be a major coach in his country; (2) Must have a good speaking knowledge of English; (3) Must not have travelled to the USA previously.

The travel schedule generally begins each year with midwestern high school, junior college and collegiate games, before moving on to the National Association of Intercollegiate Athletics (NAIA) 32-team tournament in Kansas City. Then to the National Junior College championships (eight teams) in Hutchinson, Kansas. The next stops are the National Collegiate Athletic Association (NCAA) regionals and the finals in the College Division at

BILL WALL
Former President of the NABC... Has been the only coach in the history of MacMurray College... Is head of MacMurray's physical education department and is school's Athletic Director... Has conducted many clinics in Europe... Was a member of the U.S. Olympic basketball committee... Will become the Executive Director of the NABC... Active golfer.

The 1972 NABC Foreign Fellowship recipients view the Naismith Memorial Hall of Fame, Springfield, Massachusetts. From left to right, Lucian Vasilacu, Raumania, Lee Williams, Executive Director Basketball Hall of Fame, Emmanuel Chuger, Nigeria, and Bill Wall, Chairman, NABC International Committee.

International hoops interest was fostered by John Bunn and carried on by Bill Wall and others. That is why the Olympic competition is so fierce today.
1972 NABC Foreign Fellowship

Bunn assisted Phog for nine years, enjoying a great deal of basketball success. He then took this knowledge to Stanford University where he won Pacific Coast Conference titles in 1936, 1937 and 1938. It was during this three-year run that Bunn wowed the basketball world with Hank Luisetti.

Luisetti was first noticed for his "matinee idol" looks and he single-handedly brought women out to the college games where they did not attend before. What created the stir in basketball circles was his invention of the "running one-hander." He was the first player to shoot with one hand and he would score with unbelievable ease.

Luisetti would score 1,291 points in his final three seasons, but was unfortunate to be in his prime before professional basketball was a real option for college stars. He served his country, but his career came to an unfortunate end with a wartime diagnosis of spinal meningitis. Although the disease would not alter his life, it ended his playing career when doctors insisted basketball would spread the disease and shorten his life.

Like Luisetti, John Bunn served his country during that time. Bunn was assigned as an athletic consultant to the U.S. War Department and was responsible for establishing athletic departments at many of the European military bases. This was the beginning for the "ambassador of basketball."

Bunn returned to Stanford following his service, but it was in a capacity as Dean of Men. This administrative assignment did not satisfy Bunn's competitive edge, so it was off to Springfield College to be the athletic director and head basketball coach. He was recognized for his reorganization of the department at Springfield, bringing the athletics department to the same level of excellence shared by other facets of the college.

The "ambassador" title really took hold during a period of time when Bunn would travel the world giving coaching and officiating clinics. He coached the Korean and Australian Olympic Basketball teams and would readily travel Europe teaching the game. Bunn finished a long run as an NABC Board Member with the organization presidency in 1949-1950.

Bunn took his final coaching position with Colorado College, during which time he would also serve as Editor and National Rules Interpreter of the NCAA from 1959-1967. He finally retired from coaching in 1963, after 40 years of service.

John Bunn was honored with the Metropolitan Award, the highest award given by the NABC, enshrined in the Naismith Memorial Hall of Fame, and awarded Doctor of Humanities (honorary) by Springfield College. Presently the highest award offered by the hall of fame is named after this great coach.

COACH PROFILE

PHIL MARTELLI –
ST. JOSEPH'S UNIVERSITY
(NABC MEMBER 22 YEARS)

"Many so-called experts in the business of college basketball will tell you that high school coaches struggle with the transition to coaching college basketball. Phil Martelli was not one of those. He experienced success at every level of playing and coaching and used those lessons wisely, building his career. This native of Media, Pennsylvania, is another point-guard turned basketball coach who has used his coach on the floor mentality to lead Widener College as a player and assistant coach, culminating in qualifying for the NCAA Division III Final Four."

As so many coaches did, Martelli took his philosophy to coach and teach at the high school level. He led Bishop Kenrick High School to six straight playoff appearances before St. Joseph's University in Philadelphia hired him as an assistant coach. The coaching pedigree at St. Joseph's included NBA coaches Jack Ramsey and Jim Lynam and Martelli embraced the heritage and tradition of this great program.

After filling the assistant's role for 10 years, Martelli was awarded for diligence, recruiting success and loyalty by being named the head coach. The Martelli-led Hawks reached the NIT Championship game and the progress has been steady. In 2003-2004, Martelli led St. Joe's to a number-1 ranking in the college basketball polls and a top seed in the NCAA Tournament. That team would finish in the Elite Eight with a record of 30-2 and two players were later NBA first-round draft picks.

Martelli has been the recipient of several regional and national coaching awards while establishing some impressive coaching records at St. Joe's, passing Hall of Fame Coach Jack Ramsey for second on the list for most wins and leads all Hawk coaches with post-season victories. He continues to lead the program in his very flamboyant style while sending players and assistant coaches to the NBA to pursue their personal goals.

Martelli has been a regular participant with USA Basketball, coaching the 2005 under-21 team in the World Championships and assisting with the 2001 FIBA World Championships and the 1998 Goodwill Games.

Phil and his wife Judy, a terrific college player in her own right, are very active with Coaches vs. Cancer and a number of Philadelphia programs supporting others. He is another great coach and family man, who represents his home and his community in a manner that should be an example to all of us.

HISTORY OF THE HALL OF FAME

Sadly, Dr. James Naismith died in November of 1939 before witnessing the incredible growth and development of his invention. He also did not receive any financial reward for his work. The NABC spent a year collecting change in cans at games around the country to send him to the Olympics in 1936, and this was the height of the reward for his forward-thinking attempt to solve a problem interfering with the smooth transition from fall sports to spring sports.

The National Association of Basketball Coaches of the United States raised $5,000 for the Naismith trip, and what remained after his return began a fund to plan and build a memorial to the man and the game. The NABC would champion this cause for years. Its efforts were thwarted by a lack of funds, a world war, inflation, and disinterest, but the membership marched on. Success eventually came and the inventor received his reward.

In the years following Naismith's death, Dr. Forrest "Phog" Allen referenced his mentor, coach, and friend at every opportunity. Phog's first "call to action" during the very first NABC meeting was to have James Naismith tagged "honorary president" of the organization, putting aside the fact that Naismith was always opposed to the idea that basketball needed coaching. And one of his final efforts was to address the throng at the opening of the James Naismith Memorial Basketball Hall of Fame in Springfield, Massachusetts.

One of the biggest disappointments in the Allen Legacy was the awarding of the Naismith Memorial to Springfield College.

"Twenty-five years before Dr. Naismith passed on, I went to him and said, 'Dr. Naismith, if and when somebody plans a great memorial to your honor, as they should, just where would you like that memorial to be placed?'" Allen argued to the decision-making officials. "Well, he said, I had thought some of Springfield, and then I thought of going to California to spend my latter days, but since I have lived in Kansas most of my life, my family was raised and educated here, I am determined to spend the rest of my days in Kansas, and, of course, I would like to see anything that is done for me placed at the university."

Author's Note: I cannot close this section without sharing that the comments about Allen's feelings regarding the location of the Naismith Memorial were all over the place. He wanted it in Kansas, he wanted it in Springfield, he wanted it in Canada. Each of these ideas is described as a direct quote. I can only tell you that there is a copy of a letter that Phog Allen wrote in 1941, available in the KU archives, that says, in Phog Allen's words: "I assure you (Don Spencer) that I will not stand in the way of any memorial that Springfield is intending to build in honor of Dr. Naismith, nor will I write a word against it. However, you can understand, in view of his expressed wish to me that the memorial be placed at the University of Kansas, my feeling in the matter."

The NABC continued its undying commitment to the Hall of Fame project and even moved Cliff Wells, Executive Secretary of the organization, to Springfield to run jointly the NABC and the Hall of Fame efforts. Continued failure to reach projected goals forced a re-evaluation of the project and in 1965, the project budget was halved.

In 1966, with the organization dangerously close to insolvency, the NABC removed itself from the office and returned the responsibility to the Hall of Fame Trustees. The NABC was directly responsible for providing $325,000 of the $500,000 needed to meet the revised budget.

The final portion of the budget was realized when the Hall of Fame Trustees made a serious effort after losing their NABC benefactors. When the building was finally opened in 1968, the NABC was responsible for $600,000 of the final total received for the project.

GUARDIAN

EDWARD J. HICKOX
(COACH, EDITOR,
HISTORIAN, DIRECTOR)

*"We are fortunate today that forward looking
basketball coaches had the courage and
willingness to take responsibility, the energy
and interest to give it expression, the optimism
and confidence to implement it, and the
continued forcefulness to carry on in the face of
seeming indifference of some their colleagues."*

— **Edward Hickox**

Edward J. Hickox is an intriguing study. His life raises the question of how many hours in a day one person can work. Hickox had to have started working on the day of his birth in 1878 to accomplish all that he did. He coached basketball for 40 years, beginning with a high school career that won a Colorado, Wyoming, and New Mexico combined championship in 1911; that same high school team scheduled and defeated five college teams in 1912.

Hickox's college coaching career began with the introduction of the sport of basketball at Lycoming College before he spent 26 years coaching the Springfield College (yep, the same one that keeps popping up) men's program. During World War II, Hickox would hold the NABC president's job for two years (only president to do that), and publish the *NABC Bulletin* so that the membership could maintain some contact. There was concern that the NABC would dissolve because so few members were available to participate or could afford the dues. This effort guaranteed that the NABC would survive the war and continue with little interruption.

In 1949, with the NABC struggling to keep the hope of a Naismith Memorial alive, Hickox took on the responsibility of running that operation as well. The funding was virtually non-existent. After 10 years, nearing the 1960s, Naismith was fading from memory. Hickox would run the organization, fight for funds, and work as hard as he could to keep this goal in the minds of the coaches. He was titled the executive secretary and was paid nothing for his efforts. When he stepped down in 1963, there was still no building, but the dream was alive.

During this period, Hickox also accepted the position as the first Executive Secretary of the NABC, a position that was not full time, but would be an attempt to keep the Naismith Memorial and the NABC connected in the closest possible way. He would eventually hand over the reins of the Naismith effort to John Bunn and the NABC to Cliff Wells.

GUARDIAN

ADOLPH RUPP
(TOUGH, GRUFF, CONTROVERSIAL, EDITOR, CHAMPION)

"I want to thank these men who have gone this way before. … the foundation of the National Association of Basketball Coaches wasn't laid by Adolph Rupp, it was laid by these men who've come this way before."

— Adolph Rupp

Adolph F. Rupp learned the necessary life lessons from parents who weren't from the United States. Rupp's father was from Austria and his mom from Germany. They raised a tough, no-compromise young man. Rupp was born in 1901 and was raised in Halstead, Kansas. After playing for the city's high school, he attended the University of Kansas and played for Phog Allen.

Rupp had a very uninspiring career at Kansas, but learned the game from the "father of coaching" while sitting on the KU bench. He would also spend time with Naismith as time allowed. There was never a doubt about Rupp's interest in the game or eagerness to learn.

The intention was a business career, but opportunities were slim as the last vestiges of the Great Depression were affecting employment opportunities. The first coaching stop was a bust because the school did not have a gymnasium, and then the second stop involved coaching wrestling instead of basketball. He did buy a book on wrestling and won the Iowa state championship, but his interest was not there.

Rupp finally got his basketball coaching career going in Freeport, Illinois, before interviewing for the coaching position at the University of Kentucky (UK). He would tell anyone who would listen that it was his personality that won the hearts of UK's selection committee. What really happened was the guy they wanted asked for $5,000, and Rupp agreed to work for $2,800. (Although his personality was probably important, too.)

As was the custom, multiple coaching duties were included in the job description at UK, but in four seasons of coaching basketball, Rupp went 65-9. The basketball results exploded from there, resulting in four NCAA National Championships (1948, '49, '51, '58), 25 All-Americans, 121 consecutive home victories, an NIT Championship and coaching on the gold medal staff in the 1948 Olympics.

Adolph Rupp's trials and tribulations are well documented. He was a central figure in our nation's first and worst gambling and point-shaving scandal. The NCAA has raked him over the coals regarding recruiting irregularities, even though it saw fit to give him the NCAA award for his success at Kentucky. Finally, he was vilified in the media and movies when his Wildcats lost to Texas Western in the 1966 championship game. It was identified as a major breakthrough in southern basketball integration because many thought Rupp was a racist.

"Obviously, I'm glad we beat Duke in the semis, but it would have been interesting to see if this furor about the racial differences would have been made had Duke been playing Texas Western," Larry Conley, who played on that Kentucky team, said for the book *CBS Sports Presents: Stories from the Final Four.* "Duke also had an all-white team. Would the same things about Coach Rupp and the game have been written if it had been Duke and Texas Western?

"Sure, on the court Coach Rupp was verbally tough on his players, demanding a lot of his teams and himself. I don't have a problem with a coach demanding a lot from his players if he also is working as hard as he can to be good. However, just because Coach Rupp was tough on his teams, and had an all-white team in Kentucky in the mid-1960s does not mean he was a racist."

"Coach Rupp was never a racist. In those days no one coaching basketball in the South was recruiting black players," said Jim McGary, who was at the Baron's side during most of his coaching days. "The northern schools were recruiting the black players out of the South and the southern schools were recruiting the white players out of the North.

"Coach actually recruited such great black players as Butch Beard and Wes Unseld, but when he went into their homes and talked to their mothers, he would simply be honest. He would tell them that he could not guarantee that there would not

A Glance At ... Adolph Rupp

- NABC President
- NCAA– Nation's Most Successful Coach
- National Coach of the Year - 4 times
- Coach of the Century Award
- Naismith Memorial Basketball Hall of Fame
- Helms Foundation Hall of Fame
- Kentucky Hall of Fame
- Kentucky Athletic Hall of Fame
- Kansas Hall of Fame
- SEC Coach of the Year - 4 times

Also, Rupp was active in his community, state, and region:

- President of the Kentucky Hereford Association - 12 times
- Director of the Central District Warehousing Corporation
- Board of Governors-Agricultural Hall of Fame
- State Chairman-Cerebral Palsy Association
- Nation's Outstanding Shriner
- Chairman– Shriner's Hospital for Crippled Children

COACH PROFILE

THAD MATTA –
OHIO STATE UNIVERSITY
(NABC MEMBER 12 YEARS)

"You always know that as a head coach, you get the right guys on your staff and these things are going to happen (John Groce becomes head coach at Ohio University). Now we watch another one of our family members spread his wings and I know he will do a great job. He was with me from the beginning and we were opposites."

How good of a coach or player do you have to be to live down a career playing for the Cornjerkers of Hoopeston-East? Well, for Thad Matta, the toughness he developed wearing the logo led to a terrific college-playing career.

After beginning at Southern Illinois University, Matta transferred to Butler University and led the Bulldogs in three-point field goal percentage, free throw percentage, and field goal percentage at different times in his career. He captained Butler in his senior season under the tutelage of the present director of athletics, Barry Collier.

Matta began his coaching career immediately after graduating from Butler. He worked as an assistant coach at Indiana State University, Miami of Ohio (twice), and Butler before replacing Collier at the Bulldogs' helm. In his one season at Butler, Matta set a school record for wins (24) and guided the team to the second round of the NCAA Tournament. Matta left for Xavier immediately following that season and won 26 games in each of his three seasons at the school. He would win back-to-back A-10 Championships and take the Musketeers to one NCAA Elite Eight appearance and two NCAA second round appearances.

When he was named head coach at Ohio State University, you'd have thought Matta's streak would slow some. He took over with a black cloud hanging over the program, but he didn't even flinch. Recruiting success was immediate, and Ohio State would ride two great freshmen to an appearance in the 2007 Final Four. Though he lost to the Florida Gators in the final game, and then lost point guard, Mike Conely, and the nation's best center, Greg Oden, as lottery picks in the NBA draft, Ohio State continues to be a force in college basketball. After re-tooling and competing with another group of inexperienced returning players, Ohio State appeared in the NIT in 2008.

Matta continues his pursuit of the nation's best prep players and a pipeline to Columbus is quickly forming. Recruiting the best, preparing the best and winning games is the Matta mantra, and it will continue for years to come.

be incidents or trouble concerning their race. He would do what he could to make sure that they were given every opportunity to be safe, but he could not make a guarantee."

Rupp was a hard-nosed guy who relished in the stiffness of his German and Austrian upbringing. He didn't speak to many people, and a casual conversation was unheard of. According to McGary, when entering Rupp's office, one had a very short period to make his point or he was ushered out for tasks that are more important.

It is important to remember Rupp's numerous accomplishments in basketball and community service and realize that the man survived the difficult times and moved forward in the integration of UK basketball as the times dictated. He never avoided assisting organizations or coaches around the world who asked for assistance. He made 11 overseas trips for the U.S. government, teaching the game. He was also selected as the U.S. Goodwill Ambassador to the 1968 Olympic Games.

McGary was a vital cog in Rupp's process to bring the NABC East-West All-Star Game to Lexington, Kentucky. As a member of the Junior Chamber of Commerce in Lexington, McGary was a tireless worker not only to have the game in Lexington, but also to make it the best possible event for the kids and the community.

Adolph Rupp receives his award as incoming President of the NABC from Executive Director Cliff Wells.

Rupp, with the help of other coaches and the Chamber, developed the concept and the actual presentation of the game, which began in 1962. Although other coaches, including Henry Iba and Harold Anderson, were involved with some of the planning, Rupp's dramatic personality finally brought the game to life. Rupp used his enormous influence to keep the game a part of the NABC tradition throughout his life.

This game has bounced around the country over the years, but to this day, it remains a vital part of the NABC convention and provides opportunities for seniors to showcase their skills to national and international coaches, sportswriters, and scouts.

GUARDIAN AWARDS

EDUCATION

2002 John Wooden, UCLA

2003 Robert Murrey, USA Coaches Clinics

2004 Kevin McCarthy, State University of New York-Cobleskill

2005 Herb Magee, Philadelphia University

2006 Jim Burson, NABC President

2007 Gary Smith, University of Redlands

2008 Steve Moore, College of Wooster (presented by The Hartford)

ADVOCACY

2002 Ed Bilik, Springfield

2003 Jerry Krause, Gonzaga

2004 Don Showalter, Mid-Prairie High School

2005 Chris Mowry, Santa Fe CC

2006 Bill Leatherman, Bridgewater College

2007 Jud Heathcote, Michigan State University

2008 Pete Smith, Guerin Catholic HS - Noblesville, IN (Presented by DiGiorno)

LEADERSHIP

2002 Dave Gavitt, Providence/Big East

2003 Lonnie Porter, Regis University

2004 Eddie Sutton, Oklahoma State

2005 Harry Statham, McKendree College

2006 Russell F. Booth, Glenwood City High School

2007 Steve Bankson, Baldwin-Wallace College

2008 C. Alan Rowe, Widener University

SERVICE

2002 Ron Naclerio, Cardozo H.S. (N.Y.)

2003 Hal Smith, Malone College

2004 Bo Ryan, Wisconsin-Madison

2005 Bill Van Gundy, Genesee CC

2006 Jim Kessler, Grace College

2007 Richard Reed, Sacramento State University

2008 Dave Rose, Brigham Young University

BOOK SIX

THE CHAMPIONS OF THE WORLD:

HISTORY OF OLYMPIC BASKETBALL

With the gold medal firmly in hand following the 1968 Olympic Games, the United States was sporting a 55-game winning streak going back to the first basketball competition in the Games in 1936. The U.S. had never lost an Olympic basketball game and James Naismith's invention had continued to be "America's game," regardless of the rules by which it was played.

Phog Allen was a major player in the Olympic basketball movement and was very instrumental in convincing the German Olympic Committee to officially add the game in 1936. Allen was convinced that basketball was going to be in the 1932 Games, but his effort was foiled by some last-minute, back-room politics. This time, he stayed the course until official word was received. German Olympic officials were so impressed with Allen and his years of effort, that Allen was informed of the decision even before the United States Olympic Committee was told.

Basketball actually was played in the 1904 St. Louis Olympics as an exhibition or demonstration sport. This was an Olympic tradition, allowing the different committees to measure a new sport's interest and fan enthusiasm. It was also used to gauge the level of competition around the world. Clearly, the U.S. team would have little competition from other countries participating in the event. The Buffalo Germans were so dominant in the St. Louis exhibitions that basketball would not become an official Olympic sport until years later.

"NABC leadership is directly responsible for basketball being part of Olympic competition," wrote Cliff Wells, NABC executive secretary. "Dr. Allen used his usual dogged determination to re-introduce basketball at the 1932 Olympics in Los Angeles. During the next four years this attack only intensified and, rather than an exhibition sport in 1936, Germany introduced basketball to Olympic fans everywhere."

The team from the USA would win five games that year and take the gold medal. Silver and bronze medals went to Canada and Mexico, respectively, and a 55-game winning streak had begun. James Needles from the AAU was the head coach and Gene Johnson, also from the AAU, assisted on that inaugural team.

The NABC had spent the previous year raising funds to send Dr. James Naismith to the event. After a brief discussion, the German Olympic Committee, saying they never heard he was coming, introduced Naismith to a warm greeting from the fans, players, and coaches. After being honored with tossing up the first ball in Olympic competition, Naismith returned to the United States visibly proud of what he had started.

After eight years of postponed Olympics because of the World War, the Americans dominated again in London in 1948. Omar "Bud" Browning (AAU) and Adolph Rupp (NABC) co-coached the team and an enlarged field of 23 nations competed for the medals. A gold medal after eight wins and no losses was the reward for the U.S. squad. This time around, France won the silver medal and Brazil the bronze.

A similar story was written every four years as the winning streak continued. For the next 12 years, the United States Olympic program would be in the hands of Henry Iba and the program would make history, both good and bad.

GUARDIAN

HENRY "HANK" IBA
(DELIBERATE, DEFENSE,
OLYMPIC CHAMPION)

*"I'm not against shooting; I am against bad
shooting. I want my boys to shoot. I love my boys
to shoot. But, glory be, make it a good shot."*
— **Hank Iba**

In Coach Henry Iba, there was a quiet genius. He labored for most of his Hall of Fame career at Oklahoma A & M (Oklahoma State) and was a great leader of men. A winner of 762 college basketball games and two NCAA National Championships, Iba excelled especially on the international stage. Under Iba's coaching, the United States won the gold medal at both the 1964 and 1968 Olympic Games. It was only because the United States was cheated out of the gold medal in 1972 that kept Iba from coaching his third Olympic Championship team.

Henry Iba was born in Eason, Missouri, in 1904. He remained in Eason until graduating from high school. He was an exceptional basketball player and would play on numerous teams around the Midwest. His coaching career began at Classen High School, where he won 51 games in three seasons. Iba moved on to Maryville Teachers College, winning 61 games before spending one year at the University of Colorado.

In 1934, Iba accepted the head coaching position at Oklahoma State and remained there for the remainder of his career. While in Stillwater, he won National Championships in 1945 and 1946, and was runner-up in 1949. Additionally, Iba held committee positions in many different NABC groups, served on the Board of Directors and was the NABC President in 1967-68.

Iba introduced one of the earliest seven-foot basketball players, Bob Kurland, to the college game. Kurland dominated teams on both ends of the court. He completed his collegiate career with back-to-back NCAA Championships, gold medals from the 1948 and 1952 Olympic Games, and an AAU record of 369-26.

Iba first coached in the Olympics as the United States' main man in 1964. At the time, there was a great deal of unrest in sports and even some threats of an African-American boycott. Once selected, Iba had only a short time to introduce this group of players to international competition and coach them into a cohesive unit. The team won all nine of its games and kept the gold medals on American soil.

Throughout the competition, the American teams' margins of victory were large. But the Russians were looming on the horizon. The Russian squad was thought to be the best in the competition. However, the United States beat Russia, 73-59, and continued the streak.

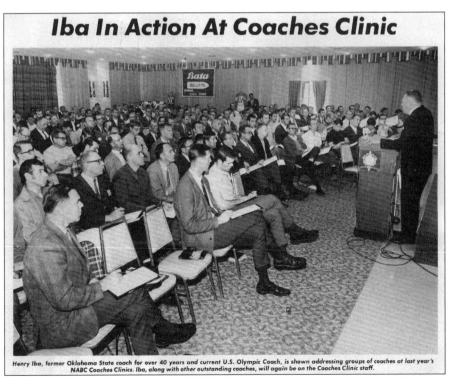

Iba In Action At Coaches Clinic

Henry Iba, former Oklahoma State coach for over 40 years and current U.S. Olympic Coach, is shown addressing groups of coaches at last year's NABC Coaches Clinics. Iba, along with other outstanding coaches, will again be on the Coaches Clinic staff.

Mr. Iba, in 1970, teaching the game to other coaches wanting to learn from the best of the era.

COACH PROFILE

BOB MCKILLOP –
DAVIDSON COLLEGE
(NABC MEMBER 34 YEARS)

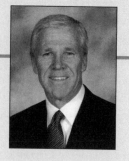

"When there is a subjective process that is married to an objective process there's going to be a lot of unhappy people. We're OK. The fact that we're in Raleigh (NCAA Tournament) makes it pretty special for us."

Bob McKillop was born and raised in New York City and played high school ball at Chaminade High School. He began his college playing career at East Carolina University and then transferred back to New York City and Hofstra University and was named team MVP before spending a short time with the Philadelphia 76ers of the NBA.

In June 2008, *USA Today* reported that Davidson College rewarded McKillop with a contract extension. McKillop has been their head coach since posting an impressive coaching record at the high school level and being recruited back to the North Carolina campus. After a one-year experiment as an assistant at Davidson, he returned to his native New York City and won five New York State Championships in 10 seasons. This success earned McKillop a return to Davidson as its head coach.

McKillop earned four post-season invitations in the first twelve years, resulting in some flak from the fans. Since then, he has gotten that post-season invitation for four consecutive seasons and brought Davidson within one point of the Final Four in 2008.

Davidson President Tom Ross said, "After 19 years at Davidson, it is clear to everyone that Coach McKillop is one of the nation's premier basketball coaches. At Davidson, we know that he is also an outstanding leader of young men and an ideal representative of Davidson, a college of excellence, both academically and athletically."

The winningest coach in school history has nine Southern Conference Championships on his resume. He also has been recipient of numerous Coach of the Year awards and received the Clair Bee Award for service outside the game.

With the return of Stephen Curry for the 2008-2009 season, the short-term future of the program seems guaranteed. McKillop is known for his aggressive scheduling that prepares his squads for post-season success. He played a who's-who of college basketball in 2008 including North Carolina, Duke, UCLA and N.C. State, and barely missed a spot in the Final Four when the game's final shot fell short against Kansas, the 2008 National Champions. It's a moment that will remain a WHAT IF memory for the coaches and players for years to come.

All streaks must end, including the Americans' domination in the Olympics. After winning in 1968, Russia beat the U.S. in the 1972 gold-medal game after a very controversial decision to put time back on the clock after the United States had won the game.

"The replaying of the video-tape, and the sworn affidavits of the game officials, document the worst miscarriage of justice in the history of the Olympic Games," wrote Olympic historian Bud Greenspan. "The documentation makes it perfectly clear that Dr. R. Williams Jones, secretary general of FIBA, usurped his authority and illegally made a decision reserved exclusively for the official working the game."

The phantom seconds added by the game's officials allowed the Russians to inbound the ball and score, defeating the Americans 51-50. The winning streak ended at 63 games.

For the first time, the United States was awarded the silver medal in Olympic basketball competition. The American team refused the medals. They remain in a vault with the understanding that they will be returned to the team only when ALL of the members agree to accept them.

The Olympic record of seven-straight championships without a defeat should stand forever. Competition has continued to improve around the world. It should be noted that this spectacular achievement was accomplished by college and university coaches, coaching college or amateur players from around the country. These NABC members have a stellar record in Olympic competition and are equally responsible for the improving play around the world.

Dave Gavitt and Marv Harshman provide the Coach of the Year Awards at the 1977 NABC National Convention. Seated and clapping is Hall of Fame Coach Nat Holman.

GUARDIAN

DEAN SMITH
(CHAMPION, TEACHER,
GUARDED, REVERED)

"I don't think any of the lettermen can really express the family atmosphere that he's built, the tradition that he's built of loyalty and camaraderie. It's a fraternity that's very much admired by basketball people everywhere. We get a lot of abuse because of our loyalty to one another, but we love being a part of it. The meaning of tradition doesn't exist in sports anymore. It's fading, from the Yankees to the Steelers to the Dodgers. North Carolina still remains very, very special. The loyalty is unprecedented. The man behind it all is Coach Smith."

— George Karl, Denver Nuggets

Maybe the greatest coach that you never see, Dean Smith learned the game from Phog Allen and set records at the University of North Carolina (UNC). He continues to be remembered for his four-corner offense and blamed for the shot clock that was introduced in 1985. Fans should remember, however, that Smith broke the racial barrier in the ACC with the recruitment of Charlie Scott and coached a team of relative unknowns to the 1976 Olympic Gold Medal.

The United States Olympic Committee selected Smith in early 1975. Although he was honored to be picked, he would often repeat many coaches deserved that opportunity more than he did. Several issues had to be dealt with in the months leading up to the Games, but first Smith had to select his coaching staff. Knowing full well that he needed veteran leadership and organizational expertise, he selected Bill Guthridge and John Thompson to be his assistant coaches.

Guthridge had been at Smith's side at North Carolina for years and was known campus-wide for his attention to detail. With everything that had to be planned from scouting to team selection, plus a certain built in confidence and loyalty, Guthridge was the easy selection.

Picking Thompson wasn't so easy. Years earlier, during Thompson's years coaching at St. Anthony's High School, Smith had come to the coach's home to recruit a player who lived with them. This young man had lost his parents so Coach Thompson and his wife had become the legal guardians. The two coaches hit it off right away and met often to discuss strategy and coaching styles. The friendship had grown, but so had the realization that the two shared a similar basketball philosophy. This shared approach would be the deciding factor in selecting John Thompson as the second assistant coach.

One of the things that complicated this entire Olympic process was a wedding date that Smith and his fiancé had selected earlier. The date fell at the same time of the NABC summer board meetings, preparations for the Olympic trials and then the trials themselves. It would be necessary for the new Smith family to honeymoon and select the Olympic players in the same period.

It was during the Olympic trials that Smith attracted some unfavorable publicity regarding the selection and make-up of the final Olympic roster. As it turned out, there were four players from UNC and seven from the Atlantic Coast Conference. Media outlets and coaches around the country, unfamiliar with the team selection process, were unkindly harsh to the head coach. Comments that the American flag must be red, white, and Carolina blue were the most hurtful.

In reality, Smith had no real power in the selection process at all. He would have one vote, equal to the other members of the selection committee. Beyond giving a pre-selection speech about the

A Glance At ... Dean Smith

- 879 Wins
- 77.6% Winning percentage
- Most Division I 20-win seasons, 30 (27 consecutive)
- 22 seasons with 25 wins
- 11 Final Four Appearances
- National Champions 1982, 1993
- 17 ACC Championships
- Finished in the ACC top 3– 33 times
- 13 ACC Tournament Titles
- 27 NCAA Tournament appearances (23 consecutive)
- 96.6% Graduation Rate
- Joined Pete Newell and Bob Knight– Won Olympics, NCAA and NIT
- 1976 Olympic Gold Medal Coach
- Joined Knight as only two to play on and coach an NCAA champion
- Coached 26 All-Americans

Awards and Accolades:
- National Coach of the Year, 1977, 1979, 1982, 1993
- 8 times ACC Coach of the Year
- Enshrined in the North Carolina Hall of Fame in 1981
- Inducted into the Naismith Memorial Basketball Hall of Fame 1983
- UNC Dean Smith Center "Dean Dome"
- Sports Illustrated Sportsman of the Year
- ESPN– All-Time Greatest Coaches
- Founding Inductee– National Collegiate Basketball Hall of Fame

characteristics he would like to see the team have, his was just the role of an observer. He even commented that he would have preferred some players who were not selected, over some who were.

"Three players that I wanted were not named to the team, while seven players made it from the ACC," Smith wrote in his book, *A Coaches Life*. "I would not have picked all of them, but some in the media still criticized me for having seven from my own conference."

With the Olympic team made up of college and university players, the U.S. team would be the youngest and least experienced in the Olympics. Complicating things that year was an unspecified refusal by several of the best players in the country to attend the trials. Players like Robert Parish and Leon Douglas on the inside and John Lucas at guard were conspicuous in their absence.

The trials lasted six days and became a bit of a survival of the fittest. Some of the players left, some failed to live up to expectations, and some were simply cut.

"Bo Ellis, great player from Marquette, didn't get past the first day," Smith reported, "when he learned that he had to run a mile under a specific time to make the squad."

From day one, the concern was the lack of candidates on the front line. Additionally and unofficially speaking, the U.S. was probably the youngest, least experienced, and smallest team in the competition.

The squad reported to Chapel Hill, North Carolina, for the final preparation. Coach Guthridge left for Europe to scout future opponents and the squad played a series of exhibition games to prepare for the Games. There was no time for the usual bonding exercises, it was just hard work to build team chemistry, and the squad came along fine. Scott May and Quinn Buckner, who had played for coach Bob Knight, set a tempo that most suffered to maintain. This lead-by-example attitude was a valuable attribute within the group.

"Ordinarily, a coach asks his players what their goals are and works to develop them over the long term," said Smith. "We didn't have time for that in putting this team together. We would live together for two months and then go our separate ways. All of us knew that our only objective was to win the gold medal."

The Olympic brackets were established and the only way that revenge over the Russians was going to become a possibility was a meeting for the gold in Montreal. The United States opened the Olympics against Italy, winning the game easily. The scare of the Games came in game two, against a tough bunch from Puerto Rico. They had lost in their opener and were playing for the right to stay in the tournament. The two guards for Puerto Rico were New York City kids, Neftali Rivera and Butch Lee, who went on to become National Player of the Year at Marquette under coach Al McGuire.

Although the U.S. beat Puerto Rico, 95-94, the Americans simply could not stop the guards from penetrating to the basket. The lack of size inside became a factor and the game was in the balance the entire time. With a sigh of relief, the Americans returned to the dorm and rested for what would become a tougher road, after some of the cracks in the armor were displayed.

The United States remained undefeated in pool play and earned the right to face the host nation, Canada, in the first semifinal game. Yugoslavia and the Soviet Union met in the other semifinal.

The American team handled Canada easily, setting up what would be a revenge game with the Russians. But, as is usually the case, the upset spoiled the fun. Yugoslavia beat the Russians. Whatever concern arose over not playing the Russians, and playing Yugoslavia, a team they had already beaten, was short-lived. Full of patriotism and determination to return the gold medal to the United States was enough to put Yugoslavia away early and easily. Although it did not completely erase the taste of being cheated four years earlier, the Americans once again owned the Olympic title.

"John, Bill, and I stood off to the side at the award ceremonies and watched our young men mount the podium to receive the gold," Smith said. "Since coaches were not considered competitors, we did not join the ceremony, which I thought was totally appropriate. College basketball could learn from that ideal. Our reward was to hear *The Star-Spangled Banner* played honoring these 12 young men who were gold medal winners."

That quote probably says more about who Dean Smith is, and how he thought, than all of the accolades that have been spoken about him.

Dean Smith was born in Emporia, Kansas, the son of a high school basketball coach. His dad was very successful, winning the Kansas state Championship in 1934. A footnote of some significance: On that 1934 team, Alfred Smith coached the first black basketball player to be permitted to participate in the Kansas State basketball tournament. Certainly, this was a precursor to what opportunity would be presented to his son later.

A terrific high school athlete, Smith excelled in football, baseball, and basketball. He earned a high school varsity letter in all four years in basketball and qualified for an academic scholarship to attend Kansas. This opportunity would mean that he would play basketball for KU coach Phog Allen, founder of the National Association of Basketball Coaches of the United States.

This relationship would last one extra year as Dean Smith would remain to assist Allen with the basketball team during the 1953-1954 season. The coaching career was interrupted with military duty in the United States Air Force in Germany. Upon returning from Europe, he would coach baseball and golf at the Air Force Academy before that one big break that the great ones all seemed to gain sometime in their

COACH PROFILE

MIKE MONTGOMERY –
UNIVERSITY OF CALIFORNIA
(NABC MEMBER 35 YEARS)

"This is all good. There's just no downside I hope for anybody. All of the rhetoric, all of the wins and accomplishments go out the window with the first loss. That's the mentality of the business for you. And our job is to get this program (California) to the top half of the conference and heading toward conference championships. We want to get to the NCAA Tournament and do it the right way."

Now here is a guy who built a coaching career as you might envision it in your head, if you had not read all of the other ways to make it in this business. Mike Montgomery coached in high school, as an assistant in college and then a college head coach, before moving on to an elite Division-I program and the NBA. This Long Beach, California, native has since returned to the ranks of elite university programs to continue what was already a stellar career.

Montgomery signed to become the head coach at the University of California in 2008. After discovering the massive differences that a coach encounters moving from NCAA basketball to the game played in the NBA. After leaving the Golden State Warriors, he took some time off and returned to the Pac 10 where he had great success at Stanford University.

After nine years coaching in the high school ranks, Montgomery would test his skills as the assistant coach at Boise State University. After a brief tenure with the Bison, he became the head coach at the University of Montana. In a true test of recruiting and scheduling to the remote reaches of the Rocky Mountains, Montgomery would win 154 games at Montana before returning to his home state of California as the coach at Stanford University.

It would be here that Montgomery began to receive some national attention and acclaim. His impressive run at Stanford included 10 NCAA appearances and earning a spot in one Final Four. Recognized with Pac 10 and Naismith Coach of the Year honors while at Stanford, Montgomery would also receive acclaim as a John R. Wooden Achievement Award winner.

As a head coach, Montgomery would post 25 of 26 winning seasons and win 20+ games his last four seasons at Stanford. He has several years of experience coaching with USA Basketball that includes work with the USA National Team and the FIBA World Championships.

career. In the Smith case, he was invited to join the coaching staff at North Carolina, working for legendary Frank McGuire.

After Smith's three-year crash course in ACC basketball, McGuire was forced to resign his position because of reported recruiting irregularities. Then UNC chancellor, William Aycock, appointed Smith as the replacement beginning with the 1961 basketball season. Dean Smith was just 30 years old and was getting ready to lead a program that had won its first national championship four years earlier.

Smith would begin his career with an abbreviated schedule and concerns that the gambling and point-shaving scandal had entered the ACC. Two North Carolina State players and one from UNC had been identified in the investigation. Looking to react accordingly, the university de-emphasized the season, playing 17 games and finishing with an 8-9 record.

If there's one question mark on Smith's coaching resume at North Carolina it would be two national championships after 11 Final Four appearances. It's easy for critics to point to that one.

One thing no one can deny is the Dean Smith Coaching Tree. It starts with his college coach, Phog Allen, who learned the game from James Naismith. Then there's Bill Guthridge, Roy Williams, Matt Doherty, George Karl, Larry Brown, Eddie Fogler, Billy Cunningham, Jeff Lebo, Buzz Peterson, Mitch Kupchak, Tony Shaver and Scott Cherry.

GUARDIAN
BOBBY KNIGHT
(WINNER: OLYMPICS, INDIANA, TEXAS TECH, ESPN)

"The selection of the Olympic Team won't be much different from the way we select our team at Indiana, which is, you've got to be able to play the way I want you to play. There are a lot of organizations that will be formed in the next year on a far more democratic basis than the U.S. Olympic Basketball Team."

— Bob Knight

It is easy to look at the career of Robert Montgomery Knight and talk about his temper, the chair throwing, and the battles leading up to his departure from Indiana. It is just as easy to forget, ignore, or never learn that Knight was never investigated by the NCAA; was before his time in the emphasis on education responsibility; and always provided a safety net for his players and fellow coaches when things went wrong.

Additionally, Knight would be selected to coach the Olympic Team and again seek revenge for the 1972 robbery.

The process of taking a team to the 1984 Olympics begins in 1982 with the selection of Knight as the head coach. This began a two-year process of evaluating the top talent around the world and selecting the best team imaginable.

The road to the '84 Games in Los Angeles began in earnest. As always, the selection process was a mixture of precedent, politics, and ability. There is always a bevy of candidates for these positions because most coaches will tell you that it is the highest honor a coach can receive. In this case, Knight's selection was championed by his long-time mentor, Pete Newell. Newell had coached the Olympics in 1960, and his selection was championed by the very first Olympic coach, James Needles, who had coached Newell in college and would be instrumental in encouraging his application.

Knight's selection meant he'd be the first basketball coach to lead the United States Olympic squad on American soil. The Games were further complicated by a return boycott by the Eastern bloc countries in response to President Jimmy Carter's decision four years earlier for the U.S. to boycott the summer Games. The competition wouldn't be any easier in 1984, just different.

Much had changed in the global development of the game in the last eight years. The Soviets had lost a great deal of talent to age and were not the powerhouse of 1976. New countries had sprung up in Eastern Europe and some were housing incredible talent. Knight made it his passion to see all of the players and the teams play. This journey would have a major impact on the selection of the players to make up the team. With a staff of coaches that included C.M. Newton from Alabama, George Raveling from USC and Don Donoher of Dayton, the process would begin on the Indiana campus in Bloomington.

"In the spring of 1984, we brought 74 very good players, almost all of them college kids, to Bloomington for the trials," said Knight. "I also asked a lot of college coaches to come for the week and work with us."

The selection process was a series of drills, teaching sessions, and scrimmages that would eventually lead to selecting the final 12 players. Knight put the players through three-a-day practices, which tested them both physically and mentally. That wasn't the only way he tested them, though.

In early May, the final 12 were set. The team was supposed to report on June 4 back in Bloomington. One of the players, Jon Koncak, was supposed to be getting married on June 22. Since that was going to interfere with practice, Koncak and his fiancé moved their wedding to Friday night, June 3.

"(On Wednesday) I got a call from Dave Bliss, who was my coach at SMU and an assistant on the Olympic team," Koncak remembered. "He said Coach Knight was flying into Kansas City and he wanted me to pick him up at the airport at 6:30. The rehearsal was at 7.

"Coach asked if we could go over to the Marriott to get something to eat. It was about 6:45. He ordered some soup. ... I kept looking at my watch. He said, 'Jon, I've been thinking about the situation with you and being on the team. ... I really don't think it's in our country's best interest for you to get married tomorrow. I don't think you can focus on the game.'

"I said, 'Coach Knight, there's nothing more that I want to do than represent our country.' He put down his spoon and said, 'That's all I wanted to hear.' And he had me take him back to the airport. To this day I don't know what the whole point of that was."

Possibly the point was to make sure the players were as focused as their coach was.

"He gave us all an 8 by 10 glossy picture of the gold medal," Koncak said. "He told us, 'These next eight weeks, I want you to spend 10 minutes looking at this picture and imagining being a gold medal winner and what it means to you and your family and this country.' We were mesmerized. ... Those next eight weeks were brutal, but we had a specific focus of what we were going to do."

The United States completed pool play with five straight wins and defeated a very tough Spanish team for the gold medal. A different player led the team stats for each game, but many would state that Michael Jordan took his first steps toward basketball stardom. According to Knight, Jordan also had an impact in the locker room.

"I had put the things that were important to us defensively on one side of a blackboard, and the offensive things we were stressing were written on the other side of the board," Knight said. "The players were already seated when I came in to talk to them. When I turned to face the board, I saw that right in the middle of it was a big yellow piece of paper off a legal pad, it said, 'Coach, don't worry. We've put up with too much shit to lose now.' And I don't have any doubt about the author. By then I knew what Michael Jordan's handwriting looked like."

Knight was born in Massillon, Ohio, on October 25, 1940. He spent his youngest days in Orrville, Ohio, with memories of little league baseball, hot-stove league baseball and a state championship won against Elyria. From his earliest days, his home was shared by his parents and grandmother and Knight would never have a room of his own. Knight slept on a pull-out couch until leaving home for college.

His fondest thoughts are the days walking the railroad yard where his dad worked.

"If you're going to accept pay for something, do it right," he'd often hear from his dad on these walks.

Knight's favorite pastime is fishing, and he was introduced to the sport when just a kid. His dad would take him cane-pole fishing right there in Orrville.

"He taught me a lot of things about life, most of them the best way—by example," said Knight. "But there's nothing I'm more grateful for when he took the time to introduce me to fishing. That was very much on my mind when I first taught my son Tim, to fish, and then his younger brother, Pat."

Like several of the other Guardians, Knight says he was most influenced by his mother, Hazel. A second grade teacher, she insisted on responsibility in school. Bob was permitted to participate in sports without restriction as long as he gave the same effort to his schoolwork.

When he was young, Knight was forced to go on Saturday shopping excursions with his mom and grandmother. During one of these Saturday trips, Knight was introduced in a way to Clair Bee, the Long Island University coach, and Naismith inductee, who would later become his coaching mentor. Bee was a very active writer with a famous series written for kids, the Chip Hilton books. Knight found one of these books in a department store and was hooked, reading the entire series. Learning the marvelous idea of losing oneself in a book introduced Knight to the library and the works of many great authors. When speaking to individuals or groups, Knight often quotes from books or refers to reading selections that he would recommend.

Besides Bee, many of the great athletes and coaches around the country influenced Knight. One of the great inspirations for Knight as a coach came when he first arrived at Indiana. Doc Counsilman, the great IU swimming coach, brought swimmers to Indiana from all over the world. These swimmers would leave IU as better athletes, and Counsilman would use each individual to become a better coach. Knight watched closely as Doc became the first coach to win six consecutive NCAA swimming championships.

Before reaching that point, however, Knight was a solid player at Ohio State University. He had attended a recruiting weekend with hundreds of other football—yes, football—recruits, but was not on Woody Hayes' radar screen. His basketball recruitment to OSU consisted of his neighbor and dentist, Dr. Don Boop, an Ohio State grad, phoning the basketball office and sending some films. Coach Fred Taylor, newly hired, visited the Knight home before he ever coached his first game at OSU. He made a favorable impression, and Knight and his dad were sold.

"He (Taylor) talked about the team he was trying to put together, but I didn't have any idea—and I'm not sure he did either—how good a first recruiting class he was going to have," Knight said. "Start off with two Hall of Fame players, (Jerry) Lucas and (John) Havlicek. How many other college basketball coaches ever recruited two of those in one class, let alone in his first recruiting class?"

Knight and the others in that first recruiting would spend the week practicing with the varsity and then watching the games from the seats. (Freshmen were ineligible for varsity competition, which meant this great recruiting class would have to wait its

COACH PROFILE

LUTE OLSON –
UNIVERSITY OF ARIZONA
(NABC MEMBER 36 YEARS)

"Our game plan will indicate the options we expect will be most successful against the next opponent. We attempt to polish these during the ensuing practice sessions."

History will look favorably upon Lute Olson when listing the best basketball coaches in the land. This seven-time Pac 10 Coach of the Year and NCAA National Champion has steadily moved up the coaching ladder, winning at every turn. He won better than 65% of the games he coached at every level and in twenty-plus seasons at Arizona, won 76% of his contests. Easily one of the greatest to coach in the Pac 10, Olson is number one in career wins and trails only John Wooden in winning percentage (.810 - .764).

Lute Olson was born in Mayville, North Dakota, and was a three-sport star at Augsburg College prior to beginning his coaching career. His career began with eleven years as a high school coach and four additional years as a junior college coach where he won 82% of his games.

He began his NCAA coaching career at Long Beach State, and immediately won a conference championship. That championship earned Olson the opportunity to lead his first elite program at the University of Iowa in the Big 10. After four years with Iowa finishing no higher than fourth in the Big 10, Olson began a streak of five consecutive NCAA berths and one trip to the Final Four. After nine seasons building the Hawkeyes into a conference championship contender, he accepted the challenge of rebuilding the Arizona Wildcats, a program that needed a complete overhaul. Still coaching at Arizona, Olson has 22 consecutive NCAA appearances, several Final Fours and a National Championship. Though he missed the 2007-2008 season to recover from personal hardship, he returned to the helm in 2008-2009.

The 2002 enshrinement into the Naismith Memorial Basketball Hall of Fame was a career milestone, but Olson obviously has not completed what he originally set out to achieve: "I think it ranks right up there with the NCAA Championships and the 1986 World Championship. This is definitely one of the special things that has happened in my career. I am very thankful for the recognition and the enshrinement. I want to thank Bobbi (wife) and my family for their sacrifices in addition to the former assistant coaches and former players that share in this honor as well."

turn.) Taylor and the freshmen watched an 11-11 season and were ready when that turn came. Twice during that season of watching, the freshmen and the varsity actually played a game. The freshmen won both times, with Lucas scoring 40 points in both games. Everyone was excited about the possibility for the next season.

During their first year of eligibility, that star-studded group breezed through the NCAA national tournament before beating California for the national title. The thing that impressed Knight about the whole thing was that Cal coach Pete Newell had tutored Taylor the previous summer, giving no thought to the possibility of playing during the year. That would be something Knight would remember as he worked his way up the coaching ranks, helping all who would come calling.

As it turned out, that was the only championship that great recruiting class would win. They would have great runs the following two seasons, but would lose in the championship game each time. It would be the first time that a Big 10 school would reach the Final Four three straight times. The first Fred Taylor recruiting class would finish its three years with a record of 78-6 and win one championship in three tries.

Knight left Ohio State thinking that he would give coaching and teaching a chance for a year or two and then try for a graduate assistantship and possibly study law. Knight ended up getting the job as assistant for Harold Andreas at Cuyahoga Falls High School.

The job turned out to be just the right opportunity, teaching Knight the difference between being a player and a coach. Learning the depth of knowledge and the myriad of questions that head coaches had to absorb was important for Knight's development. Practicing every day and then splitting off to coach the junior varsity allowed a perfect mixture of teaching and learning on the job. Depending on the source of how Knight ended up at Army, there are some disagreements. The story seems to be that Taylor had found a place for Knight as the freshmen coach at West Point if he was willing to join the Army. Knight followed through, volunteering for the draft and then George Hunter, Army coach, resigned the position. Left in limbo, Taylor would contact the new coach, Tates Locke, and the arrangement was secured. Locke had been the assistant to Hunter and was taking his first job as a head coach. Locke and Knight got along well and during the two years as the assistant coach, Knight was given a great deal of responsibility in recruiting and scouting.

Locke left Army after the second season and Knight was picked as the head coach. He would win 102 games in the next six years and gain an invitation to the NIT in four of them. Knight's Army teams reached the NIT semifinals in three of those four years, but they never made it to the championship. During his career at Army, there were job offers at Florida and Wisconsin, but in each case, the timing was just not right. During his time at Army, though, Knight recruited a point guard named Mike Krzyzewski, who eventually became the head coach at West Point.

In 1971, Knight became the new basketball coach at Indiana University. The career that Knight carved out was well documented. In his 29 years at IU, he qualified for post-season play 28 times. He never had a losing season at Indiana and would have only two losing records in the Big 10, securing postseason berths both times. There was one NIT championship in his first season at IU and three NCAA national championships in 1976, '81 and '87. Knight should have at least one more NCAA Championship, losing in the final when All-American Scott May injured his arm late in the season and could only perform at a fraction of what was expected.

While at IU, Knight spent 10 years as a very assertive member of the NABC Board. He ran his committees and provided leadership that was needed. This ended in 1986, only months before he was to become the NABC President.

As the 1986 *Bulletin* read from the July, 1986, Board meeting: "A letter of resignation from Bobby Knight was presented and read. A motion was made and seconded to accept Knight's resignation with regret. Motion carried."

Efforts to determine the reason for the abrupt change for the *Guardians of the Game* book were unsuccessful. Bill Wall, Joe Vancisin and David Berst refused to respond and all were consistent in referring the question directly to Knight. Each person added, however, that Knight's resignation from the NABC was one of the sad days in the history of the organization.

Knight would end his career at Indiana in 2000 with a well-publicized battle with university President Myles Brand. Knight left the school among student protests and alumni uprising with the following message:

> When my time on Earth is gone,
> and my activities here are past,
> I want they bury me upside down,
> and my critics can kiss my ass.

Former NABC President Gerald Myers, the director of athletics at Texas Tech University, hired Knight to lead the Red Raiders' struggling men's basketball program. There were immediate positive results in the arena and on campus. Ticket sales and donations increased and Knight donated $10,000 to a library fund that has now raised more than $300,000 with his continued support.

The basketball team showed immediate improvement as well, qualifying for post-season play in Knight's first four seasons. The Red Raiders hadn't been in postseason action since 1996. Three NCAA Tournaments and one NIT were interrupted by a poor 2006 performance, but the 2007 group rebounded and secured the fifth post-season selection under Knight. In February 2008, with 902 wins and a 138-82 record at Texas Tech, Knight retired. He handed the team to his son, Pat, and stepped away from the sideline. He and Pat sighted fatigue, plus the importance of Pat getting some sideline experience before embarking on his first full season at the helm in 2008.

Knight became a television analyst and did a terrific job. He was insightful and honest, a refreshing approach. Many, like Dick Vitale, feel that Knight will be back on the sidelines, adding to his 902 victories, before he officially hangs up his Chuck Taylors. There will always be room for a coach with Knight's body of work.

BOOK SEVEN

IT'S A SMALL WORLD

When speaking about basketball coaches, the common misconception is that the conversation centers on those who appear on television and in the national newspapers on a regular basis. Although these are the highest-paid coaches and the highest-profile coaches, they are really the smallest segment of the coaching population. Basketball coaching is visible in youth leagues, middle school, high school and every level of basketball beyond that. In post-secondary basketball coaching circles, there are seven different classifications of competition employing coaches.

Although there are countless coaches who should be recognized, the following sections identify a select few who could be considered "guardians." These great people serve in some obscurity and that service is very often overlooked. Each of these gentlemen will be the first to tell you that they share the honor with each of the competitors in their chosen division.

John Percy Page

John Percy Page is the most obscure coach in this book. He was the coach of the Edmonton Commercial Grads from 1915-1940, and compiled a record of 502-20. Depending on the source, he won 23 or 24 Canadian Provincial Titles, 15 Western Canadian Titles, 29 of 31 Canadian National Championships and 18 consecutive Underwood Trophy Tournaments in competition with United States teams. He claimed winning streaks of 147 and 78 games in his 25 years and only stopped coaching when the program ceased to exist.

Page took his teams to exhibition Olympic competition in Paris (1924), Amsterdam (1928), and Los Angeles (1932), won 27 consecutive games, and claimed the World Championship after each event.

Incidentally, the Edmonton Commercial Grads was a women's team.

COACH PROFILE

TOM PENDERS –
UNIVERSITY OF HOUSTON
(NABC MEMBER 36 YEARS)

"As previously mentioned, our pressure defenses are designed to force teams out of their set patterns. We feel we are quicker than most teams and we want these teams to play at a quicker tempo than they are accustomed to. We have basic rules and designs, but scouting and preparation for a particular opponent is essential."

Anyone working in sports has heard the term "agent of change,"—someone who overhauls a program. Tom Penders is college basketball's "agent of change."

He's another coach who played point guard, but his sports fame came in the form of baseball. He was a very talented center fielder and played professional baseball before settling in as a basketball coach. At the University of Connecticut, he played in the NCAA Tournament and the College World Series.

After a successful beginning as a high school coach, Penders began his college-coaching career with the unenviable task of rebuilding. What happened in each of these jobs was a resurgence within the program, a great deal of community support and then the inevitable move to the next needy soul to come calling.

He successfully resurrected programs at Tufts University, Columbia University, Fordham University, and the University of Rhode Island before getting his first elite program at the University of Texas.

Pender's "runnin' horns" set team records every time they took the court, and he led Texas to eight of ten NCAA appearances and one Elite Eight. He left with problems surrounding the program and accepted the position at George Washington University.

George Washington was another rebuilding job, and he matched his past results, becoming an immediate threat in the Atlantic 10 Conference. He won a western division championship and took George Washington to the NCAA Tournament in 1999. Although he would leave the Colonials with some unanswered questions by the NCAA, nothing ever resulted in penalties and Penders would change careers for a time.

After spending time working the TV and radio circuit for ESPN, he returned to coaching at the University of Houston.

GUARDIAN

JAMES PHELAN
(1,354 GAMES COACHED, 830 WINS)

"It is an honor to be selected for induction. It's a great feeling to be in such a distinguished group of gentlemen. They have all achieved so much in the realm of basketball and are all so worthwhile. I had a wonderful 49 years at the Mount with a great opportunity to contribute with a lot of fine players."

— James Phelan
(upon announcement of his induction into
National Collegiate Basketball Hall of Fame 2008)

James Phelan, the lone Guardian in this chapter, actually shows up on a hybrid list in the coaching fraternity. He stalked the Mount St. Mary's University sideline, sporting his signature bow tie, for his entire career. What makes him different is that the university changed classifications during his 49 seasons and he recorded victories at the NCAA Division-II level and later recorded victories at the Division I level.

Phelan is a native of Philadelphia and attended La Salle College High School. He was honored as All-Catholic League in 1946 and 1947 and All-City in 1947. He took his game to La Salle College where he was honored as All-Philadelphia in 1949

A Glance At ... James Phelan
- Inducted - La Salle Hall of Athletes, 1964
- 830 Wins (4th on the list)
- 1,354 games coached (first on the list)
- 5 Final Fours (Division II)
- 16 NCAA Division II tournament appearances
- 2 NCAA Division I tournament appearances
- 2 Championship Games
- 1962 NCAA Division II Championship
- 1962, 1981 National Coach of the Year
- 19 seasons of 20+ wins

and '50 and Honorable Mention All-American in 1951. Phelan's career was interrupted with military service with the Quantico Marines in the Korean War, where he was able to fit in some Armed Service basketball games during his tour of duty.

Military athletic honors and his college reputation earned him a year with the NBA's Philadelphia Warriors. Following that stint in professional basketball, Phelan returned to La Salle as an assistant coach and was on the bench when it won the 1954 national championship. In 1954, he headed off to Mount St. Mary's

University as the coach and remained in that position until retirement in 2003. He would lead his team to the 1962 NCAA Division II National Championship and set many other benchmarks during his incredible career.

According to the Mount Saint Mary's Sports Information office: "(Phelan) got his 800th win in the Northeast Conference Championship Game on March 1, 1999. He became just the fourth coach in NCAA history to get 800 career wins; currently, he resides fourth on the all-time list behind Bob Knight, Dean Smith, and Adolph Rupp. On January 19, 1998, he became the second coach in NCAA history to coach in 1,200 career games following Clarence Gaines; he holds the record in games coached with 1,354 across all divisions."

Phelan coached through illness and injury and even continued to coach while battling cancer later in his career. His biography notes that his training in the United States Marines was responsible for this mental toughness. It also notes that Phelan is the only college basketball coach with over 800 wins who is not enshrined in the Naismith Memorial Basketball Hall of Fame, which has since been rectified. (He was chosen for 2008 induction into the National Collegiate Basketball Hall of Fame and will represent the hundreds of coaches who toil daily for the love of the game, and service to their schools and their student-athletes.)

Jim Phelan, will be forever remembered with a banner hanging in the arena and his signature bow tie painted clearly on the basketball court that bears his name. The Northeast Conference has aptly named the Conference Coach of the Year Award in his name.

Executive Director Cliff Wells introduces NABC President Fred Taylor of Ohio State (1972).

NCAA Division II

The coach with the second most wins in this division has already been identified in the book. Clarence "Big House" Gaines won 828 games at Winston-Salem State University. But then there's Herb Magee.

Herb Magee, Philadelphia University, 855-340 and Counting

Herb Magee prepped at West Catholic High School in Philadelphia with two other coaching fraternity brethren as teammates: Jim Lynam, future Philadelphia 76ers' coach, and Jim Boyle, St. Joseph's coach. Each of the three has gone on to carve out his separate niche in coaching.

Magee began his college basketball experience at Philadelphia Textile as a player. His four-year statistics included scoring more than 2,200 points and averaging 24.3 points a game over his career. He left Textile with a degree in Marketing and went on to earn a Masters in Education from St. Joseph's.

The Boston Celtics picked Magee with the 62nd pick in the 1963 draft, but he opted to return to Textile as an assistant coach to his mentor, Bucky Harris.

At the age of 25, Magee took over as head of the Rams and continues as the head coach today. Through the 2007-08 season, he had compiled a record of 855-340 in 41 seasons. Magee's coaching resume includes 23 NCAA National Tournament appearances, three regional championships, and one national championship.

Recognized around the country as a shooting expert, Magee tutors players from all levels in the art of the perfect form. A popular clinic and camp speaker, he includes NBA Hall of Famer Charles Barkley and the Orlando Magic's Jameer Nelson as pupils of his teachings.

NCAA Division III

Glenn Robinson, Franklin & Marshall University, 710 and counting

Similar to seemingly a plethora of other incredible coaches, Glenn Robinson was born in Pennsylvania, where he became a star in baseball and basketball at Aldan Lansdowne High School. Following his prep career, he moved his sports talent to West Chester University, graduating in 1967 and obtaining a Master's Degree only a year later.

Robinson joined the coaching staff at Franklin & Marshall, working for the legendary Naismith Hall of Fame Inductee, Chuck Taylor. Three

A Glance At ... Glenn Robinson

- 10th among active coaches for victories
- 24th on the all-time list for victories
- NCAA Division III Final Four in 1979, 1991, 1996 and 2000
- 12 Coach of the Year Honors
- 8th for career winning percentage

seasons later, Robinson took over for Taylor. The 2007-08 season marked his 37th as the head coach at F&M.

It was not a smooth beginning as the Diplomats struggled to end a string of losing seasons. The team improved, winning a few more games each season, until the breakout season in 1976 that ended eight years of frustration.

The program continued to thrive and Robinson and the Diplomats set team victory records in 1977, 1979, 1991, culminating with a school-record 29 wins in 1999.

"If you look at F&M over the years, you'll see that there's rarely a player with an average of more than 17 points per game," said F&M All-American player Jeremiah Henry. "The best way to play basketball is for all five people on the floor to function completely as a unit. We really stress teamwork and the ability to play together and that comes through Coach Robinson's system."

In addition to Glenn Robinson's record of wins and his outstanding string of basketball seasons, it should be noted that the F&M Web site reports that only one player who was awarded a varsity letter in basketball has failed to gain a degree during Robinson's 37 seasons. That alone qualifies him for this list.

National Association of Intercollegiate Athletics
NAIA Division I

Harry Statham

Harry Statham of McKendree University in Illinois completed his 42nd season in 2008 as the athletic director and head basketball coach with a collegiate-record 965 victories. That puts Statham at the top of the list of all coaches competing at four-year colleges or universities. Legendary coach Bob Knight is second on that list with 902 wins.

Statham is an alumnus of McKendree and actually began his coaching career while a student. He would coach at O'Fallon Junior High School and work his class schedule around his team's schedule. Upon graduation from McKendree, he accepted a graduate assistantship at the University of Illinois in basketball and track & field. After completing

A Glance At ... Harry Statham
- NAIA Men's Basketball Coach of the Year 2002
- Post-season Play 37 of 42 seasons
- 12 NAIA National Tournaments
- 32 20-win seasons
- AMC Coach of the Year, 7 times
- District Coach of the Year, 6 times
- NABC Guardians of the Game Award 2005
- NAIA-Illinois Coach of the Year, 11 times
- United States Sports Academy–Distinguished Service Award
- 1998 NAIA Hall of Fame Induction
- 1987 IBCA-NAIA Hall of Fame Induction

COACH PROFILE

RICK PITINO –
UNIVERSITY OF LOUISVILLE
(NABC MEMBER 32 YEARS)

"According to Winston Churchill, victory comes only to those who work long and hard, who are willing to pay the price in blood, sweat, and tears. Hard work is also the basic building block of every kind of achievement. Without it, everything else is pointless. You can start with a dream or an idea or a goal, but before any of your hopes can be realized, you truly must deserve your success."

Rick Pitino is the epitome of the college basketball coach. The successful college coach is a recruiting/retention mastermind. Pitino was that guy. He had more future lottery picks on his teams than anyone else in America. His players stayed with him and even returned to coach with him when their playing careers were over. He built the family and the family did not get too far away from the godfather.

Pitino became a standout guard for St. Dominic High School in New York City and set team records in assists at University of Massachusetts. He began his coaching career as a graduate assistant at the University of Hawaii, and was promoted to full-time assistant at Hawaii before becoming an assistant for Jim Boeheim at Syracuse University.

During his first head coaching position at Boston University, Pitino had his players wrap athletic tape around two red bricks, and carry those when working on defensive drills. Keeping your hands in the correct position and charting tips and deflections was always a prime target and the bricks emphasized both. The brick trick must've worked, because in two seasons at BU, Pitino led the Terriers back to the NCAA Tournament after a 24-year absence.

"At Boston University, I motivated negatively and I found that although it can work at first, by the end of the year everyone was dying for the year to end, and you have lost them," he said. "The last two years at Boston University, I motivated positively and got much better results."

The Pitino "way" did not equate to wins in the pros, but has been the answer at three of America's elite basketball programs. "The only way to get people to work hard is to motivate them," he says. "Today, people must understand why they're working hard. Each individual in an organization is motivated by something different."

Twenty-win seasons, NCAA tournaments, Final Fours and National Championships are always just a moment away. If the folks at Louisville are a patient group, he will find the trophy at least once more before the final buzzer sounds.

the requirements for a Master's of Science in Physical Education, Statham returned to coaching at the high school level.

Two successful tours at Manito Forman High School and Dwight High School prepared Statham for his return to his alma mater. His return required a job description of athletic director, head coach of baseball and basketball, and physical education teacher.

Statham has achieved a great deal of coaching success, but has also garnered awards as an athletic director. The present athletic department at McKendree supports 20 varsity sports. Statham was recognized by the National Association of Collegiate Directors of Athletics as a NAIA Regional Athletic Director of the Year. He has been recognized for his coaching success locally, state-wide, regionally and nationally on a number of occasions.

NAIA Division II
Danny Miles, Oregon Institute of Technology

Danny Miles of Oregon Institute of Technology has a record of 847-362 after 37 years at the helm for the Hustlin' Owls of the Cascade Collegiate Conference. This division of the NAIA provides very limited scholarship opportunities for student-athletes, and financial aid comes to those with high academic results and showing a family need. Miles has thrived in this environment, recruiting athletes for the football, baseball and softball programs at times during his much-diversified career at OIT.

A life-long resident of Oregon, Miles was a standout performer in high school. Medford's Outstanding Athlete in 1963 would attend Southern Oregon College of Education and establish a remarkable three-sport career, winning All-American honors in football, All-Conference in basketball and finishing with an All-District selection in baseball. During his very productive football career, he led the nation in passing percentage twice and led the nation in total offense as a senior.

A Glance At ... Danny Miles
- 2008 National Coach of the Year
- 2004 A.T. Slats Gill All-Sports Coach of the Year
- Conference All-Sports Coach of the Year, 4 times
- Conference Coach of the Year, 8 times
- Northwest Coach of the Year, 2 times
- West Coast Coach of the Year
- Two NAIA National Championships
- One National Runner-up
- 25 teams ranked in the top 20 Nationally
- OIT Basketball Court named Danny Miles Court
- NAIA Hall of Fame
- Oregon Sports Hall of Fame
- Southern Oregon Distinguished Alumnus Award

This very versatile coach has been a staple of the OIT coaching staff for many years. He assisted in football and included head coaching stints in baseball and softball to his resume. Miles recorded some excellent seasons in baseball, but would shine in softball, leading the program to six conference championships and one trip to the World Series. Additionally, Miles passed the time in the summer coaching American Legion baseball, winning two Oregon State Championships in 1974 and 1987.

Believe it or not, however, the best results came in the Hustlin' Owls basketball program. The 2008 National Coach of the Year has taken 13 teams to the NAIA National Tournament and received numerous accolades for his service.

National Junior College Athletic Association

Junior college and community college coaches are so important to the basketball coaching profession. These are the coaches who provide the next levels with players who have overcome maturity issues, character issues, legal issues, academic issues, and/or playing-out-of-position issues. These coaches have become experts at creating program environments that allow for student-athletes to meet their potential as students, athletes, and citizens.

Gene V. Bess, Three Rivers Community College, 1,056 wins and counting

In 2008, Gene Bess completed his 38th season as Three Rivers' athletic director and head basketball coach. Although in most cases this would be a career, he first spent 12 years as a high school coach and compiled 250 wins at that level. Bess served a one-year apprenticeship as the Three Rivers' assistant to Bob Cradic before taking over the program himself.

Bess, who coached future NBA star Latrell Sprewell, has won 1,056 games while losing only 278. He has won two national championships and been honored in most every way a coach can be honored.

A Glance At ... Gene Bess
- Regional Coach of the Year, 18 times
- National Coach of the Year, twice
- MCCAC Conference Coach of the Year, 17 times
- Poplar Bluff Hall of Fame
- Missouri Basketball Coaches Hall of Fame
- National Junior College Hall of Fame
- 15 National Tournament Appearances
- 37-22 record in the NJCAA National Tournament
- NJCAA Tournament Final Four, 8 times
- NJCAA National Champions 1979 and 1992

There are so many coaches with superlative records who deserve to be mentioned in this chapter. Frankly, identifying just a few is a disservice. Coaches at all levels, including high school, with career victories at the 200, 300, 400, 500, 600 and 700 levels are no less important than the coaches identified.

BOOK EIGHT

THE UGLY STUFF

Not everything the NABC has been involved in is a winning combination. Going back to the 1920s when basketball was America's newest fascination, Phog Allen was pontificating about a black cloud on the horizon. Coaches and players were becoming more visible and more popular, and with fame came the vestiges of crime. Without question, there was money to be made in the basketball business and that would attract the event managers, promoters, and fans. It would also attract the criminal element looking to make a fast buck and take advantage of those novice, unsuspecting participants.

When Allen returned to the University of Kansas to take the job of athletic director and basketball coach, he brought with him several years of mixing with the regular world. He had built relationships across the country and had become less naive in regards to the sports industry. The Allen advantage was becoming a "healer" and having added contacts in professional sports and with media personalities across the country. He was never shy about his opinions, and was willing to repeat unsubstantiated information, while always protecting the original source.

"Horse racing, former king of sports, is a sideling, boxing is in the gutter, and baseball, America's great national game, is kept alive only by its soul, living in the breast of a 6- and 7-year-old child," he said. "All this is the result of gamblers. And now they are after our greatest intercollegiate sport—football. Don't bet on your team, don't bet against your team, assure them of your support by your undying loyalty to them."

This concern for gambling was a vision of the future for college basketball. In 1944, World War II was over and the country was able to take a deep breath and begin to repair the physical and mental damage that the war imposed on the nation. Sports fans could reflect back on the last four basketball championships, the growth of the NIT, and the continued interest in intersectional games. Teams were gaining a loyal following, soldiers were returning to institutions to continue their athletic careers and the feeling of patriotism was felt across the land.

Phog Allen continued his verbal barrage against sport governance while telling anyone who would listen that if there was not a strong personality put in the position

COACH PROFILE

**BO RYAN –
UNIVERSITY OF WISCONSIN
(NABC MEMBER 32 YEARS)**

"In Bo Ryan's seven seasons as Wisconsin's head coach, the Badgers have compiled a 107-7 record at Kohl Center, including a 54-3 (.947) record in Big 10 games. UW's three losses in conference home games are the fewest of any team in a BCS conference."

Bo Ryan built his coaching career the "old fashioned way," he earned it. When you read about the "guardians" in the book, they all started somewhere, won games, went somewhere else, won games and then got that great opportunity to coach. That is not the way it goes any more. If you start in high school, you rarely get a shot up the ladder. If you begin coaching at the small college or university, that elite program only comes along on very rare occasions. Bo Ryan did all of that. Then, when the chance came, he grabbed it.

As is common in the profession, Ryan went directly to graduate school after graduating from Wilkes College. After graduate school at Villanova, he began coaching at Racine College and then returned to Pennsylvania as the head basketball coach at Sun Valley High School. He was conference coach of the year and then accepted an assistant's position at the University of Wisconsin and worked for Bill Cofield and Steve Yoder.

Ryan moved from assistant at Wisconsin to UW-Platteville as the head coach. He won 113 games as an NAIA coach, and then UW-Platteville moved to NCAA Division-III and Ryan won 240 games and four national championships. He took the head coaching job at NCAA Division-II UW-Milwaukee for two seasons and then returned to the University of Wisconsin as an NCAA Division-I head coach. Ryan and Wisconsin have had seven highly successful seasons. The fewest wins were 19 and the most, two monster 30-win seasons in 2006-07 and 2007-08. All seven teams qualified for the NCAA Tournament and made the Elite Eight in 2005.

Bo Ryan has been THE dominating force in Wisconsin basketball for a long time. Maybe this kind of dominance has not been since in the State since Dr. Walter Meanwell went 44-1 his first three seasons as the Gophers coach and won the Helms Foundation National Championship in the first season that he ever coached basketball.

for cleansing collegiate sports, it would be in serious trouble. As was becoming a habit, his crystal ball was working overtime.

"Judge (Kennesaw Mountain) Landis (Major League Baseball Commissioner) is fighting betting on professional baseball in his vigorous manner, but the colleges are doing nothing about it, and as sure as you live the thing is going to crack wide open sometime when they lay bare a scandal that will rock the college world," Allen preached in a letter in 1944. "It has already happened in Madison Square Garden, but the newspapers have kept it quiet."

Allen warned the country about the perils of gambling that were hovering on the horizon, but he also would provide a suggestion to reduce or eliminate the problem. The NCAA was already in position to govern the problem within college athletics, but Allen was obviously not confident that they were taking necessary steps.

"More money is bet on collegiate football and basketball than on horse racing," he told the *New York Times*, "but all the trouble it causes could be eliminated if college presidents would get together and appoint an absolute czar over all college sports. If they don't, some of these college boys who have never seen big money are going to sell out and it will cause a scandal that will stink to high heaven. It could ruin intercollegiate sports."

Sports writers and other authorities scoffed at Allen's charges and even resorted to calling him a buffoon and other less printable accusations. Maybe, like the boy who cried wolf, Allen had been talking too much and then the realization set in that he might be right.

As much as everyone wanted to deny the possibilities, Allen was speaking the truth. The gambling problems appeared in New York, but they were spreading to other hotbeds of intercollegiate competition.

A *New York Times* article from February 24, 1945, pointed out how big the problem was perceived to be.

Police Commissioner Lewis J. Valentine told Kings County Judge Samuel S. Leibowitz in Brooklyn yesterday that even if college basketball games went back to campus gymnasiums gambling could not be stopped. The Jurist, sitting as a committing magistrate, was told that such a move, however, might aid in the drive to end corruption.

"Commissioner, do you feel that amateur basketball would be safer if confined to the gymnasiums of the colleges?", Mr. Cohen asked.

"Unquestionably," the Commissioner answered. "If confined to the campus, it would reduce and maybe entirely do away with any possible corruption, but it would not prevent gambling. At present there are two sheets published, one in Philadelphia and the other in Indianapolis, that give the names of the players of all the colleges and their past scores. That information is used by gamblers."

Ned Irish and others in and around Madison Square Garden were trying to step in and correct a problem long ignored. It was too late and college basketball in New York City would soon be crushed under the weight of major scandals from which they would never recover.

The country, the college and university presidents, the media, and all the coaches had been warned by Allen that the day was coming. Then in 1950, when college basketball had reached an unparalleled level of popularity, the shoe dropped on the sport. Great players across the country were being scooped up and charged with "fixing" games. Gamblers were paying college players thousands to alter scores. The earliest reports were that the problems were in New York City only and could be contained. However, *"Three former University of Kentucky basketball players, two of them All-American stars, admitted yesterday they had accepted $1,500 in bribes to 'throw' a National Invitational Game at Madison Square Garden on March 14, 1949 ... The two All-American players, Ralph Beard and Alex Groza, were among the modern 'greats' of the game ... The involvement of the University of Kentucky brought to seven the number of leading colleges figuring in 'fixed' games at Madison Square Garden in the last several years."*
— *New York Times, October 21, 1951*

GUARDIAN

NAT HOLMAN
(MR. BASKETBALL,
GRAND SLAM, TRAGEDY)

"The stories you read about champions getting weary of winning are so much nonsense. No champion ever wins so many contests that he doesn't mind losing one."

— Nat Holman

Nat Holman arrived on the coaching scene after completing a superb prep career and during a professional basketball career that had—and still has—no peer. He was the greatest player in the early years of the game, being nicknamed "Mr. Basket Ball" during his tenure. He was born in New York City as one of 10 children. He embraced the game early in life and even though he would star in many sports, his destiny would remain in basketball.

At Commerce High School, Holman starred in football, soccer, basketball, and baseball. He was offered a professional baseball contract out of high school, but chose college and professional basketball instead. That began an incredible balancing act between attending Savage School of Physical Education and playing on numerous teams in numerous leagues. One could argue that he was the first schoolboy to turn professional out of high school. He rode so many trains to games and cities, he would occasionally get on the wrong train and arrive in the wrong city and miss a scheduled game.

From his earliest days in the city, Holman was a basketball wizard. He would introduce different skills in shooting, scoring, ball handling and passing. Feinting or faking with the body and/or the ball was his specialty. Many players who followed Holman emulated his techniques to get clear of clinging defenders.

The Holman legacy really took off with his joining of a great barnstorming team called the Original Celtics. The group was so spectacular that they are one of the few teams that have been enshrined in the Naismith Memorial Hall of Fame. During his years of stardom with the Original Celtics, the team record was 720-75—in only seven years! You don't need an abacus to figure that's about 100 wins per year.

During this run of excellence, Holman was introduced to New York City as the head basketball coach at City College of New York. At the time, "City" would offer a free education to any student in the metropolitan area of New York who could meet the very high entrance requirements.

The great players went other places and Holman coached the smart kids. An advocate of the deliberate style of play, Holman is often quoted as wanting his clubs to emphasize poise, ball-handling, fitness, shooting and elusive movement.

"I teach my players to recognize situations and know what will develop from a particular floor pattern," he said. "All basketball is a pattern. Get in that pattern and then you're going."

Many say Holman revolutionized the play in the post, particularly on defense. Never having the opportunity to coach a big player, Holman implemented the "switch" in his man-to-man defense, a defensive strategy that is very prevalent in the college game today.

CCNY's greatest accomplishment under Holman came in the 1949-50 season when they were selected to play in the National Invitation Tournament (NIT). After a 17-5 campaign, they were the last team invited and placed in the bracket as an unseeded entry. This would require a tougher challenge to reach the finals, but the Beavers were ready for the task. CCNY reached the finals after beating San Francisco, Kentucky and Duquesne. Bradley was the competition in the finals and, at 26-3, a prohibitive favorite. Against all odds, however, the CCNY Beavers prevailed 69-61 and qualified for entry into the NCAA National Championship.

Holman's Beavers shockingly made it to the championship game after defeating Ohio State and North Carolina State. This would mean a rematch with the Braves of Bradley for the NCAA Championship.

CCNY would make basketball history that night, beating Bradley for the second time, 71-68. This would be the only time a team won both "big" season-ending basketball tournaments.

Holman and his great CCNY program would be rocked, though, with scandal the next year as a point-shaving and gambling enterprise was uncovered. Three CCNY players—Ed Warner, Ed Roman and Al Roth—were arrested on February 18, 1951, on bribery charges. Nine days later, Floyd Layne was arrested. Then, on March 26, the final three CCNY players involved in the scandal—Herb Cohen, Irwin Dambrot, and Norm Mager—were arrested. (By the time all of the investigations ended nationally, more than 30 players from seven schools were arrested for fixing games from 1947-50.)

CCNY officials suspended Holman with accusations of an "inability to control" his players. Holman was never one to back down and this time was no different. He appealed his suspension and the New York State Education Commissioner reinstated Holman a few weeks later.

Nat Holman, "Mr. Basketball" in New York City, Helms Award winner, National Coach of the Year (1950) and Naismith Hall of Fame inductee, was forever marked by the scandals that killed his program. Even after reinstatement, the CCNY program

The NABC would always record their past-presidents and board to present to non-attending members in the Bulletins to follow the convention. Shown sitting (L to R): Barry Dowd, Bill Foster, Abe Lemons, Bob Polk, Ned Wulk and Joe Vancisin. Standing: Marv Harshman, Bill Thomas, Tex Winter, Lucias Mitchell, Dean Smith, Scott Knisley and Will Renken.

COACH PROFILE

BILL SELF –
UNIVERSITY OF KANSAS
(NABC MEMBER 22 YEARS)

"I love my job. I love working with these guys. I love being in a tradition-rich place that I get the opportunity to work at every day."

Not a bad thought shortly after winning the NCAA National Championship in a mild upset over John Calipari and the University of Memphis. Bill Self started coaching the minute he finished playing. There was no hesitation when he accepted an assistant coaching position with Larry Brown at the University of Kansas. Who would have guessed at that time, that Self would also bring the national championship to Lawrence?

Maybe the best player of all the profiles in the book, Self was the Oklahoma Player of the Year while in high school. He took his award-winning game to Oklahoma State University and earned a varsity letter in each of his four seasons. He received All Big 8 honors following his freshman year.

Self returned to Oklahoma State as an assistant before accepting his first head coaching position at Oral Roberts University. After a run of NIT appearances, he led the program at the University of Tulsa. Self earned two NCAA bids in three years and his first Elite Eight appearance there, and took the next step in the progression to coaching an elite program. Illinois named him their coach where he again built a program that competed at a consistently high level with a return trip to the Elite Eight.

Without skipping a step in between or failing to win at any level, he was now ready to be a head coach at one of the nation's premier programs. When Roy Williams disappointed the Jayhawk faithful and returned to North Carolina, the opportunity was there. Fully understanding the frustration of all who wore the crimson and blue, he set out to win that championship. In five seasons at KU, Self continued the efficient stepping-stone approach he used in his career. In the first five years, he qualified for five NCAA appearances, one Elite Eight and won a National Championship in 2008. Finally, for all concerned, the frustration was lifted and Bill Self situated himself smack in the middle of Kansas Jayhawk basketball history.

After a tense courtship by the Cowboys of Oklahoma State, Self chose to stay at KU and try to win another national championship. The reports out of Lawrence said that Self was compensated so that he would remain in the coaches' seat until his career was over, just like those other guys named Phog Allen and Ted Owens.

never approached the success that was seen prior to the gambling problems in college basketball.

Holman retired in 1960, but only after his health prohibited his continuing in the only job he had ever had. He would never have allowed the game to get the best of him.

Years later, CCNY, in one final effort to heal the hurt inflicted by the scandal, brought back one of its own to replace Holman.

As reported in the *New York Times* on September 5, 1974: *"Floyd Layne, a star who rose and fell at City College, is returning 23 years later as the Beavers' basketball coach. Layne, a wiry backcourt man and floor general of the City team that won the 1949-50 National Invitation Tournament and the National Collegiate Athletic Association championship, was later involved in the widespread college basketball "fix" scandal.*

City College has called a news conference for today to introduce Layne, who will be the Beavers' first black head basketball coach ... Robert Marshak, the President of City College, said, 'Floyd Layne's rehabilitation is a remarkable success story that holds many valuable lessons for the youth of this city.'"

GUARDIAN
CLAIR BEE
(AUTHOR, LEADER, MENTOR)

Photo courtesy:
Long Island University Athletics

"In a fast game, I believe teamwork is paramount. You cannot get precision teamwork with a large number of men; it has to be achieved with the same men practicing and working together as much as possible. I realize there is grave danger in lack of depth—we pooped out that way one year—but if I can get seven good ones, I will go with them all the way, counting on their teamwork and conditioning to stay the season."

— Clair Bee

This scholarly basketball coach was another of the greats who was responsible for the development of college basketball in the 1930s. He led Long Island University to college basketball's elite levels with unprecedented victory streaks before finishing his 20-year career with a 357-79 record and recognition as one of the best.

Clair Bee grew up in West Virginia and a bout of tuberculosis spurred him into sports activity. The doctor ordered young Clair to spend as much time as possible outdoors to fight the disease. So, he would engage his slight frame into whatever activity was available on any given day. After his mother died of the same disease, he lived with his uncle in Kansas part-time and bounced around to different locations in West Virginia.

As a youngster, Bee and others would sneak into the church and play basketball. It did not take long for the authorities to figure it out, but he would always comment that, "The priests caught on, but they turned their heads … They were happy to see us in church even though it was only for basketball."

These activities would be the basis for many of his "Chip Hilton" series of sports books written for youngsters throughout much of his life.

After some coaching experience at Waynesburg and Rider colleges, Bee headed for LIU. The five-year stint at Rider included working in accounting and business departments and coaching football and basketball. His job description at LIU included leading the business department, teaching in the physical education department, and coaching baseball and basketball. It was not long after his arrival that his talent in the game of basketball would become evident.

Under Bee, Long Island University set a standard that all others in the game would shoot for. He was a pioneer in the introduction of African-American players into the segregated world of college basketball. His teams achieved a 139-game home winning-streak and additional winning streaks of 20 and 43 games. The end of the Blackbirds' 43-game winning streak became a legendary game, an "instant classic," if you will. The streak ended in Madison Square Garden in 1936, when John Bunn brought Stanford and the great player Frank Luisetti in and beat the Blackbirds.

Bee led LIU to the NIT championship two times. (During this particular era, the NIT was THE tournament in college basketball, and a championship would carry a great deal of significance.)

After 20 years of excellence, Coach Bee was shocked to learn that his boys were involved in the point-shaving scandal of the late 1940s.

According to the *New York Times* on February 21, 1951: *"Three Long Island University basketball players, including the high scorer among the country's major teams, admitted yesterday that they had taken $18,500 in bribes to "fix" seven games, four this season and three last year."*

With that news, the university's administration shut the program down.

Of all the coaches with players involved in the scandal, Clair Bee was the most affected.

"I guess I was too concerned with my own doings," Bee said. "Each coach says it couldn't happen to him. I refused to believe it when it happened, because I never suspected a player. You know, in my opinion, a coach is like a father. He is the last to recognize the weaknesses of his son, and if he recognizes imperfections, he can't believe it because his hopes for the youngster are so high. When it happened, I tried to block it out of my mind, I wanted to wrap myself up in something else."

That was nearly impossible.

"He is done," commented one of his assistants. "If he lives through this and lives to see another basketball season, I will be surprised."

Although Bee tried to coach some professional basketball after the mess, his heart was never in it and he retreated to his duties as an athletic administrator and author.

His remorse was obvious. When speaking to a group of coaches he said: "We—you and I—have flunked. We have not done the job that was expected of us in training the young people. I am not bitter. I am hurt, hurt desperately. When I was told that three of my boys had sold themselves it was a deep bereavement. I am not ashamed to say that I wept ... It was then that something died within me."

Everyone had a solution for the gambling problem. The NABC took a hard line against the schools and stated emphatically who they thought was at fault. This was not the first time, nor will it be the last, that sports organizations are warned against the WIN AT ALL COST attitude.

When asked in 2008 if he felt there was a chance college basketball could experience another incredible scandal, Walter Byers, the long-time executive director of the NCAA said: "Very real, and the NCAA's review of the chosen officials is inadequate."

BOOK NINE

THE NCAA: THE EMPIRE

GUARDIAN
WALTER BYERS
(LEADER DICTATOR, POLITICIAN, INNOVATOR)

"I was charged with the dual mission of keeping intercollegiate sports clean while generating millions of dollars each year as income for the colleges. These were compelling and competing tasks, and, in my enthusiasm for sports, I believed it possible to achieve both."

— **Walter Byers**

Photo courtesty: NCAA

Since the beginning of sports competition between colleges and universities, the NCAA has ruled the roost. Theodore Roosevelt waved the magic wand when trouble in football was increasing with the "flying wedge." Out of that, in 1906, the Intercollegiate Athletic Association of the United States (IAAUS) was officially chartered.

The IAAUS became the National Collegiate Athletic Association (NCAA) in 1910 and began the slow but steady march to control all of the sports and sections of the country that were enjoying intercollegiate competition.

Throughout the NCAA's existence, it has been very aggressive in crushing athletic organizations that have gotten in the way. The NCAA pushed aside the YMCA and the AAU in the basketball rules battles, and crushed the AAU a second time when the AAU would not grant the wishes of the NCAA concerning the Olympics. The organization has been given widespread powers by the institutions in membership and has never shied away from the authority that it has held and presently enjoys. There have been numerous attacks, both in the media and in the courtroom, but the NCAA has conceded very little.

The one group the NCAA didn't push aside—early on at least—was the NABC. The basketball coaches association worked closely with the NCAA in several critical areas specific to college basketball, and would join the NCAA in the development of the National Championship Tournament. As stated earlier in the book, the tournament was created by the NABC, which sold it to the NCAA to partially pay a past debt and to relieve the coaches of having to operate their own tournament while trying to qualify for the same.

When the NABC handed the tournament to the NCAA following the 1940 event in Kansas City, the NABC washed its hands of the troubling administrative duties of operating such an event and breathed a sigh of relief. In return, the NABC asked for the right to have a permanent committee presence, to have tickets for dues-paying members at each subsequent event and the right to petition the NCAA for a portion of the profits.

A decade later, in 1951, the NCAA needed a steady hand to help guide the organization and collegiate athletics through both growth as well as the betting and point-shaving scandal that was rocking basketball. That ruling hand was Walter Byers, who had been splitting his work time between the Big Ten Conference and the NCAA.

With a new sheriff in charge, the NCAA had now begun the process of becoming a police force to ensure that the member schools and personnel would abide by all legislation passed into NCAA Law by the member institutions (560 members in 1961).

The very first enforcement case conducted by the NCAA investigators arrived on Byers' desk as a result of the gambling and point-shaving scandal of the late-1940s and the early-1950s. Taking center stage in that investigation was the University of Kentucky and Adolph Rupp. Rupp's Wildcats had won the 1948 NCAA Championship, were the core group of the 1948 Olympic team that won the gold medal and then went on to win the 1949 NCAA Championship. This was also a group whose two biggest stars were arrested for point shaving games in return for major cash returns.

Due to Rupp being familiar with some of the gamblers in Lexington, the NCAA put the entire UK program under a microscope. After the federal authorities were finished, the enforcement group found flagrant violations of the rules and regulations set to govern scholarship limits and eligibility.

In what became the first "death penalty" handed down by the NCAA, the Southeastern Conference suspended Kentucky from playing any basketball for one entire season. Kentucky fans will argue that all the NCAA did was suggest that Division I schools not schedule UK for that year, but the university officials made the decision to suspend the program as directed. Since then, there have been no death penalty decisions in basketball.

Of course, that doesn't mean everyone has lived happily ever after. The other major challenge facing schools and the NCAA was illegal recruiting. Suddenly, students coming out of high school were being offered extra gifts by colleges. More than anyone, this was hurting the traditionally black schools because, as the legendary Grambling football coach Eddie Robinson explained: "It would be real hard for me to tell a boy, living in a shotgun house with five sleeping in one room, to turn down a new house, car, and a better job for his daddy. I know it's wrong, but it's hard for a man to walk in another man's shoes."

Walter Byers hired David Berst to assist the NCAA in building a bridge between basketball and the NCAA. Berst's NABC membership and familiarity with Cliff Wells and Bill Wall was paramount in that decision. Berst had actually played and worked for Wall at MacMurray College. Byers designated that relationship as a focus for Berst. This personal knowledge went a long way in creating an opening for the NABC to begin eliminating the recruiting problems.

"More than one-eighth of the 229 major colleges and universities that play basketball—about 29 or 30 institutions—are making illegal offers to athletes in order to recruit them, according to a year-long survey released by the National Association of Basketball Coaches," *New York Times* writer Gordon S. White Jr. wrote in 1974. "The study indicates that of the colleges trying to attract high school athletes with improper inducements, all are offering money, 80 percent are offering automobiles, and more than half are offering clothing. Forty per cent of the youngsters interviewed were offered illegal inducements.

Walter Byers

The NCAA certainly has changed from its days more than 100 years ago as the IAAUS, and that's thanks largely to Walter Byers.

1. The NCAA sponsors 88 National Championship events in 23 sports
2. The NCAA presently sponsors 33 individual committees
3. The NCAA provides instant access to all statistics, polls, rules, records, research and eligibility for every sport which it provides sponsorship
4. The NCAA employs 350-380 full-time staff
5. The yearly expenditure for Sport Science is $4,913,000
6. The NCAA no longer operates the U.S. Olympic or Pan American programs
7. The NCAA annually spends $19,609,000 on membership services and governance
8. The NCAA pays an annual insurance premium of $11,530,000
9. The NCAA annually pays $7,552,000 for membership education and outreach
10. The NCAA program for scholarships and education programs has an annual budget of $4,779,000
11. Assisting national coaches organizations
12. The library facilities of the NCAA are extensive. The available documents, forms, videos, DVDs and other research, instantly available on the NCAA website. Everything regarding the governance of the organization is also readily available.

"The survey was conducted by 10 college head or assistant coaches on a committee headed by Frank Arnold, an assistant to John Wooden at the University of California, Los Angeles. Arnold submitted the report to the NABC at its annual convention. ... Arnold said 12.8 percent of the institutions in America were making illegal offers to youngsters."

As explained in detail earlier, this is when the NABC proposal on self-reporting was presented to Walter Byers by then-NABC Executive Director Cliff Wells, Bill Wall, and Henry Iba. There was considerable hand ringing and starts and stops as the program was implemented. Berst said that the program "definitely helped" because the coaches were "more willing to talk to other coaches than the NCAA."

When Berst took over NCAA Enforcement, "We had one full-time enforcement person, and the NABC gave us information that led to infractions cases that we processed."

Wells, Wall, and Joe Vancisin all participated in this program to varying degrees of enthusiasm. The relationship changed when Vancisin took charge. Berst and Vancisin did not know each other.

"Joe had more reluctance to being involved in the enforcement activities than Wall," Berst said. "The information exchange continued for awhile because some members of the board had become confident in me, but as they were moving on, the cooperation on enforcement ended."

Berst, however, felt that the NABC was very instrumental in streamlining issues in recruiting by mandating calendars, limiting entertainment, and curtailing the unrestricted use of school boosters in the recruiting process. When asked to rate their effort in legislative issues, he said, "Contrary to the shared opinion that football people get the most done because they can attend the NCAA convention in January, the truth is that the NABC has been the most effective in getting their issues discussed and in many cases implemented."

That might be where the niceness—at least for a time—between the NCAA and NABC ended. The strained relationship, which has been discussed throughout the book, deals with the NABC "selling" the cash cow, the men's national basketball tournament, to the NCAA.

Look at it this way. Walter Byers responded to a question about the NABC and the tournament by stating emphatically: "The NABC had no role in the start and early development of the NCAA Tournament."

Tom Jernstedt, the architect of the modern tournament and the director of NCAA Division I basketball, doesn't necessarily see the relationship between the two organizations as strained. He said he would characterize it differently. Over the years, the NCAA and the NABC would have different personalities leading their efforts. Some were more difficult and some were easier, but as far the as the relationship between the two organizations, the relationship has always been professional.

As the NCAA's director of basketball, Jernstedt has been involved with the tournament committee and decisions surrounding the tournament since the 1960s.

"The basketball committee was made up of six people and then we moved to 10," he said. "While there has always been an effort to have basketball people on the committee that was not always the case. In fact, sometimes we had basketball people with strong personalities and sometimes less aggressive. Sometimes we had no basketball people, very strong athletic administrators, but no direct connection to the game. One committee had Vic Bubas and Dave Gavitt, both great coaches, who could not agree."

The committee makes all decisions about the tournament and anything that has changed over the years was the result of a committee vote. Jernstedt said: "I can tell you that when basketball people are on the committee, the decisions are more readily accepted."

The committee's decisions to expand the tournament have always been met with concern. People are always voicing their opinions. But the present product seems to have been built on a solid foundation.

In the days of the UCLA dynasty, J.D. Morgan, UCLA's athletic director and a member of the committee, and coach John Wooden were opposed to tournament expansion. Wooden was convincing in his arguments that, "a team should win its conference before it can win a national championship."

During the writing of this book, Wooden pointed out—as he has often since retiring—that the tournament should be cut to 36 or include every team.

"When you consider expansion from 64 to 96, and I don't think that is very far off, the conference tournament will become less important," said Jernstedt. "Right now the conference tournaments are actually the first rounds of the tournament, but the conferences get all of the revenue. That would change with expansion, while we are really only adding the sixth, seventh and eighth-place teams from the major conferences to the field. We can keep the tournament the same and if any of those teams win the conference tournament, they qualify for the next round."

Until then, any chance of somehow taking the best 64 teams instead of winners from small conferences?

"The system of automatic qualifiers is an essential aspect of the tournament," Jernstedt said emphatically. "We don't want to legislate out the David vs. Goliath aspect that can be very enjoyable."

The NCAA is very aware that coaches such as Jim Boeheim and Bob Knight are calling for expansion. But like all other decisions, there will have to be concrete evidence that a change is needed. The only reason that Jernstedt can point to today is that since the last expansion, the membership numbers of Division I schools have increased. The committee has to determine whether the correct percentage of those members is being selected.

BOOK TEN

THE MEDIA SAYS IT ALL

There have been references to the media's influence throughout *Guardians of the Game*. There can be no doubt that coaches, players, rewards, rules and popularity can be the result of media coverage going back to the days of Phog Allen. It was the media that informed Allen that the Joint Rules Committee discontinued the dribble, and it was the media that carried Allen's battle cry back to the coaches across the country.

It was also the media that accused Allen of being an idiot when pontificating about the gambling. And, it was the media that would become intimately paired with the NABC running the East-West All-Star game and selecting the All-American teams.

HISTORY OF THE NABC COACHES' ALL-AMERICAN SELECTIONS

The coaching members of the National Association of Basketball Coaches were always involved with selecting All-Americans when teamed with sports writers or broadcasters.

Cash motivated the organization to select NABC All-America teams. *True* magazine, which was published from 1937-74, offered the NABC $1,000 to evaluate the national talent and select the members of the teams. In 1947, the NABC provided the magazine with the first groups of players selected solely by the coaches' organization.

The NABC provided first, second and third All-America basketball teams using the district format designed by the NCAA. The committee charged with this challenge presented a first-class product, worth every penny of the payout. The selection results were so successful that the organization was able to negotiate a contract with *Collier's* magazine for a yearly fee of $5,000. The one interesting caveat to the contract was that the selected teams had to be ratified by the active coaches within the NABC membership. This contract remained in place until *Collier's* ceased distribution in 1957.

From 1957 until 1970, the Coaches All-America selections were published in the *NABC Bulletin* and were sponsored by the Wheaties Sports Federation, owned and operated by General Mills. Wheaties would occasionally print the teams in *American Weekly*, but they were always released to the national wire services. This new arrangement paid the NABC an annual stipend of $6,000.

COACH PROFILE

TUBBY SMITH –
UNIVERSITY OF MINNESOTA
(NABC MEMBER 27 YEARS)

"We expect graduation to be the norm for our student-athletes in this program. We were glad, but not surprised, to see these four meet the expectations that we will always have for our athletes at the University of Minnesota."

Can it ever be a mistake to win a national championship? Maybe Tubby Smith should have waited a year or two before winning the NCAA Championship at the University of Kentucky. Maybe it was enough to be the first African-American head coach at Kentucky that first year. What should have been received as an incredible run of success at UK was always compared to that first season and eventually enough was enough.

After college, Smith retuned to Great Mills HS to begin his coaching career and then moved to Hoke County HS before joining J.D. Barnett as an assistant coach at Virginia Commonwealth. He would assist at South Carolina and Kentucky before getting his first opportunity to lead a program.

Smith began his tenure as a head coach at Tulsa, earning two NCAA bids, Coach of the Year, and a sweet 16 appearance. He then took over at the University of Georgia where he led the Bulldogs to two NCAA Tournament appearances and once again won the conference Coach of the Year award.

Smith had worked for Rick Pitino at the University of Kentucky, and when Pitino left for his second stint in the NBA, as president and coach of the Boston Celtics, Smith was the perfect choice. He was 10 for 10 in NCAA bids at Kentucky, but that second championship eluded him.

With the fans getting restless, and the scrutiny relentless, Smith took his coaching prowess to Minnesota to rebuild a team that had fallen on hard times. His first Gopher team earned a bid to the 2008 NIT. It will not be long before the Gophers are back at elite status within the basketball ranks. Recruiting will be successful, the team will be victorious and the fans will be ecstatic. Smith joined Roy Williams, Nolan Richardson, Denny Crum, and Jim Boeheim as the only coaches who won 365 games in 15 years or less.

Bill Wall, who later would be the second full-time NABC Executive Secretary, initiated the first All-America selections for the college division players across the country. In addition to the added selections, the NABC Board of Directors provided each selected All-American with a laminated certificate and sent a laminated plaque to each represented institution. The very democratic voting system required by *Collier's* remained in place. The membership has the final vote on who gets put on what team, which encourages active voting. If a coach wants his players supported in the future, he realizes that it is imperative that he vote for the players representing his district.

The coaches were adamant that players be treated as fairly as possible and the voting system that emerged was a weighted system that would take into account the number of votes available in each district and then adjusted accordingly so that every vote carried exactly the same impact. This may have been—and may remain—the fairest selection process in all of sport. For 11 years of the process, (1961-1972) players would gather and be filmed and photographed in uniform for release to TV. These short clips would have the players' coach describing the player's skill with the player demonstrating some of the same. Since 1972, a suitable sponsor has not been found, but the plaques to player and school continue. State Farm sponsored 2007-08 All-America teams and has a 3-year contract.

BROADCASTING BOOMS BASKETBALL

Regional radio created hotbeds of rabid fans from Lexington, Kentucky, to Eugene, Oregon, and everywhere in between. The increasing fan support, the gaudy gate-receipt income and cash from many of the other resources goes back to the days when people sat as a family listening to the game's radio broadcast and many of those early broadcasters became as legendary as the coaches with whom they worked.

Television's arrival, although a concern in the beginning, became the next catalyst for the growing fan base and income possibilities for college basketball. Early on, the NCAA and the NABC worried that televised games would encourage fans to stay away from the arenas and watch the games in the comfort of their homes. The opposite was the actual result and fans flocked to the games while TV ratings soared. This popularity spurt and industry growth increased the speed that TV basketball coverage advanced from local, to regional and then to national broadcasts.

Finally, with increasing interest in college basketball, and the cult-like embracing of the NCAA National Tournament, television broadcasters were becoming a part of the raging popularity that was sport in the United States. Howard Cosell was boxing; Keith Jackson was college football; Curt Gowdy the Olympics and Wide World of Sports; John Madden the NFL; Dick Enberg college basketball; and many more than could be named in these pages.

During the past 30 years or so, two very different personalities have become staples of the college basketball broadcasting scene. First is Billy Packer, who is the main analyst for CBS Sports' coverage of NCAA men's basketball. He has been calling the games since the rush to popularity began. In 2008, Packer called his 34th consecutive national championship game.

The other, Dick Vitale, is another story altogether. In the span of 30 years, he became the face and the voice of college basketball, mainly through ESPN. This was evident in the minutes of the 1986 NABC Board Meeting, when former coach and athletic director C.M Newton said: "There has been a shift in basketball experts. It used to be Rupp, Wooden, Iba, and other notable coaches. Now the recognized experts are Packer, (Al) McGuire and Vitale."

GUARDIAN

BILLY PACKER
(PLAYER, COACH,
"THE VOICE OF THE FINAL FOUR")

"I'm probably the most misunderstood person that people have opinions about."

— Billy Packer

There are numerous views of Billy Packer. If you review blogs and opinions written all over the Internet, you see quickly that in almost every case he has touched someone's last nerve. His opinions are often controversial and have embroiled him in racial issues, gender issues and partner issues throughout his career, but like some, he endures because he is good. Jim Nantz, CBS broadcast teammate, says, "He has been the voice, he is the voice, of college basketball." That might be a stretch, but Packer certainly is the voice of March Madness and the Final Four.

Tom Jernstedt, Director of NCAA Basketball, was very positive about the role Packer has played in the calling of tournament games. "His passion and love for the college game was displayed by the magnificent analysis when early tournament games carried some significant importance." Jernstedt went on the say, "I have worked in one capacity or another with Billy Packer for 36 years and it is my opinion that Dick Enberg, Al McGuire and Billy Packer were the best three-man broadcast team in college or professional basketball history."

Packer was born in Wellsville, New York, in 1940. The family later moved to Pennsylvania, where his dad was a coach at Lehigh University. Billy attended Liberty High School in Bethlehem, and earned All-State honors in basketball and was twice selected Pennsylvania Player of the Year in baseball. While his parents were looking at Ivy League opportunities, Billy's college of choice was Duke University. That's where he was headed until the coaching staff there asked him to wait until another player made his decision. Packer was immediately off to Wake Forest University to compete against the school that did not want him.

Packer had a solid career at Wake Forest, leading the Demon Deacons to their only Final Four in 1962. He was a two-time All-ACC selection, and helped Wake beat the Duke Blue Devils five out of six games. An economics degree and a business career in the offing, Packer was immediately out of basketball and in the corporate world. It took a couple of years working away from the sport before he realized at some level that he needed to be back in the game.

Never one to float along, he returned to Wake Forest as an assistant coach with a four-year plan to make it in coaching or return to the business world and never look back. With one near miss as an applicant for the head coaching position at Memphis State University, where he lost out to Gene Bartow, Packer was once again out of basketball and into radio ad sales. As he promised himself, he never gave coaching a second thought. It was during this time working in radio that he was asked to fill in as an analyst for a game between North Carolina State and the University of Maryland.

Curt Gowdy, long-time NABC convention master of ceremonies, controls the dais at the 1977 National Convention.

He was off and running. After successfully calling the game, he and his wife Barbara went off to Hawaii. He never thought of broadcasting as a career, so the calls from network officials went unanswered.

With games rarely televised nationally, different groups were vying for the best games and the best TV personalities. The ACC Network searched for Packer while he was in Hawaii, and at the same time negotiating with TVS and Eddie Einhorn to televise a game between No. 3 UCLA and No. 5 Maryland. When Packer was finally available to take a call, he agreed to work the game as part of the broadcast team. Since this was a split telecast, he would be working with Jim Thacker (ACC) for one half and Dick Enberg (TVS) for the other half. Expecting the worst, Packer found the arrangement to be workable and did not get in trouble until the post-game interview with losing coach Lefty Driesell, when Packer commented on national TV: "For a guy who we all know can recruit, but can't coach..." This would not be the last time Packer would provide fodder for the tabloids.

Packer worked his first NCAA Tournament in 1975 and was assigned a Hall of Fame partner. Packer was excited to be teamed with Curt Gowdy, and the two were successful in their initial outing. As a result, Packer was offered a game in each of the ensuing rounds and would eventually be chosen to work the championship game. Packer would begin his string of tournament championship games with the last one that John Wooden would coach.

"Coach Wooden had resigned and knew it was going to be his final game," Packer said in 2008. "If someone had listened to that broadcast, they wouldn't know I was rooting, probably, but I knew I was rooting for him to win."

That game became the first of what would become 34 straight championship games for Packer. He has teamed with a who's who of partners, including Enberg, Gary Bender, Brent Musburger, and finally, Nantz.

Packer controversies have included battles with CBS brass over the popular show "60 Minutes" in 1998 and 2002.

Then there was his very public battle with Phil Martelli, coach at St. Joseph's of Philadelphia. Commenting on the quality of the St. Joe's tournament resume, Packer disagreed about whether St. Joe's belonged in the tournament. There was an ugly exchange being conducted in the media, but in the end, Packer and Martelli discussed their issue on national television and ended the discussion with a handshake and an agreement to disagree.

In another incident, Packer publicly accused Larry Bird of being overrated and was very critical of his 1979 Indiana State team, their weak schedule and the Sycamores' No. 1 seed in the tournament. Packer had seen Bird play that summer and found him to be uninspiring. These comments added a great deal of interest to the '79 Final Four.

Packer offered no public explanation after the Sycamores justified their presence by qualifying for the championship game.

The most serious controversy occurred during a game broadcast including the Georgetown Hoyas, when he referred to Allen Iverson as a "tough monkey" on national television. Packer was saved from public disgrace by coach John Thompson of Georgetown when Thompson reported to *USA Today* that he didn't "have to explain to anybody about Billy being a racist because he's not."

Fellow journalists are always pointing to the list above and marveling at the staying power Packer enjoys. Analysts with more experience and less baggage have been unceremoniously dismissed when making unfortunate remarks involving race or gender. Packer simply addresses those issues directly and moves on.

"And it's not like Packer is Mr. Popularity, an astonishing number of fans across America fervently believe Packer has an ax to grind against their favorite team," wrote ESPN's Bill Simmons. "At the 2005 ACC Tournament in D.C., Packer was honored for his body of work at halftime—and the arena booed him as if he was a WWE Villain. In retrospect, this might have been the only time Duke fans and North Carolina fans agreed on anything."

Packer's reaction to all of his critics is simple.

"Since everyone thinks I hate their team," says Packer, a 2008 inductee into the National Collegiate Basketball Hall of Fame, "that has to prove that I am impartial."

The man just continues to roll along, Final Four after Final Four.

"The string has ended in the Packer analysis of Final Four Championships. After 34 years of excellent, yet controversial, broadcast journalism Billy Packer has been replaced by Clark Kellogg (July 2008). "These are really good circumstances, he said, this decision was made by myself and CBS over a year ago."

For those fans that grew up listening to Packer dissect the NCAA Tournament games, there is doubt now. Whether or not Clark Kellogg can carry the day is for future fans to determine. Many of us close to the game share the feelings expressed by Big East Commissioner Mike Tranghese; "The only word to describe Billy is a giant, he said, his passion for the game and presenting in the way he presented it is, I think unrivaled. This creates an incredible void. Those of us who have a passion for the game of college basketball are going to miss him."

Clark Kellogg, responding to the media, concerning his new assignment left little doubt that he was not intimidated by the new responsibilities, yet he understood the size of the shoes that he is intending to fill. "His excellence as an analyst is Hall of Fame worthy, he said, his knowledge of the game and its history is unparalleled. That, along with his passion and keen insights, enable him to do his work as an analyst better and longer than anyone in the game's history. His Legacy is one of enduring excellence and keeping the focus on the game. That is the foundation I aspire to build on."

GUARDIAN

DICK VITALE
(COLLEGE COACH, NBA COACH,
PHENOMENON)

"I'm living the American Dream. I learned from my mom and dad, who didn't have a formal education, but had doctorates of love. They told me that if you gave 110 percent all the time, a lot of beautiful things will happen."
— **Dick Vitale**

Photo courtesty: Rich Arden, ESPN

The question that no one seems to ask is "how did this happen?" Dick Vitale is unquestionably the face and voice of college basketball across America. He has replaced the "rock star" coaches and all other personalities associated with the game and has taken center stage. He is a walking advertisement and is *always* in peacock plumage when college basketball is the topic of the day. He wasn't a great player, and compared to many others, he wasn't a great coach. His resume highlights a couple of New Jersey State Championships, but the list ends with a victory over Marquette during Al McGuire's championship season and one NCAA Tournament appearance. How did this happen?

Guys are not simply born in New Jersey—they are Jersey guys. Vitale is a Jersey guy. Richard J. "Dick" Vitale was born in Passaic in 1939. His parents, Mae and John Vitale, toiled in the garment industry and his dad would moonlight as a security guard. After an uneventful childhood, high school found him tooling around in his 1955 red Ford convertible.

As most Jersey guys did, he went to Seton Hall University and graduated with a degree in business. He later earned a Masters Degree in education and took his first job at Mark Twain Elementary School in Garfield. He did some coaching in football and basketball, while working his way into the head basketball position at Garfield High School. After one season, he was offered the same position at his alma mater, East Rutherford High School, where he would win two New Jersey State Championships in his seven years there.

Rutgers University coach Raymond Jones hired Vitale to his staff in 1970, where he found recruiting to be his forte. He was responsible for recruiting many talented players for Rutgers, highlighted by Phil Sellers and Mike Dabney, who would take Rutgers to the Final Four in 1976. The high school championships and recruiting success got him an interview for the head coaching position at the University of Detroit. He was hired in 1973.

A Glance At ... Dick Vitale

Awards

- Cable Ace, 1994 and 1995
- Honorary Alumnus, University of Detroit
- Man of the Year, Detroit Athletic Club
- Greater Detroit Community Award
- Honorary Citizen, Boy's Town
- Sports Personality of the Year, Sportscasters Association
- Sports Personality of the Year, NIT Metropolitan Media
- John Domino Award for Professional Service
- Phil Rizzuto "Scooter Award" for most caring broadcaster
- Black Coaches Association Award, dedication to youth
- Man of the Year, Make-a-Wish Foundation
- Honorary Degree, Notre Dame University
- Ronald Reagan Media Award
- Curt Gowdy Media Award
- Lifetime Achievement Award, Sons of Italy
- NABC Cliff Wells Appreciation Award
- Jake Wade Award, COSIDA for contributions to college athletics
- President's Humanitarian Award, State of Florida
- Ethics and Sportsmanship in Sports Media Award
- National Pathfinder Award

Inducted into

- National Italian Sports Hall of Fame
- Sarasota Boy's and Girl's Club Hall of Fame
- Five-Star Basketball Hall of Fame
- University of Detroit Hall of Fame
- Florida Sports Hall of Fame
- New Jersey Sports Hall of Fame
- College Basketball Hall of Fame
- Naismith Memorial Hall of Fame

Philanthropy

- Scholarships, Boy's and Girl's Club, Sarasota, FL
- Dick Vitale Physical Education Health and Training Center
- Board of Directors, Jimmy V Foundation
- Jimmy V Foundation Golf Classic

Vitale did relatively well at Detroit and later added the athletic director's position to his duties at the university. His efforts at Detroit would result in several honors, such as the United Fund's Detroit Man of the Year. His community effort, effervescent personality and coaching success would not go unnoticed.

In May 1978, the NBA's Detroit Pistons came calling and Vitale answered. He finished his first NBA season with a 30-52 record. Unfortunately, after a slow start (4-8) in 1979, he was replaced.

Maybe it wasn't so unfortunate. In fact, it turned out great for Vitale. Just weeks after being let go, Vitale negotiated an opportunity for the time between coaching positions.

ESPN had just started broadcasting 24-hour sports and was in need of on-air personalities to broadcast the games. Vitale would call his first game for the ESPN cable network and what started as a stop-gap measure between coaching jobs turned "Dickie V" into an entrepreneurial masterpiece. He has broadcast close to 1,000 college games and turned his personality into a pop-culture icon.

No other sportscaster has endeared himself to the college students like Vitale. He arrives on the campus early, parades and parties with the students on campus, and then does it all again when the arena doors open hours before tip-off. He conducts shooting contests and other events with the kids. He is warmly welcomed and rarely disappoints on campuses around the country.

Vitale has taken this popularity and expanded his brand. He actively advertises for a restaurant chain, a frozen pizza company, and he does a variety of shows with ESPN, in addition to the games that he is calling for the sports network. Vitale has even done the NBA playoffs and the Olympics for radio and been involved in many other projects for ABC and ESPN.

While many of us are familiar with Vitale's college basketball shtick, we are not as familiar with his heart. Always remembering where he came from and the positives that he has received from sports, Vitale actively provides money, time and support for numerous causes, charities and individuals around the country. Dick Vitale has used his fortunate opportunities to influence, assist and mentor others. People of all ages have been supported by Vitale's generosity.

It is this philanthropic attitude, exhausting work ethic and his connection to generations much younger than himself that go a long way in answering why Dickie V has become the face of college basketball.

After the Vitale brand is a thing of the past, it will be for historians to decide the magnitude of his impact on basketball. Fans of all ages hang on his every word. Often his opinions are controversial and in some circles he's even accused of having favorite teams or favorite coaches. Still, people listen. Probably the most important achievement of a television personality is connectivity and Vitale certainly has achieved that, and with several different demographics. A television producer's All-American, baby!

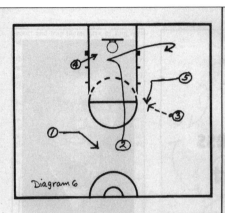

Diagram 6

No. 5. In Diagram 6, notice the path of No. 1 to the top of the circle—this is usually taken to receive a pass from No. 3 when he is not able to pass to No. 5. In this case, No. 1 will try to hit No. 5. If No. 1 succeeds in this, all action will be the same as explained in the No. 3 passing to No. 5 action—No. 1 will go down that weak side.

In Diagram 7, No. 3 passes to No. 2. It is an important fundamental for No. 3 to pass to No. 2 only when he has established a shooting position facing the basket—he must not pass if No. 2 is still moving toward the sideline. If this fundamental is followed, No. 2 will be able to shoot as soon as he receives the ball chin high from No. 3. No. 2 must be aware of the fundamental and make it a point of establishing his shooting position as soon as he can. No. 3 cuts to the basket after passing to No. 2. He does this to get a return pass, a rebound, or to screen a defensive man near No. 4 who will try to take advantage of this screen by looking for an open area. No. 5 then looks for an open area—usually the vacated spot of No. 3. No. 1 should balance out to a defensive position at the top of the key. The move may end with No. 5 getting the ball from No. 2 and then passing out to No. 1 while No. 2 and No. 3 return to the outside to begin the 3-2 attack again.

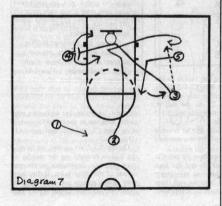

Diagram 7

Original NABC Coaches Clinic "Faculty"

In a rare photograph three of America's greatest coaches, Henry Iba, John Wooden and Adolph Rupp, are shown together.

These three outstanding men were on the original NABC Clinic speaking panel five years ago. All three were scheduled to speak again this year, but Kentucky's Rupp is sidelined by illness and in his place will be the colorful Guy Lewis, of Houston, like the others in the photo, a former Coach of the Year.

A rare photo from the 1971 NABC Program of the greatest ever known. Iba in the Midwest, Wooden in the West and Rupp representing the East. They come in all sizes.

BOOK ELEVEN

THE GREATEST OF THEM ALL

GUARDIAN

JOHN R. WOODEN
(HUSBAND, FATHER,
TEACHER, COACH)

*"A coach can only do his best, nothing more,
but he does owe that, not only to himself,
but to the people who employ him and to the
youngsters under his supervision."*

— John Wooden

John Wooden's coaching record at UCLA was an impressive 620-147, which equates to a winning percentage that tops a stunning 80 percent. But the road traveled, to be in a position to win those games, is an intriguing tale that needs to be repeated as often and as accurately as possible.

Wooden addresses the 1977 NABC convention. He would use these opportunities the express his views on the state of the game.

Wooden proudly carries the title of UCLA Head Basketball Coach Emeritus and will for perpetuity. Anyone who ever had the privilege of speaking with Wooden or anyone who has ever studied Wooden the man, know that his story, his passion, goes beyond the impressive winning percentage and the championships that his UCLA teams won.

"The rapport and association I have with all my players is what I am most proud of," Wooden told the *Indianapolis Star* in 2006. "In your earlier days of teaching, you don't see it that way, but when you get older, and you reflect, those are the things that give you the most pleasure."

Anyone remotely familiar with college basketball would understand a reference to the "Wizard of Westwood." The UCLA Bruins' run of 10 championships was magical, but certainly John Wooden (Coach) did not use some magic potion to succeed. Winning championships at any level is wonderful, but winning 10 NCAA Division I basketball championships in 12 years, including seven consecutive, is just simply unheard of. It hadn't happened before then, and likely never will be duplicated. Unbelievably, Coach is still the face of college basketball more than 30 years after retiring from UCLA. When asked to try to reflect on that exact idea, he responded simply that, "Championships is not what identifies success."

A study of John Wooden and his techniques offer a plan that embraces great depth. He believed in talking to anyone who would listen about the importance of personal preparation and becoming the best possible person, before he ever begins discussions about coaching. Swen Nater, former Wooden player, says it better than anyone does.

"To not celebrate, to fail to take notice, would be unthinkable," Nater said. "It has been 28 years since he stopped coaching UCLA's basketball team, 28 years since the last of those magical 10 national championships. And it has been 28 years of his growing on us, the sports community of southern California. Of his teaching us perspective, showing us how character counts, patting us on the hand to assure us that, whatever it is we are all hyped up about, the sun will come up tomorrow. For 28 years, long since the basketball buzz has gone away, he has remained our older statesman about life."

No coach in the history of the game has threatened comparison to Wooden's remarkable accomplishments. Coaches Henry Iba, Dean Smith, Bob Knight, Adolph Rupp, and Mike Krzyzewski have won two or more championships and been called great. What verb do we then select to describe Wooden's success on the nations' largest stage? He has set levels of coaching achievement that many have tried or will aspire to match. More importantly, he has established a level of commitment, integrity and selflessness that coaches today should never even consider. The task is too tough and the challenge too severe to continuously place your family, your faith and your personal integrity on daily public display.

During an especially significant period of accomplishment, there have been coaches who have accepted college basketball's leadership role for a year or two, but the hallmark of the game may always be Wooden.

"I knew when I retired I'd be in demand for clinics and speaking engagements because of my name," Wooden said in 1986. "But I am very surprised that I am still in demand. I'm not sure I'd want to go listen to a coach who hadn't coached in 11 years."

Coach Wooden took the reins at UCLA in 1948 and upon his retirement had never experienced a losing season. Actually, the only losing season he ever experienced was his very first year coaching basketball. His high school team in Dayton, Kentucky, went 6-11, but a similar experience was never repeated. He returned to Indiana to coach high school basketball, then two years at Indiana State and then, with little fanfare, he was coaching at UCLA.

There was a 14-12 record in his 12th year and five seasons with double-digit loses, but there were also four conference championships in the years leading up to that first NCAA title. When coach "finally" learned to win the big game, he won 10 national championships in 12 years. Quite a lesson learned.

"I think I learned more my first year of teaching than I did of any other year," he said. "The second year I think I learned more than any other year following that, and the third year and so on … I hope I learned a little bit each and every year. As I like to say, if I'm through learning, I'm through."

Wooden was born in 1910 and grew up in Centerton, an Indiana farming community, on a 60-acre farm his mother Roxie Wooden had inherited. The family remained there until they lost the farm to the devastation of the Great Depression and the family moved to Martinsville, Indiana. It was on the farm that Johnny Wooden honed his skills when his parents went looking for an outlet for his excessive energy. His dad nailed a hollowed-out tomato basket to the barn, while his mom turned old rags and stockings into a ball.

His father, Joshua, supported the family by taking different jobs around the area. John helped when he could between studying and playing basketball and baseball for Martinsville High School. Wooden led the Artesians to the final game of the high school championship tournament three consecutive seasons, winning the Indiana High School State Championship his junior year.

Wooden ended up attending Purdue University. A trip with a buddy, however, actually could've altered that.

After his junior year, with life for his family difficult because of the Depression, Wooden and his friend hitchhiked south to Kansas to work the wheat harvest as a summer job. They arrived in Lawrence, home of the University of Kansas, a little early for the start of the harvest. So, the school's basketball coach and athletics director, "Phog" Allen, put them to work on the crew building KU's new football stadium, in exchange for a place to sleep in the gymnasium. Meals were provided at the local restaurant and they spent a week waiting for the wheat harvest to begin.

So, did Allen discuss with Wooden the idea of finishing high school in Lawrence and then attending KU, as the story goes?

"There was some discussion," Wooden said with a grin, "but never any pressure."

After a week of working on the stadium, the wheat harvest was beginning so the two boys headed farther south and began the arduous task of following the harvest that began in southern Kansas and ended in southern Canada prior to returning to school in Indiana.

"We were originally wearing our high school letterman's sweaters so that we might have better luck getting rides, but the heat was just too much," Wooden said. "Shortly after beginning the harvest work, my teammate returned to Indiana, but I remained because the money was so good. I could not make near this amount in Indiana and so I stayed and followed the harvest north.

"I was surrounded by characters who gambled their earnings away, so I immediately sent my paychecks home so that the family had what they needed."

In spite of Allen's potential offer, Wooden became a legend in Indiana with the combination of high school championships and all-state honors, plus his three-time College All-American career at Purdue. The notoriety led to a short professional career with a team sponsored by the Kautsky grocery chain in Indianapolis. Wooden's National Basketball League career ended when a late arrival at a game required immediate entry into competition and a severe muscle tear sent him to the sidelines permanently.

The Wooden legacy, similar to many legends,

A Glance At ... John Wooden

- High school and college coaching record, 801-196
- 15 conference championships in 27 years
- 7 NCAA Championships in a row (1967-1973)
- 88 regular season game winning streak
- 38 game NCAA tournament game winning streak
- 30-0 undefeated seasons four times
- .938 winning percentage for last 12 years at UCLA
- 10 NCAA Championships in final 12 seasons

Executive Director Joe Vancisin gives Coach of the Year Award to John Wooden in one of his very first NABC National Conventions.

had some very significant occurrences that could have changed the flow of history. When asked about a seemingly unconnected series of personal events, Wooden repeats Lincoln's words, "Things work out best for those who work best with the way things turn out." Wooden could have easily attended Indiana or Kansas instead of Purdue; could have stayed in high school coaching; could have been lost in World War II with his ship in the Pacific; could have taken the job at the University of Minnesota and could have left UCLA for Purdue, but he didn't. He built a championship program that many have admired, but none have replicated.

In picking a college, Wooden had decided that he wanted to study civil engineering. Purdue had a program and the University of Indiana did not, so the decision to attend Purdue was an easy one. It wasn't until Wooden was enrolled in the program that he learned that a degree in civil engineering required "summer work to support the book learning" during the traditional school year. With summer commitments already in place, he switched to English. Since civil engineers did not coach, while teachers often did, the first step had been taken on the road to immortality.

While teaching and coaching high school basketball in Dayton, Kentucky, and then at South Bend Central High School in Indiana, Wooden decided that this was his calling and was happy and comfortable with marriage to Nell and young children.

"I would still be coaching at South Bend Central if not for the war," he said.

Wooden never considered college coaching and he loved teaching English as much as he loved coaching his boys. His father taught him to "never look back after a decision was made," but he was certain in his heart that South Bend is where he would have remained.

The Navy and World War II interrupted the happy Wooden family. While on assignment staging for duty in the South Pacific, with orders to board the USS Franklin, Wooden became seriously ill.

"It was impossible for me to maintain my responsibilities," he said, "and a medical examination determined that I had a burst appendix."

An emergency appendectomy caused him to miss the sailing of his assigned vessel and he remained behind for rehabilitation. While in service in the Pacific, the Japanese bombed and sank the Franklin, killing 724 sailors in March 1945. Coach said: "A fellow student from Purdue was assigned to the Franklin and was killed in the attack."

Did the Good Lord already have a plan for Wooden's life?

"It is too complicated to try to understand why things happen," he responded. "Life offers good and bad and we have to be prepared for both."

Upon his return to South Bend, Wooden returned to his duties and coaching in college was still "never a thought." As seemed to be the case with Wooden, fate would step in again and someone he knew and respected would change the course of his life. His high school coach, Glenn Curtis, retired from a coaching and administrative position at Indiana State University (ISU) to try his hand at coaching professional basketball. Asked for a recommendation for his replacement, Curtis nominated John Wooden to fill the position. Without warning or prior discussion, a deal was on the table to become the athletic director, basketball coach and baseball coach at ISU.

Using much of what he had learned from Glenn Curtis at Martinsville High School and Ward "Piggy" Lambert at Purdue University, Wooden went to work on building a competitive collegiate basketball team. Curtis left a solid group at Indiana State and Wooden was able to win the conference championship in his first season. The National Association of Intercollegiate Basketball (NAIB) invited the Sycamores to participate in the national tournament, but the invitation would be rejected. The tournament was played annually in Kansas City, and the city had yet to be integrated. Coach had Clarence Walker, an African-American, on his bench and refused to participate without his entire squad.

Indiana State repeated the needed record to qualify again in 1948 and the NAIB again issued the invitation and this time with fewer restrictions.

"Clarence still was not playing much, but they let us stay in the downtown hotel this time and although we had to eat our meals in seclusion, we were able to attend as a team," he said.

He added later: "It was more difficult to find services on the road to Kansas City. Finding places to eat often required us to eat in our vehicles or in the restaurant's kitchen, but I was determined to do things together. At one stop, they did not notice Curtis until the meals were being delivered and they said he could not eat. We all got up and left the food on the table."

The Sycamores won several games and Walker didn't play more than a couple of minutes, but he did help to integrate the national tournament. ISU would meet Louisville in the final game and would be defeated, and Wooden would finish his two-year career at Indiana State with a record of 47-14, two national tournament invitations and, more importantly, an assist in the integration of college basketball.

After reaching the NAIB National Championship game in 1948, the "big time" was calling and a decision had to be made. Minnesota and UCLA were vying for Wooden's services and, initially, the Gophers won the contest, "I really wanted to coach in the Big 10," but when they failed to meet the deadline for a formal offer, Wooden was off to UCLA.

"I wasn't sure anyone was going to accept the way I wanted basketball to be played. I had ideas that weren't being used elsewhere," he said.

Later it was learned that a severe snowstorm in Minnesota crushed the phone systems and efforts to hire him were squashed by a higher power.

COACH PROFILE
JOHN THOMPSON III –
GEORGETOWN UNIVERSITY
(NABC MEMBER 12 YEARS)

"I say this every year and it's extremely important, but everyone in this community has been extremely supportive and they come out and cheer for us. The biggest point of this is thanking you, thanking everyone who supports us; from the students to the fans; to the bands and cheerleaders, and thanking you for helping to accomplish the little that we accomplished, and what we will accomplish. We are extremely appreciative and I cannot express that enough."

Toughness is often misinterpreted in the coaching ranks. Winning is tough, recruiting is tough and the NBA raiding your best players is really tough, but following Hall of Fame coaches Pete Carril and John Thompson Jr. on the sideline is just impossible.

John Thompson III did just that—and has a terrific record to show for it. Thompson's players are graduating at an amazing rate, and some of his players are in the NBA. Learning the Princeton University system under Carril was a great opportunity for Thompson. There was no program that was more polar-opposite from his father's.

After four seasons playing at Princeton, Thompson III returned to as an assistant coach for both Pete Carril and Bill Carmody before taking control of the Princeton program himself. In four seasons as the head coach, Thompson III won three Ivy League championships and qualified for post-season invitations three seasons.

In 2004, he accepted the position of head coach at Georgetown University—the program his father, John Thompson Jr., had built and coached to national prominence for many years. With obvious wisdom beyond his years, he meshed portions of the Princeton system with some of the traditional characteristics of the Georgetown program—with examplary resutlts. Thompson III qualified for the post-season in each of the first four seasons, winning two Big East Championships, earning one Sweet Sixteen and one Final Four berth. Additionally, John Thompson III has shown a great affinity for recruiting and has had first-round picks in two NBA drafts.

Although he does not resemble his father in stature, he sends his players into real life just as his father did: prepared. Jonathon Wallace, speaking at the Hoyas banquet expressed it this way, "Coach always preached about the baby-step process, about how we should go about things and how he goes about things. You can apply that to life; nothing happens overnight."

Wooden had several West Coast contacts who assisted his securing the UCLA position, but the beginning of his tenure in Los Angeles wasn't the smoothest for the family. Not long after that first season at UCLA, Purdue was looking for a coach and the first stop in their search was at UCLA. There was still a great desire to coach in the Big 10, but Wooden would remain to coach the Bruins.

"I had insisted on a three-year contract to move to California and UCLA had provided the family security I had requested," he pointed out.

Being true to his teachings and to the security that UCLA had acquiesced to provide, Purdue went away empty handed.

One would think that the obstacles were finally set aside and the career could move smoothly forward. One additional event guaranteed something special was in store for the man from Indiana. Annually, Wooden would attend a clinic in North Carolina, flying to Atlanta and then connecting on a flight to the clinic. There was a year when Wooden was ready to leave, but as he said, "there was an incident at UCLA that required my attention, so I re-booked for the next day." The airplane that Wooden was holding a ticket for crashed and killed all aboard.

Incredible as this all sounds, if any one of those scenarios had happened differently this chapter might not be in the book because the result might have turned out completely different or not at all.

With reams of written material about every inch of the basketball phenomenon that was the Wooden-led UCLA Bruins, there are some very obvious elements that seemed to be missing from this most impressive of coaching resumes. Wooden continued his 58-year membership in the NABC, but he never held a leadership position within the NABC. When asked about that, he sat and looked off into space for a little while and commented that, "Many of my peers politicked and maneuvered for those positions and I did not operate that way. If I had been asked to serve, I would have, but no one ever asked."

Later, when discussing the NABC in general, he stated, "I had the feeling that many of my contemporaries did not agree with my decision to include (his wife) Nell in the convention events. As a lifetime teetotaler, they often commented that I did not mix and mingle at the important events."

Research on the history of the NABC did uncover a record of Wooden's participation on the NABC Officiating Committee for a couple of years. Coaches and officials were asked how to improve officiating and the relationship between coaches and officials. The following are Wooden's suggestions:

1. *Officials who never decide in advance how they are going to call a game or what they are going to be especially looking for, or strict about, or lenient about.*
2. *Officials who understand all coaches and realize that the game is the vocation of the coaches and only the avocation of themselves.*
3. *Officials who know the rules, but do not hide behind the technicalities of the rulebook and officiate according to the purpose of the rules.*
4. *Officials who keep all personality conflicts with coaches, players, or fellow officials completely apart from anything related to the game or their officiating.*
5. *Officials who command, rather than demand, the respect and cooperation of all those associated in any way with the playing or viewing of the game.*

"I can understand most of the rules changes," Wooden said during the writing of this book. "I don't always agree, but I understand. I think the rule change that had the most positive effect on the game was eliminating the jump ball. I don't know if you know this, but the game used to have a jump ball after every score and this just slowed the game down. Many felt that I was opposed to the dunk being eliminated, but truly, I think the mistake was putting the dunk back into the game. I am opposed to anything that promotes showmanship and that is exactly what the dunk does."

When asked to comment on one change that he would make to improve the college game today, he answered by saying, "The officials have to officiate the games based upon the rules as they are written. Prior to every dunk the players take extra steps and could be called for traveling. The official must stop the extra steps and also the dribbler must be restricted to using the top-half of the basketball."

As confusing as Wooden's absence from NABC leadership during his career, is his lack of participation with the U.S. Olympic basketball program. The Amateur Athletic Union was providing the head coaches for the different teams and there was a national committee made up of basketball people making suggestions to the group ruling Olympic team selections. When asked about the Olympics coached by Rupp, Iba, Knight and Smith and why possibly the greatest coach in college basketball history was not involved, his response was short and surprising: "I would have loved to have been the Olympic coach, but I was never asked."

Bill Wall, NABC Executive Director during Wooden's tenure at UCLA and a member of the committee in those days, said: "I can't honestly remember if John's name was ever placed in nomination. We were in the minority on the committee, I think there were 38 AAU members and 12 from the NABC, so we never won any arguments, but I cannot really remember John's name being mentioned and I really don't know why. Quite possibly, when Iba was selected for the second time, Wooden and Smith may have been our choices and Adolph Rupp was the choice of the AAU.

Rupp was terribly frail and so a compromise candidate may have been selected, but that is just speculation."

There is one interesting story about Wooden's lack of participation in the Olympics. Lew Alcindor (now Kareem Abdul-Jabbar) was picked for the U.S. Olympic team, but decided not to play. "Behind the scenes," the Olympic committee approached Wooden.

"I was offered a position on the Olympic staff if I could persuade Lew to change his mind," Wooden said. "I spent hours teaching the UCLA players the value of getting an education. I spent hours monitoring and mentoring them about academic responsibility. Lew wanted to graduate with his class and playing in the Olympics would interfere with that. They were not specific about my position, towel boy, equipment manager, I don't know, but I was not going to the Olympics on the coattails of anyone else and I was not going to do anything that would delay the graduation of one of my players."

That mentality is one of the many ways in which Wooden was unique. But what separated John Wooden from the other coaches in his era?

"I was a very unexciting man whose teams played exciting basketball," he said. "We were a very easy team to scout, but a very difficult team to stop."

"I am not a strategy coach," Wooden added. "I do my coaching in practice. I don't feel that players can take things from a paper and transfer the information to the court. They must repeat the activity until they can do it quickly and efficiently."

Hence, the reason he did away with playbooks at UCLA, because he realized they just sat in lockers and "gathered dust."

Still, with an unorthodox coach, the UCLA Bruins dominated. Several coaches have won more games but there is not a single coach or program that has achieved anything near Wooden's 10 national championships in 12 years.

"The UCLA record in tournament play was truly amazing," said long-time Wooden assistant Denny Crum. "I believe there were a number of reasons. One, basketball is a game of conditioning, fundamentals and team play. The practices were very demanding, which insured the conditioning. At least one hour a day was spent on the fundamentals, right up to, and including, the day before the championship game.

"Coach was a big believer that the best five players did not always make the best team. A perfect example of that was Kareem's senior year when Lynn Shackleford started at forward on the wing and Kareem played in the low post. He could and would pass the ball into Kareem, where it should go most of the time, and he was a better outside shooter than Sidney Wicks, who was, overall, our most talented player at that time except for Kareem. Another factor was that we used a switching man-to-man defense, which allowed us to not have to spend our practice time on what our opponents were doing and allowed us to work more on the things that we needed to improve on."

"Coach Wooden was the best teacher I have ever seen. He was also the best organized. His attention to detail was also second to no one. Coach Wooden was also the smartest person I have ever known. He knew what his strengths and weaknesses were and made sure he surrounded himself with people who were good at the things he either couldn't or did not want to do. Things like making changes during games and recruiting."

The reverberating message throughout Wooden's career was that the successful coach was a teacher first.

"Everyone, everyone is a teacher," he said. "Everyone is a teacher to someone; maybe it's your children, maybe it's your neighbor, maybe it's someone under your supervision in some other way, and in one way or another, you're teaching them by your actions."

One teaching tool Wooden used—one which has had books written about it—is his "Pyramid of Success," which was a 14-year labor of love. It was actually designed as a teaching tool in his English classes rather than having anything to do with coaching.

His father always stressed that a person should strive for integrity and character and that would result in success.

"I can still visualize several ladders of success that I had come across," he said, "but that was not exactly what I was looking for."

"Years later, after the building blocks were in place," Wooden added, "I realized that the core of my pyramid—Condition, Skill, Team Spirit—were the three things that Coach (Piggy) Lambert stressed for all those years I played basketball for Purdue."

Wooden never put a copyright on the Pyramid because he wanted it to spread on the merits of the message. He never intended to profit from

John Wooden and the media, always then and always now!!

what he constantly preaches are the steps to succeed in whatever goals you have set for yourself.

Tying in with the Pyramid is Wooden's love of and appreciation for poetry. During any conversation with Wooden, the listener likely will receive an insightful saying or poem, many of the same ones Wooden passed along to his Bruins. In fact, Coach Wooden's "business" card contains his father's "two lists of threes" and a favorite poem:

Never cheat	Don't whine
Never lie	Don't complain
Never steal	Don't make excuses

Four things a man should learn to do
If he would make his life more true:
To think without confusion clearly,
To love his fellow man sincerely,
To act from honest motives purely,
To trust in God and Heaven securely.
—Reverend Henry Van Dyke

Wooden's interests remained in the details of his life and in the game of basketball. He taught stressing the smallest details of his program and was not satisfied until skills could be performed flawlessly and at top speed. He often repeated his mantra "be quick, but don't hurry" in so many aspects of his philosophy, that it seems to be the crux of the program.

The adaptation of Wooden's discipline and his expectations for the players changed gradually each year, but with no sacrificing of his program or personal principles. Silent team meals and coats and ties were set aside to soften the relationship-building processes between both teammate to teammate, and players to coaches. Wooden, however, always took each situation on its own merits.

The *NABC Bulletin* reprinted an interview with former *Kansas City Star* editor Joe McGuff, where Coach was direct in his decision-making process:

"When I met with my squad this year before the start of practice I told them that I was opposed to long hair because I think it is detrimental to their performance. It holds perspiration and the sweat can get in their eyes and on their hands. Long hair requires a lot of care to keep clean and looking presentable. When we finish practice, they immediately go out doors and wet hair makes them more susceptible to colds."

"I told them there would be no beards, mustaches or long side burns. While I have reasons for being opposed to long hair, I do not have reasons for being opposed to beards, mustaches and side burns. I told my players that I simply do not like them. I told them that these are the rules and that if anyone could not accept them to say so, that we would part friends and that they would not lose their scholarship. I told them if they stayed then they were agreeing to abide by the rules."

Always the psychologist, by giving the players a choice to play or not, with the scholarship NOT an issue, the softer Coach Wooden allows the athlete to make the decision regarding adjusting his principles, rather than the coach forcing an unpopular decision on the group.

A very modest man whose actions spoke much louder than his words, Wooden was constantly recognized for his expertise and continues to be honored across the country:

- Presidential Medal of Freedom, George W. Bush, 2003; highest civilian honor available in the United States
- Presidential awards from Gerald Ford, Ronald Reagan, George Bush
- NCAA Theodore Roosevelt Award; highest NCAA Award Available
- Naismith Memorial Basketball Hall of Fame as a player
- Big 10 Medal of Honor for Athletic and Academic Excellence
- Naismith Peach Basket Award (first recipient, 1974)
- Coach of the year 1964, '67, '69, '70, '72
- Naismith Memorial Basketball Hall of Fame as a coach
- Outstanding Coach of the United States, Christian Church
- 1970 Sports Man of the Year, *The Sporting News*
- Coach of the Century– Friars Club, Beverly Hills California
- Helms All-Time All-American team, 1943
- Indiana State Basketball Hall of Fame
- California Father of the Year, 1964

There are detractors who have attempted to demean or deface Wooden's accomplishments, but in every case, the antagonist has been aggressively turned aside. There were years of dominant teams, with the country's greatest players donning the UCLA uniforms, under interesting circumstances. There were rumors of unlimited scholarships, allowing Wooden's staff to stockpile talent, keeping it away from the competitors. There were stories about glad-handers and godfathers, but the truth was that Wooden was able to teach the game better than anyone else was.

"There are always detractors in life and that is just part of being successful," he said. "A man knows in his heart (at this point he taps the center of his chest) the level of his integrity."

For every championship won by a team led by Lew Alcindor or Bill Walton, there were teams led by unknowns and lesser talents that bought into the UCLA way and won unexpected championships. Although Wooden was reluctant to compare teams,

COACH PROFILE

GARY WILLIAMS –
UNIVERSITY OF MARYLAND
(NABC MEMBER 36 YEARS)

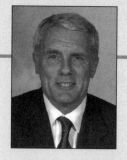

"I always feel that you can do more, Williams said. It's like coaching. You always think you can win another game. Nobody's satisfied – we're always looking for ways to increase the amount."

The Williams scouting report is simple. Run the flex offense, show patience and get good shots, and then press, attack and demoralize on defense. Some nice thoughts, but easier said than done. Teaching a team to play at different speeds, changing attack to patience in a single possession and being tough with finesse are characteristics of the Williams school of coaching. There are not many that can get that done on a consistent basis.

Gary Williams was born in Collingswood, New Jersey, and parlayed his high school basketball career into a basketball scholarship at the University of Maryland. Once again, a tough-minded point guard who went into coaching, where have we seen that before?

Williams began his coaching career at the high school level. His first job was as an assistant at Woodrow Wilson High School and he then became the head coach at the same school. From there he worked as an assistant coach at both Lafayette College and Boston College before getting his first chance at being a head coach at American University. After two NIT appearances in four years at American, Williams would accept the head coaching position at Boston College and would lead the Eagles to three post-season appearances in four seasons including a sweet 16. Moving to Ohio State University, Williams was three-for-three in post-season appearances and then took his talents to the University of Maryland, where he has won almost 400 games, earned spots in two Final Fours and winning one NCAA National Championship.

Known for his intense coaching style, Williams is often shown on the sideline perspiring through his suit jacket, using everything about him to motivate his players to success. Former Maryland player Jason McAlpin may have said it best: "The biggest thing I learned from playing basketball at Maryland was that you have to be tough and you have to be a competitor…There are going to be setbacks and things are not always going to go your way, but you have to be mentally tough and put those things out of your mind so you can accomplish what needs to get done."

he says there were two teams that achieved the most from the first day of practice in October until winning the title.

In 1964, his first championship team was a mess of personalities that "just simply did not get along." Wooden would mention Jack Hirsch and Gail Goodrich specifically when asked about the difficult personalities.

Walt Hazzard, Hirsh and Goodrich each had their own ideas of how the game should be played, and each added strong feelings about keeping their individual lifestyles intact while competing for the Bruins.

According to a 1973 *New York Times* article: "Wooden brooks little criticism. when Jack Hirsch, on a team back in the early nineteen-sixties, once said of the food, 'I can't eat this slop.' Wooden told him to stay away until he could, which meant suspension from the team. Hirsch stayed away two weeks, and then came back and apologized, and was silent when he ate the slop, which was usually a juicy steak or prime ribs."

Wooden and his staff recognized that the group had excellent talent, but lacked in size with no player taller than 6'5", and certainly in team chemistry.

"The more talent that a team has increases the difficulty of developing team chemistry," he said. "(But) I will always take the talent and put in the extra work to build the team unity."

The 1964 Bruin team was unranked in the preseason and was the smallest of any in the conference. In spite of these shortcomings, they led the conference in rebounding, finished 30-0 and won Wooden his first national championship.

The second example Coach identified as "over-achievers" was his final team in 1975. He had just graduated Bill Walton and Keith Wilkes, two of the greatest in UCLA Bruin history. He also lost his starting backcourt, so he could have described 1974-1975 as a rebuilding year for the program. Coach commented, "I knew we had talent ready to step in, but to replace four, two being Walton and Wilkes, well it was going to be tough."

Inside newcomers Richard Washington and Marques Johnson teamed up nicely with guards Andre Carter and Pete Trgovich and stabilized the Bruins. Led by lone returning starter and "great leader" David Meyers, UCLA had a magnificent run, finishing 23-3 and winning Wooden his 10th NCAA Championship.

The 1975 Tournament began with the NCAA expanding the field to 32 teams. The party line was that this would eliminate byes and be a more representative bracket. The truth was that the 1974 tournament had to leave three of the top ten teams (Maryland, North Carolina and USC) home because they did not win the conference championship and television was not going to let that happen again.

The Final Four paired Louisville and UCLA in the opener and Kentucky and Syracuse in the late game. UCLA won a hard-fought game against Louisville, and Kentucky pummeled the Orangemen. The final game would be a classic pairing that would determine a winner between the old school approach of Wooden and the new school approach of Joe B. Hall.

The Bruins took the pounding presented by the new style and prevailed. The Wooden system would once again prove superior in the face of the game's newest approach. Even with Meyers hurt and Johnson slowly recovering from a bout with hepatitis, the finely tuned squad took all that Kentucky had to offer. To offset some of the interior pounding by the huge Wildcat postmen, Wooden substituted rarely used center Ralph Drollinger in the post. Drollinger responded with his greatest game as a Bruin.

That was John Wooden's final game. He had surprised everyone on the eve of the championship game by announcing that the game for the NCAA crown would be his last.

"If someone had asked me before the semifinal game against Louisville, I would have said that I was prepared to coach three or four years longer and that would be it," Wooden said in 2007. "After a great hard-fought victory against Louisville and friend Denny Crum, I felt an emptiness inside. I had no interest in speaking to the media because it was a shame that either team had to walk off of that court feeling like a loser.

My immediate thought was that if I can't enjoy this great victory then it is time to leave the game. I went into the locker room, called the players out of the shower and gathered the staff and the trainers and informed them of my decision. No one knew of this because until the game was over, I didn't know myself.

"Since then, I have enjoyed reading about my retirement. There have been many different opinions, even people quoting me, but I just told you how my retirement actually occurred."

Of course, the difficulty for UCLA after that was trying to find a successor. Gene Bartow got the job, but he wasn't necessarily Wooden's first choice.

"Denny Crum," Wooden finally said when prodded about

Denny Crum sporting the Leisure Suit while working the sidelines at the University of Lousiville.

whom he would have selected, "but I knew what he was making at Louisville and I did not think J.D. Morgan (UCLA Athletic Director) would pay that much."

Upon his retirement in 1975, Wooden was making $32,500 and he knew that UCLA would be reluctant to pay more than that. Apparently it was more than just money that kept Crum from returning to attempt to keep the Bruin dynasty alive, and reading between the lines, the opportunity had actually been on the table.

"When I left UCLA to take the Louisville job, my intention was to prove I could be a successful Division I head coach and then come back to UCLA when Coach Wooden retired," said Crum. "However, I grew to love Louisville, especially the people there, and I could not bring myself to leave when the opportunity came."

"He was such a good influence on everyone he came in contact with," Crum added. "I cannot begin to tell you what he has meant to me both personally and professionally. He has not only been my coach and friend, but he has been like a father in so many ways. I have been truly blessed to have him in my life."

Athletic directors across the nation should note that Wooden coached the Bruins for 15 seasons before winning the first national championship. It was the patience of the UCLA administration that allowed a coach to grow and a program to develop the character needed to win on the big stage. There were detractors out there as a series of NCAA first-round losses plagued the Bruins, and the favorite criticism was "he can't win the big one," when UCLA was eliminated in the NCAA first round in 1950, '52 and '56. It wasn't until 1962 that a Wooden team reached the second round. As in almost every case, Wooden responds to his detractors simply.

"Once you're number one," he said, "people are never satisfied with anything less. I'm not crying. I'm just saying what it's like."

Much of what we know about John Wooden goes to the beginning of his UCLA career and the building of the championship dynasty. For decades, sports fans talked about the Babe Ruth home run record of 60 in a season being untouchable. That's been broken several times since. Baseball's consecutive-game record of 2,130 set by Lou Gehrig would never be surpassed, they said. That was before Cal Ripken Jr. In recent years, both records have passed into history, but Wooden's record of 10 NCAA Championships in 12 years, with seven consecutive (1967-1973), remains an impossible dream for college coaches. No coach came close before Wooden and no coach has come close since.

Indeed, at 97 years old when interviewed for this book in 2007, Wooden showed the physical signs of aging, but his memory, his voice and his opinions were strong and clear. Nell Wooden, Coach's late wife, said it best in 1973, when responding to a reporter's query:

"I don't know if he'll ever really retire. I don't know if he will ever retire in the truest sense—leave basketball entirely. I'll see him after one season ends, sitting in a chair and jotting down on a piece of paper his lineups for next year. He doesn't feel he'll miss the excitement, but I don't know."

The coaching mentor to thousands has a real message, one that continues to be very relevant today. His emphasis on education, teaching, character and integrity are all issues with which coaches and administrators constantly struggle. There is no question that college basketball was blessed to have Coach Wooden in its midst for so long, but the commitment goes far beyond the efforts of one man. For those who will look beyond his 97 years and listen closely, amazingly clear and precise advice is still available about basketball, coaching and achieving a successful life.

The coach was simply before his time in so many facets of the game and of life. It is the responsibility of the NABC membership to share this message for however long the game goes on.

BOOK TWELVE

THE FUTURE IS UPON US

When you are selecting the anchor man for your winning relay team, you do not always select the fastest, or the strongest, but you always select the finisher. You select the one who you know would get the team to the finish line regardless of the barriers placed before him. So it is that Duke University's Mike Krzyzewski has been chosen to anchor the conclusion of this book. The final Guardian is not the fastest or the strongest, but he will get us to the finish line regardless of the cost.

GUARDIAN

MIKE KRZYZEWSKI (SERVICE, LEADERSHIP, CHAMPION, INNOVATOR)

"During the season, your team should be led with exuberance and excitement. You should live the journey. You should live it right. You should live it together. You should live it shared. You should try to make one another better. You should get on one another if somebody's not doing their part. You should hug one another when they are. You should be disappointed in a loss and exhilarated in a win. It's all about the journey."

— **Mike Krzyzewski**

Mike Krzyzewski, or Coach K as he is fondly referred to in and around basketball circles, is the final installment in this Legacy of Leadership. He opened the book with his words of wisdom for both those who are involved in coaching as a profession and those who use coaches as role models in their lives, regardless of what they do for a living. The final section will be dedicated to following his lead into the future of the game of basketball, the profession of basketball coaching and the responsibilities that come with accepting the title "coach."

Born February 13, 1947, Krzyzewski (pronounced sha-shef-ski) was raised in the Polish section of northwest Chicago. His parents, Emily and Bill, worked very hard to provide a comfortable living for Mike.

Mike embraced characteristics from both parents. His dad was a quiet, hardworking man with an intense work ethic, while his mom shared her toughness in other ways, but could provide compassion when needed.

ATTACKING ZONE PRESS

(1) lines up head on the ball so that he can go either way to free himself. This maneuver is difficult to defend but,

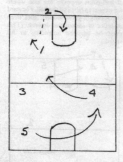

Diagram XVI

even more important, the second line of the press is unable to anticipate where the ball will be inbounded. The best ball handling forwards (3) and (4) line up in the mid-court area while the strongest rebounder (5) goes deep.
N.B. We designate these three methods of inbounding the ball as FIELD GOAL, FOUL SHOT, or INFRACTION. There is flexibility provided in that we may decide to use the INFRACTION method after an opposing field goal late in the game if we prefer to have the guards doing most of the handling.
HALF COURT PRESSURE
Since we operate from a two-three front court offense we have very little

difficulty in adjusting to a half-court trap or zone press. The same principles apply in terms of "DRAGGING A GUARD" as a safety valve or pitch back man and "ROTATING THE FORWARDS" in a triangular fashion.
N.B. The only new principle is that the guards (1) and (2) have to make a decision before they reach the ten second line. If they decide to dribble over, they must be able to penetrate deep enough to make room for a pitch back.

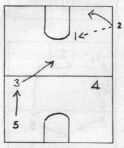

Diagram XVII

In Diagram XVIII be aware that the lob pass to the weak side corner is now a good calculated risk since the back defensive men have to be more conscious of the goal than the steal. In addition this one pass gives us a good percentage shot without a great risk of losing the ball. The rule against half-court pressure is the same—"YOU MUST SCORE TO BEAT A PRESS".
Staff Offense—"Four Corners"
We are convinced that a team cannot

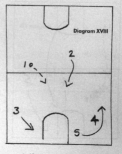

Diagram XVIII

use a half-court trap or half-court zone press against a good stall offense. The only rule is to keep the ball ahead of the double team. Always look to hit the man whose man is attempting to double team the ball handler. We use either our best ball handling guard or our best ball handling forward as the post man. The post man is the safety valve and should only be one pass away from the ball at all times.
Note that we have intentionally neglected to use defensive men in our diagrams. In our opinion it doesn't matter what kind of a zone press or where its point of attack will originate! Our team is drilled to take up an original offensive position that is designated not as a spot on the floor, but a position relative to the press. The routes taken are unimportant but everyone has to organize at the same time so that the principles of (1) DRAG THE GUARD and (2) TRIANGLE THE FORWARDS are in effect at all times in order to always assure the ball handler three passing outlets.

Presidents of the National Association of Basketball Coaches

Years	Name	University	Years	Name	University
1927-1929	Dr. Forrest C. Allen	University of Kansas	1951-1952	Bruce Drake	Oklahoma University
1929-1930	J. Craig Ruby	University of Illinois	1952-1953	Franklin C. Cappon	Princeton University
1930-1931	Lewis P. Andreas	Syracuse University	1953-1954	Edward S. Hickey	St. Louis University
1931-1932	Arthur A. Schabinger	Creighton University	1954-1955	Paul D. Hinkle	Butler University
1932-1933	Harold G. Olsen	Ohio State University	1955-1956	Harold E. Foster	University of Wisconsin
1933-1934	Roy M. Mundorff	Georgia Tech	1956-1957	Ray Oosting	Trinity College
1934-1935	Howard B. Ortner	Cornell University	1957-1958	Amory T. Gill	Oregon State University
1935-1936	Arthur C. Lonborg	Northwestern University	1958-1959	Clifford Wells	Tulane University
1936-1937	H. Clifford Carlson	University of Pittsburgh	1959-1960	Everett Shelton	Sacramento State College
1937-1938	George R. Edwards	University of Missouri	1960-1961	R. E. "Bill" Henderson	Baylor University
1938-1939	William S. Chandler	Marquette University	1961-1962	Wilbur Stalcup	University of Missouri
1939-1940	Brandon T. Grover	Ohio University	1962-1963	Harold Anderson	Bowling Green University
1940-1941	Nat Holman	City College of New York	1963-1964	Lee Williams	Colby College
1941-1942	Nelson Norgen	University of Chicago	1964-1965	Forrest F. Twogood	Univ. of Southern California
1942-1944	Edward A. Kelleher	Fordham University	1965-1966	Ben Carnevale	U.S. Naval Academy
1944-1946	Edward J. Hickox	Springfield College	1966-1967	Alvin F. Julian	Dartmouth College
1946-1947	Blair Gullion	University of Connecticut	1967-1968	Henry P. Iba	Oklahoma State University
1947-1948	Howard A. Hobson	University of Oregon	1968-1969	William C. Gardiner	Catholic University
1948-1949	Herbert W. Read	Western Michigan University	1969-1970	Adolph Rupp	Brigham Young University
1949-1950	John Bunn	Springfield College	1970-1971	Stanley Watts	Kentucky
1950-1951	Vadal Peterson	University of Utah	1971-1972	Bill Wall	MacMurray College

38

Clinic notes and the NABC Past Presidents from the 1971 NABC Coaches Clinic Program, what could be more appropriate for this book?

"The person who inspired me my whole life was my mom, because she taught me commitment," Krzyzewski said. "She sacrificed. We weren't dirt poor, but we weren't real rich or anything. I would always have what I needed, and when I looked in her closet, she would have two dresses. She taught me to be outside of myself, to get outside of yourself, and be committed to somebody. That's the same thing that I try to teach."

Krzyzewski was into sports from a very early age and learned the game of basketball and the game of life on the playgrounds. His parents did not really understand this fascination and did not necessarily approve of his activities.

"At the time, we were in a Polish community in the inner city of Chicago, and I was the youngest of a bunch of cousins. Polish families are real big, with cousins and aunts and uncles," he said. "My older brother is about twice as big as me, he's about six-foot-six, 250 pounds. He didn't play sports. Being in the band, or other things, those were things that you did. They were not frivolous. Playing sports was somewhat frivolous, but I liked it. I rebelled a little bit, and wouldn't go to music lessons and things like that, but I would go and play ball. My parents learned to love it because they saw how much I got out of it."

Reflecting back on his childhood, he would often comment that he had a tendency to lead whenever there was a group looking to make a decision. Never one to sit still much, he quickly became angered at indecision and would just simply make a decision and the group would follow. This was certainly the personality trait that would later lead to coaching greatness.

Krzyzewski attended the all-boys Weber High School in Chicago. He tried out for the football team, but was cut. He then gravitated toward basketball and realized quickly that he had a passion for the sport.

As with most of the Guardians, there was someone who was easily identified as the role model for what would come later. In Krzyzewski's case that was his high school basketball coach, Al Ostrowski, who pushed Krzyzewski to levels that he could not have imagined achieving. Although Ostrowski had never been a player himself, he recognized the depth of potential in his young player and would always ask for more. In the beginning, Krzyzewski would react poorly, worrying about his teammates when coach wanted him to take more shots or make more decisions, but soon the light went on and he would push ahead.

"If success or talent were on floors, maybe I saw myself on the fifth floor," said Krzyzewski. "He always saw me on the twentieth floor. As a result, I climbed more floors when I was with him."

Krzyzewski the player dreamed of the day he would become a high school teacher and coach. His relationship with Ostrowski would become his motivation to find his place in that world. Krzyzewski said: "He was only in his 20s, and he wasn't even a former basketball player, but I really believed in him, and that had a huge impact."

Ostrowski pushing and Krzyzewski begrudgingly responding finally resulted in a breakthrough game against Loyola, when Krzyzewski scored more than 30 points and directed his team to a convincing victory. The coach of that Loyola squad, Gene Sullivan, was so impressed with Krzyzewski that he called a friend who was coaching at the United States Military Academy. Bob Knight took the call that day and began to review the career of Mike Krzyzewski and how he might be able to contribute to the Army program.

"I went to Weber, found Mike, and took him to lunch at the school cafeteria," said Knight. "I made arrangements to meet with him and his parents at their home. I visited, and talked about what we had to offer. His Dad didn't say much, but when I was all done, he said, 'Well Mike, I think West Point is where you ought to go to school.'"

Knight's visit to the Krzyzewski home was a big success in the eyes of Mike's parents. They were shocked that basketball could lead to a free education and a job after graduation.

> ## A Glance At ... Mike Krzyzewski
> - Five consecutive Final Fours
> - 69 Career wins in NCAA Tournament (#1)
> - 3 National Championships
> - 10 Final Fours
> - 11 ACC Regular Season Titles
> - 10 ACC Tournament Titles
> - 800+ Career Wins
> - *Basketball Times* Coach of the Year, 1986 and '97
> - Naismith Coach of the year, 1989 and '99
> - NABC Coach of the Year, 1991 and '99
> - 1992 *Sporting News* Coach of the Year (1st college coach named)
> - 2000 CBS/Chevrolet Coach of the Year
> - ACC Coach of the Year– 2000, 1999, 1997, 1986, 1984
> - Naismith Memorial Basketball Hall of Fame, 2001
> - 2001 America's Best Coach by *Time* and CNN (non-sport specific)
> - 2004 Clair Bee Award

Mike had different ideas and was not so excited about leaving the neighborhood, his friends and his dreams. In the end he would accept the offer and attend West Point, but it was not without a steady push from the folks at home.

Krzyzewski's first experience was not at all pleasant at Army as the city boy and the expectations at West Point did not always mesh. Krzyzewski was behind from the outset because he had never been out of the confines of the city of Chicago, and camping and swimming were foreign to him.

COACH PROFILE

ROY WILLIAMS –
UNIVERSITY OF NORTH CAROLINA
(NABC MEMBER 28 YEARS)

"With what we face nowadays, with the stresses, the expectations, the pressures created by so many different media outlets, call-in shows, internet sites, the off-the-court things somebody faces now make the longevity [of coaching] so much more challenging."

Roy Williams is one of the few coaches with direct connections to Dr. James Naismith. Williams' long-time mentor Dean Smith played for Phog Allen—who played for Naismith. Williams worked for Smith for years, then became the head coach at Kansas, before returning home to lead the Tar Heels. Williams was rumored to walk to the grave of James Naismith in Lawrence on bad days to discuss how things might get better. Those direct links to the founder of this game are fading into history very quickly.

Williams lettered all four years in basketball and baseball at T.C. Roberson High School in Asheville, North Carolina. Williams cites his high school coach, Buddy Baldwin, as one of the most influential people in his life. Williams then went to North Carolina and played junior varsity basketball while studying the coaching techniques of Dean Smith.

Williams took his first coaching job at Charles D. Owen High School where he coached basketball, golf, and football, as well as serving a term as the school's athletic director. Williams returned to North Carolina as an assistant to Smith and would remain in that position for 10 years. He got his first head coaching opportunity at the University of Kansas following Larry Brown. During his 15 seasons at KU, he led the Jayhawks to 14 consecutive NCAA tournaments, reaching the Final Four four times. The national championship eluded the Jayhawks during his tenure, and this gradually became a problem for the KU fans. Williams would move to his alma mater in 2003 and win the coveted national championship in his second season at the helm of the Tar Heels. Williams has continued to keep North Carolina at the top of the polls and been incredibly successful in recruiting the best talent in the land, but continues to be one of the quietest and most genuine people in the land.

If one single event could define a person, for Roy Williams, that event would be sitting in the stands during the championship game in 2008, wearing a Jayhawk sticker. Though the Jayhawks had just beaten N.C. in a heart-breaking game to gain a spot in the final, the former KU coach still rooted for those kids and the program that was once his.

Things weren't much easier on the court. The style of basketball Knight preached was not comfortable. Where shooting was Krzyzewski's strength, Knight wanted defense. And more defense. Passing the ball was a mandate, not just an option.

The Army career was better after he learned the ways of the Infantry and the ways of Knight. Knight was never one to counsel or comfort his players and there were difficult times during Krzyzewski's four years playing basketball. With the natural recruiting restrictions, a great season was never an expectation, but one could take great pride in gaining a winning record and an NIT invitation. During his senior season he was awarded with a second-team All-NIT selection.

Toward the end of that season, however, as Army was trying to secure an NIT berth, Krzyzewski learned after a game that his father had suffered a massive cerebral hemorrhage. By the time Krzyzewski, accompanied by Knight, made it to Chicago, his dad had died.

Krzyzewski spoke at length about that night in Knight's autobiography, written with Bob Hammel, *Knight: My Story*.

"Anybody that has been around him (Knight) knows how much a practice meant to him--let alone one in this situation, when we were playing for the whole season, really," Krzyzewski said. "But he came out to Chicago that night, and he came right to the house. He came in and loosened his tie. He sat around the kitchen table—Polish people sit around the kitchen table and eat all the time. My mom had some polish food on the table and Coach would just grab it with his fingers. It was very relaxed—just the sort of thing my mom needed. He stayed around till Wednesday, when we had the funeral. He talked with my mom after the funeral, and he ate another meal with us. He didn't get away until that afternoon, and we were leaving for Colgate Thursday.

"I'm captain of the team and I'm starting at guard, and he told me to stay with my mom and take all the time I needed. People say, 'Boy it was nice of him to come out,' but they don't realize just how nice. The NIT is what the coach and the whole team look for at Army. I know how much work had gone into it, but it was important for him to come out there and visit. I got back in time to make the bus up to Colgate. We won both games and we got a bid to the NIT, so everything worked out great."

After his post-graduation military commitment, Krzyzewski joined Knight's staff at Indiana for one season. Krzyzewski then returned to West Point as the head coach and would serve for five years. His record at West Point was 73-59 with one appearance in the NIT.

In 1980, Krzyzewski had opportunities to become the coach at two schools: Duke and Iowa State. After a couple of interviews and the media giving the Duke job to everybody else but him, Krzyzewski was announced as the new head coach at Duke University. There were doubts that he was ready—plus a concern from people at Duke that they had gotten another Bob Knight.

After a three-year struggle that resulted in a 38-47 record, the program needed to change direction quickly. As with most college programs, the answer came in recruiting. A terrific recruiting class resulted in the first of what would become a yearly event: an NCAA berth. The Blue Devils received 24 consecutive invitations.

During the writing of *Guardians of the Game*, Krzyzewski offered the following thoughts on various topics. As easy as it would have been to place a few of these comments throughout the text of this chapter, it seems more appropriate to present them in a Question/Answer format.

Who were your early mentors?

Coach Knight has always been and remains my mentor. What is important for people to realize, it is the other people that you meet because of your mentor that is important. I have several relationships because of him. Coach (Hank) Iba and Coach (Pete) Newell, who have always been mentors of Coach Knight, have also assisted me. My fondest memories as a young coach is sitting around a table and listening to these three dissect the game. I never said anything, just took it all in and asked questions later.

When I was working for Coach Knight, I used to marvel at the teaching skills of the coaches teaching stations at summer camps. I learned a great deal from those sessions.

How has coaching changed during your career?

I think the biggest change is the amount of auxiliary things coaches have to do that have nothing to do with basketball. The media scrutiny is so intense that coaches have become isolationists. In the earlier days of the ACC, coaches would share thoughts about their program and issues within the conference. Today they are more focused on what is happening with them.

We do not have time to do clinics anymore. It used to be that when you did a clinic, you would sit and visit with the other speakers and even stay and go to dinner. Now we fly in, present the session on the schedule and fly out. Sometimes you do not even see another coach in the transition. Clinics started the coaches sharing and we have gotten out of the habit now.

Finally, how much time can we give to other coaches when we are struggling to have enough time to spend with our players? The NABC has to figure out a way to teach the game and keep these values going.

How did you become a member of the NABC Board?

I started working for Coach Knight while he was a board member. I was always doing the gopher work for him. We didn't have computers then so there were always surveys to do and mailings to get out. It was a natural thing for me. I did not politic for it, it was just a natural transition. Coach Knight was so passionate in the '70s and '80s that I was convinced that it was a part of my duty.

There were a lot of people who did not want to be on the board. I think it is important to be involved in what happens when you are a coach–what happens during your watch. Nobody is bigger than the game.

The year you were NABC President, Duke went 32-2. Was the presidency a distraction?

To become president you have to spend years on the board. As a board member, you succumb to the extra work involved with serving the NABC. Meetings and conference calls become part of your calendar. Being president was no different. Being the NABC President was never a distraction, it was an honor. Being a coach is wonderful, to be president of all coaches is living a dream.

Your first three years at Duke were a struggle. What changed?

I was given time. Today a three-year record of 38-47, I don't know if I would still have my job. I never worried about my job. I would get messages from different levels of the administration, letting me know they were pleased with the direction of the program. Duke certainly has benefited from the notoriety that resulted from that patience.

I always appreciated that level of commitment from Duke. It is why I would never consider another college job. There were opportunities for me to go into the NBA, but the final decision was always based upon the support and commitment that Duke has given me.

I wish that the NABC could speak directly with university presidents about having that patience and making that commitment.

What are the characteristics necessary for sustaining program success?

A coach must have honest and open communication with team, staff, and administration. At West Point we had the honor code and it relieved so much stress because you knew you were being told the truth. There was just never a doubt. It is also important to re-create this relationship with every team, every staff change and every change in administration. It is the coach's responsibility to create the relationship and it is the coach's responsibility to re-create it. You cannot ever overlook that responsibility.

The other element that must be created and preserved is trust. As much as possible you have to eliminate doubt from your program.

Coach John Wooden spoke of talent and chemistry. How do they fit in the equation?

Talent is important, but remember, everyone has talent. I think you must recruit talent and character. Everybody remembers Wooden's teams with Jabbar and Walton, but he won with teams less talented and that was because of chemistry.

The goal is to recruit talent with character; kids who will fit in your school and who want to be part of something bigger than themselves. The really good people want to be part of something bigger than themselves–most people do! To sustain success you have to have talent and character, and then develop both.

How did you get involved with the Olympic Games?

Again, it started with Coach Knight and the 1979 Pan-American Games. He gave me an opportunity to be an assistant coach. I always remained involved with U.S. basketball at different levels and was given the opportunity to be assistant coach with the "Dream Team", coached by Chuck Daly. I am convinced that it was the correct decision to go with NBA coaches during that time and I was honored to be asked to assist. It was a great experience working with those players and learning every day from Chuck Daly, Lenny Wilkens, and P.J. Carlesimo. After the Olympics, I was convinced that my tour of duty was over.

I was contacted and asked to consider the head coaching position for the 2008 Olympics and I said of course I would consider it. When I was selected, I said, how lucky am I? There is no greater honor in our profession! There is nothing in coaching more important than coaching for your country!

It was a historical decision to create a U.S. National Team. This was the first time that the United States attempted to do this. No matter what happens, Jerry Colangelo and USA Basketball made the right decision to do what the teams around the world have always done. I am very proud to be the first National Team coach.

What has been your greatest day in coaching?

It wouldn't be a win! I think my greatest day is the first day of practice every year. You are starting everything new. What you are going to do the next six months begins on that day. I have 33 best days in coaching.

What advice would you give to young people entering coaching today?

First, continuous learning– learn to love to learn.

Second, listen to others teach, and teach yourself; get involved.

Third, maintain and increase your passion to coach; value each part of that youngster and don't judge based upon the scoreboard.

Finally, balance your life; Family, Faith, and Game.

Photo courtesty: AP Images

Mike Krzyzewski and the 2008 United States Olympic Team return the gold medal to American soil where it all began. Coach K joins a very exclusive club of NABC coaches who have won a National Championship and coached the Olympic team to the gold medal. This achievement emphasizes why he is identified as a Guardian of the Game.

After studying the final two Guardians, John Wooden and Mike Krzyzewski, it is apparent that the two are very similar. Both have a strong commitment to teaching and team chemistry. They share the importance of character in themselves, their staff, and their players. They both teach that the essence of basketball is holding the team above individual needs. As many great coaches as this game has seen, and continues to see today, it would behoove a young coach today to study Wooden and Krzyzewski at length. There is something in their methods that equates to success.

CONCLUSION

More than 115 years have passed since Dr. James Naismith invented basketball. Incredibly, the foundations of the game are still dominated by most of the 13 original rules. Worldwide, the game has surpassed every game except soccer in attendance and popularity. In almost every facet of basketball, the NABC has had a vital role in that popularity.

Eighty-one years ago the NABC was officially chartered by a group of coaches who cared deeply about the game and the future of basketball coaching. Gradually the NABC was able to erase regional boundaries and create an atmosphere where the profession embraced those entering and those leaving, and encouraged a sharing during the period between. The profession has flourished, but the original staples of the constitution have suffered in the transition.

In the decades that have passed, coaches participated in the game for the love of basketball and the relationships with players. No one got wealthy financially. During those times, the coaches had the attitude that whatever needed to be done, would be done. That is why so many of our predecessors had such broad and involved resumes. Some of the greatest coaches in the land were enshrined in halls of fame as *contributors*. Their span of influence was so broad that to applaud the coaching while ignoring all of the other achievements would be incorrect.

This attitude embraced by our coaching forefathers is a dying characteristic. Many of the elite coaches—whether because of popularity or wealth—have become invisible. They have turned away from the responsibility of teaching basketball coaching to the next generation as it was taught to them and to me.

"With more money comes more paranoia," said David Berst of the NCAA. "Coaches have become more selfish, more cautious, more controlling over what they are doing, unwilling to share the secrets that they have somehow uncovered."

Back in the day, a phone call to Indiana, West Point or Boston University was answered or returned. An offer to teach was always on the minds of those who had achieved a superior level in the profession.

I was shocked at the difficulty of getting input for this project. The levels of protection surrounding coaches today were very discouraging. Even with this book being sponsored by the NABC and a portion of the proceeds directed into the NABC programs, many coaches remained unavailable. I cannot imagine the reaction to a 25–year-old coach calling to get help with his practice plans or principles of zone defense.

So, on behalf of those 20-somethings looking for advice, or guys who have been in the business for 25 years, this is a plea to the coaching fraternity that claim NABC membership. Co-existence between the retired, acting, and young coaches is possible if we use what we have to support each other.

To the youngest, who are just beginning or are hoping to be coaches, study in detail what the coaches in this book teach. Learn the lessons of coaching history and how each facet of the game has evolved. Develop your personal philosophy embracing a little of each of the greats that have come before. Then when you feel ready to branch out, ignore the rock-star coaches and review the list of coaches at other levels who have won 600, 700 or 800 games. These guys have it figured out and will answer the phone. When I called for information about someone during the research for the book, there were no passwords or secret handshakes required. Also, take advantage of the retired coaches who still love to talk about coaching. I was never turned away, regardless of how many halls of fame a particular coach was enshrined in. I promise you that their message is still vital.

To the active Division I coaches who are becoming wealthy because of the game, share your knowledge. Since it is difficult for you to answer when the calls come in, provide DVDs and downloadable material that will teach the young coaches what you know. Share practice plans and the intricacies of the parts of the game that you have become famous for. Reviewing an NABC convention program from the past, the great coaches took their turns at the dais. Rupp, Holman, Knight, Smith, Allen, Wooden, Iba, and all the others could be found on the schedule. Don't just give back– give back to the profession.

To those active coaches who toil year after year at levels below the elite, your message is important, but the vehicle of delivery more difficult. For you the responsibility is simple ... answer the phone!

Finally, to the retired coaches across the country, your input, and support for this book have been wonderful. Although it was impossible to share comments from each coach, my hope is that I preserved the message that you share with so many of your peers.

I would like to suggest that you put your energies together and provide coaching mentorships for the young coaches searching for assistance. Sure, some of you tire a little more easily than before, but a group presentation would be tremendously informative. The youngsters still need help with teaching the fundamentals of every aspect of the game and who better than you to teach them? I have a tape of a roundtable discussion from my younger coaching days when Wooden, Rupp, Foster, Drake, Holman, Iba, and Lemons shared their feelings about the game. It is one of my personal treasures.

Finally, during your retirement or in your will, leave your important documents, books, and personal basketball treasures to the NABC. Force them to collect, preserve, and display the history of this great game and this great profession.

THANK YOU! YOU ARE HOOPS HISTORY!

"Perfect technique, perfect team work, good conditioning and the building of a tradition are not enough. The truly successful coach must go with his men, individually, beyond the field of conditioning and beyond the field of competition. He must get into their hearts; he must know their folks; he must find what interests them most; he must study their different temperaments, as he would study the temperament of his own sons."

—Dr. Forrest "Phog" Allen

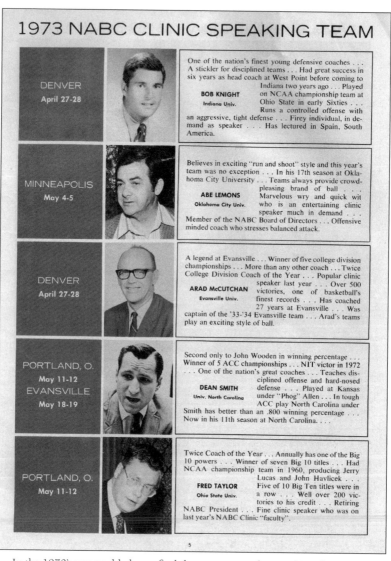

1973 NABC CLINIC SPEAKING TEAM

DENVER
April 27-28

One of the nation's finest young defensive coaches . . . A stickler for disciplined teams . . . Had great success in six years as head coach at West Point before coming to Indiana two years ago . . . Played **BOB KNIGHT** on NCAA championship team at Indiana Univ. Ohio State in early Sixties . . . Runs a controlled offense with an aggressive, tight defense . . . Firey individual, in demand as speaker . . . Has lectured in Spain, South America.

MINNEAPOLIS
May 4-5

Believes in exciting "run and shoot" style and this year's team was no exception . . . In his 17th season at Oklahoma City University . . . Teams always provide crowd-pleasing brand of ball . . . **ABE LEMONS** Marvelous wry and quick wit Oklahoma City Univ. who is an entertaining clinic speaker much in demand . . . Member of the NABC Board of Directors . . . Offensive minded coach who stresses balanced attack.

DENVER
April 27-28

A legend at Evansville . . . Winner of five college division championships . . . More than any other coach . . . Twice College Division Coach of the Year . . . Popular clinic speaker last year . . . Over 500 **ARAD McCUTCHAN** victories, one of basketball's Evansville Univ. finest records . . . Has coached 27 years at Evansville . . . Was captain of the '33-'34 Evansville team . . . Arad's teams play an exciting style of ball.

PORTLAND, O.
May 11-12
EVANSVILLE
May 18-19

Second only to John Wooden in winning percentage . . . Winner of 5 ACC championships . . . NIT victor in 1972 . . . One of the nation's great coaches . . . Teaches disciplined offense and hard-nosed **DEAN SMITH** defense . . . Played at Kansas Univ. North Carolina under "Phog" Allen . . . In tough ACC play North Carolina under Smith has better than an .800 winning percentage . . . Now in his 11th season at North Carolina. . . .

PORTLAND, O.
May 11-12

Twice Coach of the Year . . . Annually has one of the Big 10 powers . . . Winner of seven Big 10 titles . . . Had NCAA championship team in 1960, producing Jerry Lucas and John Havlicek . . . **FRED TAYLOR** Five of 10 Big Ten titles were in Ohio State Univ. a row . . . Well over 200 victories to his credit . . . Retiring NABC President . . . Fine clinic speaker who was on last year's NABC Clinic "faculty".

5

In the 1970's you could always find the greatest coaches teaching the game... Something that has not continued into the 21st Century.

ABOUT THE NABC

The National Association of Basketball Coaches (NABC), located in Kansas City, Missouri, was founded in 1927 by Phog Allen, the legendary University of Kansas basketball coach.

Since its beginning, the NABC has continually worked to further the best interests of the game of basketball as well as the players and coaches who participate in the sport. In doing so, the NABC has established the following goals and objectives to pursue its mission:

- To promote the ideals of integrity, sportsmanship and teamwork among men's basketball coaches and the players whom they coach;
- To unify coaches on issues pertaining to basketball at all levels;
- To provide member services which address the needs of the coach professionally, emotionally, financially, physically and spiritually;
- To encourage basketball coaches to serve as community outreach agents who elevate moral, ethical and educational values;
- To enlighten the general public, media, institutional educators and athletic administrators to the fact that coaches are good for the sport and the young people whom they serve;
- To work with the legislative arm of the NCAA on issues that affect basketball and intercollegiate athletics, in particular identifying issues that not only benefit the student-athlete but also the ability of the coaching staff to work effectively and beneficially within the institution.

Guardians of the Game is a national awareness and education program led by the NABC that focuses attention on the positive roles coaches play in the lives of today's student-athletes, the game of basketball and the community. The program includes the association's four core values: advocacy, leadership, service and education. Each core value provides coaches with a platform to effect positive changes within the game, among student-athletes and their communities.

BASKETBALL FANS:

If you have enjoyed *Guardians of the Game – A Legacy of Leadership* and the wonderful CD, then you are sure to enjoy the College Basketball Experience (CBE) in Kansas City, Missouri. This two level showcase of college basketball has attractions for all ages of sports fans.

On the first floor is a full basketball court and many action stations where kids of all ages can test their basketball skills, compare their dimensions to the great players and compete among themselves in shooting the "3" or performing some flashy dunks.

The lower level is an "eye popping" display of the game from the beginning to present day, and even some thoughts about the future. You can track the great basketball personalities through their mentors and see how each has inspired others to become coaches. Maybe the most inspirational piece of the entire Experience is to wander through the National Collegiate Basketball Hall of Fame, see the names of those pioneers who came before and in many cases hear them expressing thoughts about their careers and the great game of college basketball.

The CBE is housed inside the beautiful, state-of-the-art Sprint Center and with a little planning, the concert or rodeo attendee can get to the Sprint Center a little early and enjoy the Experience before the regularly scheduled event.

ENJOY THE COLLEGE BASKETBALL EXPERIENCE AND THANK YOU FOR SUPPORTING THE NABC AND COLLEGE BASKETBALL BY YOUR PURCHASE OF *GUARDIANS OF THE GAME – A LEGACY OF LEADERSHIP.*

NOTES

Unless otherwise noted, direct quotes were taken from personal interviews conducted by the author.

Introduction

"I Believe..." *Original NABC Constitution 1927* – University of Kansas Archives

"For over forty years..." 1994 Speech delivered at NABC Convention by incoming President George Blaney, Head Coach, Holy Cross.

"200 people watched from a balcony..." *Springfield Republican*, March 12, 1892.

"Do not be afraid..." Phog Allen quoted James Naismith in the Eulogy for Naismith found in the University of Kansas archives

"Going into Physical Education in 1890..." James Naismith Speech, 1932

"There was a revolt against..." James Naismith letter to T.J. Brown, 1898

"In 1890, when I first entered the institution..." James Naismith, *The Origins of Basketball*, 1932

"YMCA originated it..." Dr. John Brown, 1940 National Council of the YMCA, reprinted in *The Golden Jubilee of Basketball*

"13 Original Rules" – James Naismith, onion skin copy of typed rules found in KU archives, unnamed and undated.

"Dr. Naismith taught us more than just basketball..." John McLendon interview, *NABC Bulletin* 173, pg 43

"Basketball is especially adapted..." James Naismith, early letter to the NCAA, reprinted in the 1954 *NABC Bulletin*

Book One – The Beginning

"The Year I graduated..." Dean Smith, Forward, *Phog Allen, The Father of Basketball Coaching* by Blair Kerkhoff

"Forrest was ten..." Ibid, pg. 2-3

"We played for five years and only lost one game..." Hubert Allen, *Illinois Telegraph*, 1974

"The convention hall series..." James Naismith, *Kansas City Star*, March 1905

"I was much delighted..." James Naismith, *Kansas City Star*, March 1905

"With a merry laugh..." Phog Allen, *Phog Allen's Sports Stories*, 1947, pg. 174

"Dr. F. C. Allen, Miracle Man..." *Champaign Daily News*

"I sure wouldn't be here..." Johnny Mize, *Topeka Daily Capital*, July 23, 1950

"The National Association of Basketball Coaches was..." Edward Hickox, NABC Archives (Bulletins of several different years)

"The Objects and Purpose of this Association..." *Original NABC Constitution*, University of Kansas Archives

"The college administrators from around..." Peter Bjarkman, *The Biographical History of Basketball*

"I think this would be a very interesting experiment..." Allen to Everett Morris, University of Kansas Archives

"If Naismith is the founding father..." Peter Bjarkman, *The Biographical History of Basketball*, pg. 260

"It is entirely fitting that the 'prestige'..." *1939 Basketball Guide*, pg. 8

"Luckily, I had been working as a ..." Howard Hobson, *Shooting Ducks*

Book Two – The Rules

"The responsibility of the Coaches is even…" James Naismith, 1913, reprinted in *NABC Bulletin,* 1956

"Thirty Years ago there were three…" Oswald Tower, *Golden Jubilee of Basketball*, 1941, pg. 13

"It is believed that by this means…" *New York Times*, March 1907

"So the secret is out…" Timothy Duncan, *Boston Sunday Post*, 1947

"Old Timers, many young men and women, too…" *Boston Herald*, December 9, 1945

"For the first time in history…" Oswald Tower, *New York Times*, December 1914

"There are critics who say…" Dr. Walter Meanwell, *The Science of Basket Ball*, 1924, pg. 6

"Skill in catching and passing the ball…" Ibid, pg. 72

"Back in April of 1927…" Handwritten notes by Allen, Bill Wall Archives

"As Editor, national interpreter and guardian of rules…" Edward Steitz to Charles Hollinger, *New York Times*, December, 1988

"Five basketball seasons ago…" John Feinstein, *Washington Post*, 1984

"Coaches Opinions, Sutton – Brown", *USA Today*, April 3, 1986

"The first thing you've got to talk about…" Ed Steitz, *Boston Globe*, 1987

Book Three – The Parallel Universe

"Here was a man…" Dr. Milton S. Katz, *Breaking Through*

"Dr. Naismith taught us more…" John McLendon, *NABC Bulletin*, 1973, pg. 43

"Basketball finally go to the Olympics…" John McLendon, Interview tapes provided by Joanna McLendon and Dr. Milton S. Katz

"It would be impractical…" Tug Wilson letter, NCAA Archives

"You may rest assured…" Walter Byers letter, NCAA Archives

"It's sort of like being…" John McLendon to Finn, *Springfield Union*, 1979

"He is one of two legendary…" Chris Dempsey, *Denver Post*, March 2008

"Our role as mentors, monitors and…" Clarence "Big House" Gaines letter to NABC membership, *NABC Bulletin*, 1989

"I've never seen anything bigger than you…" Winston Salem Archives

"Dick Shultz, in his remarks…" Clarence Gaines, Letter re-printed in *NABC Bulletin*, 1989

"The most bothersome and misunderstood…" Interview 2007

"For me, clearly, he's…" Karl Hobbs, *Washington Post*, 2005

"There wasn't a parent out there…" James Donaldson, Russell Houghtaling, *Four-Fathers of Cougar Basketball*, January 17, 2006

"I view this as coming home…" George Raveling, 1986, *NABC Bulletin*

"I want to be a winner…" John Thompson Jr., *The Washington Magazine*, 1990

"I'm a basketball coach…" Thompson to Krause/Pim, *Lessons from the Legends*, pg. 263

"I don't think there is another coach…" Richard Lapchick, Center for Sports & Society, Northeastern University, *NABC Courtside*, pg 16

"I'm not sure why…" John Thompson Jr. to Ken Davis, *NABC Courtside*, 1999, pg 16

Book Four – The Moral Compass

"Hank Luisetti, at Stanford…" Cliff Wells to Gorman, *Winningest Coach of All*, pg. 14

"Lost Luggage…" Cliff Wells, *NABC Bulletin*, 1965

"I do not believe that anyone…" Adolph Rupp letter to Bill Wall, Wall personal papers, November 1975

"…and there are other ills…" Bill Wall, *Sports Illustrated*, 1972

"Our stated position indicates…" Wall letter to United States Congress, 1972

"It has been the perfect fit…" Herb Kenny speech, Vancisin Retirement

Book Five – The Connectors

"Start out in the morning…" Dr. H.C. Carlson, *Spiritual Side of Basketball*, 1928
"While there are many theories…" John Bunn, *Scientific Principles of Coaching*, 1955
"We are fortunate today that forward…" Edward Hickox, Letter to the NABC members, asking for additional funds for the Naismith Memorial
"I want to thank these men…" Adolph Rupp, Convention Speech, reprinted in the *NABC Bulletin*

Book Six – The Champions of the World

"NABC leadership is directly responsible…" Cliff Wells, *NABC Policies Manual*
"I am not against shooting…" Henry Iba from speech delivered at NABC convention in the 1970s
"The replaying of the video tape…" Bud Greenspan, *We WUZ Robbed*, pg. 11
"I don't think any of the letterman…" George Karl, Foreword, *A Coach's Life*
"Bo Ellis, a great player…" Ibid
"Three players that I wanted…" Ibid, pg.165
"John, Bill and I stood off to the side…" Ibid, pg. 170
"The selection of the Olympic team…" Bob Knight to Steve Alford, *Playing for Knight*, pg. 112
"I had put the things that were important…" Knight to Hammel, *Knight, My Story*
"(On Wednesday) I got a call…" John Koncak to Matt Fulks, *"Where are they now?"*, *The Kansas City Star*, June 15, 2005
"He taught me a lot of things…" Ibid
"When my time on earth is gone…" Knight Speech at Indiana, ESPN video archives

Book Seven – It's a Small World

"It is an honor to be selected…" James Phelan, Mount St. Mary's Website, 2008
"If you look at F&M over the years…" Jeremiah Henry, All American, Franklin and Marshall, Website

Book Eight – The Ugly Stuff

"Horse racing, former king of sports…" Phog Allen, *Daily Kansan*, 1920
"Judge (Kennesaw Mountain) Landis…" 1944 Phog Allen Letter to Sam Smith, University of Kansas Archives
"More money is bet on collegiate football…" Phog Allen, *New York Times*, October 21, 1944
"The stories you read about champions…" Nat Holman, *Basketball's Hall of Fame*, pg. 28
"I teach my players…" Nat Holman, *Holman on Basketball*
"In a fast game, I believe…" Clair Bee, *NABC* Basketball *Bulletin*, 1947
"The Priests Caught on…" Clair Bee, Ibid
"I guess I was to concerned with my own…" Clair Bee, *New York Times*, 1951
"We, you and I, have flunked…" Clair Bee, *NABC Bulletin*, 1951

Book Nine – The NCAA: The Empire

"I was charged with…" Walter Byers, *Unsportsmanlike Conduct*, pg. 5
"It would be real hard for me…" Eddie Robinson, Ibid
"More than one-eighth…" Gordon White, Greensboro, NC, March 24, 1974

Book Ten – The Media Says It All

"I'm probably the most misunderstood…" Billy Packer to John Akers, *Basketball Times*, April 2008, pg. 32
"I'm living the American dream…" Dick Vitale, Vitale Official Website

Book Eleven – The Greatest of Them All

"The rapport and association…" John Wooden, *Indianapolis Star*, 2006

"To not celebrate, to fail to…" Swen Nater, *You Haven't Taught Until They Have Learned*, pg. XVII, 2006.

"When I met with my squad this year…" John Wooden to Joe McGuff, *Kansas City Star*

"I always considered myself a teacher…" John Wooden, *You Haven't Taught Until They Have Learned*, pg. XV, 2006.

Book Twelve – The Future is Upon Us

"During the season…" Mike Krzyzewski, Academy of Success Website

"If success or talent were on floors…" Mike Krzyzewski to Gregg Doyel, *Building the Duke Dynasty*

"I went to Weber and found Mike…" Bob Knight to Bob Hammel, *Knight, My Story*

Conclusion

"Perfect technique, perfect team work…" Phog Allen, *My Basket-Ball Bible*, 1924